A Spiritual Right of Passage

CONVERSION AND DIGNITY
IN THE
JEWISH TRADITION

Richard F. Kaufman

EDITED BY
PAUL MENDES-FLOHR
&
KELLY JAMES CLARK

Copyright © 2020 by Richard F. Kaufman

First Printing, 2020
ISBN 978-163625816-4

All rights reserved. This book or any portion thereof may not be reproduced or used in any manner whatsœver without the express written permission of Richard F. Kaufman except for the use of brief quotations in a book review.

Printed in the United States of America

Typesetting by Wahid M. Amin

*To Dick's many cherished mentors,
recent and over the ages,
who have helped illuminate
human dignity in these pages*

Contents

Introduction — 1

1. Human Dignity in the Hebrew Bible and the Talmud — 5
2. The Prooftext for the Rabbinic Conception of Human Dignity — 23
3. Social Mitzvot and Human Dignity Prevail — 36
4. Two Rabbinic Paradigms of Conversion — 57
5. A Reform Responsum on Conversion — 91
6. American Reform Judaism: History and Demographics — 114
7. Circumcision and Moral Universalism — 135

Epilogue: Reflections — 150

Appendices

1. Memories and Metavalues — 155
   Paul Mendes-Flohr

2. Should Conversion be Promoted in Judaism? — 157
   Donniel Hartman

3. Does Love Require Christians to Convert their Neighbor? — 163
   Richard Mouw

Bibliography — 175

A Spiritual Right of Passage:
Conversion and Dignity in the Jewish Tradition

Introduction

This study of conversion and converts in traditional and contemporary Jewish thought and practice proposes that human dignity is the metavalue[1] determining the overarching ethos of Jewish tradition and that it is the preeminent metavalue of Reform Judaism in the United States. The book argues, further, that American Reform Judaism is an authentic expression of Jewish tradition, both in theology and in religious-cum-ethical practice. Reform Judaism's openness to change and its concern with the lives and dignity of contemporary Jews is characteristic of the tradition.

A review of the tradition indicates that during most of the period from 500 CE to the present the views about conversion that predominated were to welcome the proselyte, minimize the importance of motivation, and ignore future lifestyle as considerations for conversion. I will also review current thought on cultural value—the conscious, the unconscious, and methods to modify behavior—in order to help those who wish to understand and possibly to change their views concerning conversion and converts.

The conception of human dignity in the Jewish tradition is founded upon the creation narrative in the Hebrew Bible. Accordingly, humans have inherent value because they are created in the image of God; humans are created from the same mold, with the same forebears, Adam and Eve, and yet each is different. God engages in dialogue with humans about moral values and actions, prompting them to develop their ethical and spiritual sensibilities.

I have written in a style intended to be accessible and engaging to all Jews—whether familiar or unfamiliar with the subjects considered. In choosing historical, theological, psychological, anthropological, and sociological frames of reference, I have sought to contribute to the understanding of the intersection in Judaism of the metavalue of human dignity and the treatment of converts.

***

Chapter 1, "Human Dignity in the Hebrew Bible and the Talmud," reviews the two stories of the creation of humanity (Genesis 1 and 2), the narrative of Abraham before the destruction of Sodom and Gomorrah (Genesis

---

[1] Editor's note: For background to the term *metavalue*, see the Appendix 1.

18), the book of Job, and the account of the sacrifice of Isaac (Genesis 22). It focuses on the texts as they privilege human dignity and moral behavior. The texts are from the Bible; the *haggadah*, the nonlegal texts in the Talmud; and *halakhah*, the legal texts in the Talmud. Biblical texts and haggadic texts are primary references in American Reform Judaism, which, contrary to other denominations, does not consider halakhah obligatory.

Chapter 2, "The Prooftext for the Rabbinic Conception of Human Dignity," explores the story of the Oven of Aknai, in Babylonian Talmud, Bava Metzi'a 59a–b, a text many scholars consider to be the prooftext for rabbinic Judaism. A plain or literal reading concludes that God was displeased at having his interpretation of the text ignored and that God was angry with Rabbi Gamaliel for humiliating his brother-in-law, Rabbi Eliezer, who interpreted the Oven of Aknai in accord with its divine meaning. The text illustrates the conflict between God's meaning, on the one hand, and human interpretation of God's word, on the other. It illustrates the tension between rabbinic authority and intellectual autonomy, which I hold to be an essential dimension of human dignity.

Chapter 3, "Social *Mitzvot* and Human Dignity Prevail," reviews Daniel Sperber's *On the Relationship of Mitzvot between Man and His Neighbor and Man and His Maker* (2014). An exhaustive exegesis of biblical and Talmudic texts supports the precedence of social *mitzvot* (sglr.: *mitzvah*) — actions directed at fellow human beings — over ritual *mitzvot*, actions directed at God. Sperber (b. 1940) is a leading Orthodox scholar who demonstrates that there are certain basic ethical values upon which halakhah is based. The dignity of the individual is the predominant value, followed by the sanctity of life, the positive nature of mitzvot, and the foundational notion of moral rectitude.

Chapter 4, "Two Rabbinic Paradigms of Conversion," reviews *Transforming Identity: The Ritual Transformation from Gentile to Jew; Structure and Meaning* (2007), coauthored by Avi Sagi (b. 1947), an Israeli scholar of philosophy and ethics, and Zvi Zohar, an Israeli Talmudic scholar. The book is an encyclopedic study of belief and practice concerning conversion to Judaism from 500 CE to the present. Sagi and Zohar posit that the canonical text for conversion from the Geonic period (589–1038 CE)[2] until recently was the baraita[3] cited in Yevamot 47a–b. They found that converts

---

[2] The Geonim were the heads of the academic centers in Babylon that were the center of Jewish learning during the Jews' exile from Judah.

[3] A baraita is an oral tradition of religious law that was not included in the Mishnah, the

were welcomed during most periods in Jewish history, motives were not questioned deeply, and a future lifestyle was not dictated.

Chapter 5, "A Reform Responsum on Conversion," reviews *Pledges of Jewish Allegiance: Conversion, Law, and Policymaking in Nineteenth- and Twentieth-Century Orthodox Responsa* (2012), by David Ellenson (b. 1947), a leading Reform Jewish scholar, and Daniel Gordis (b. 1959), a leading Conservative Jewish scholar. They consider those who wrote these Orthodox responsa *not as legal arbiters* but as *framers of public policy*—on Jewish identity, status, and conversion—who are faced with the problems of increasing intermarriage and lack of observance of Jewish ritual traditions. They also discuss the influence of personal values on halakhic decisions.

Chapter 6, "American Reform Judaism: History and Demographics," begins with a brief history of Reform Judaism and Jewish identity. Next, it discusses data from the 2013 Pew Research Center study *A Portrait of Jewish Americans*. Pew found that American Jews said they were proud to be Jewish and had a strong sense of belonging to the Jewish people. According to the survey, ancestry and culture were the most important determinants of identity. Eighty-three percent of Jews of no religious affiliation belonged to this category, whereas 55 percent of Jews by religion regarded themselves as Jews of ethnic descent and culture. The chapter continues with an account of a critical analysis of the accuracy and meaning of polls and surveys written by the dean of survey scholars, Robert Wuthnow of Princeton University. Wuthnow's *Inventing American Religion: Polls, Surveys, and the Tenuous Quest for a Nations Faith* (2015) argues that the public's views of American religion are a construct of studies of religion that have gained currency during a century of polling. This observation applies to surveys of American Judaism. The accuracy of these surveys is questionable. Less than 9 percent of those contacted responded to the surveys. Multivariate analysis and statistical methods cannot rationalize or summarize the varieties of human experience and human meaning that are expressed in polls. Chapter 6 concludes by discussing two of the most influential sociological studies in the last half of the twentieth century, Will Herberg's *Protestant, Catholic, Jew: An Essay in American Religious Sociology* (1955) and Robert D. Putnam's *Bowling Alone: The Collapse and Revival of American Community* (2000).

Chapter 7, "Circumcision and Moral Universalism," reviews the cultural

---

first authoritative codification of religious laws.

and psychological anthropologic views of Richard A. Shweder, the Harold H. Swift Distinguished Service Professor of Human Development at the University of Chicago. First, I present some of his research on circumcision. Then I present some of his thoughts on moral pluralism, in which values in different cultures are different but equal. Third, I present his "Big Three" nexus of values: autonomy, community, and divinity. These values are prevalent, with different valences, in most societies. Autonomy is characteristic of the United States. Fourth, I present Shweder's views and those of Jonathan Haidt, author of *The Righteous Mind* (2011), on cognitive intuitionism, in which emotions are the gatekeepers to the ethical universe. Fifth, I explore Shweder's notion that human rights are objective and inalienable: moral absolutes of the sort I have in mind are self-evident in the sense that reason requires of them no justification or deliberation. The chapter concludes with a sober reflection written over thirty years ago by Robert N. Bellah, the principal author of the celebrated *Habits of the Heart: Individualism and Commitment in American Life* (1985).

I conclude with an epilogue that reflects on what I have learned about conversion and converts and about a prudent way forward for American Reform to create a meaningful and sustainable Judaism for the future.

CHAPTER 1

Human Dignity in the Hebrew Bible and the Talmud

Reading and Interpreting Texts

Much of Talmudic discussion is in the form of conversations between rabbis. Halakhic texts may be thought of as both spoken and written. The Written Torah, called the Bible or the Five Books of Moses, is believed by the ultra-Orthodox to have been given to Moses at Mount Sinai. They also believe that the Oral Torah was spoken by God to Moses at the same time. The Written Torah preceded the Oral Torah, although many scholars believe that during the later period of the development of the Written Torah, the Oral Torah was being developed in parallel.

The Oral Torah was not committed to writing until early in the third century CE. The first part is the Mishnah, which was compiled by numerous scholars (called Tannaim) over a period of about two centuries and redacted by R.[1] Judah ha-Nasi between 200 and 220 CE. The Mishnah supplements the written, or scriptural, laws found in the Pentateuch. It presents various interpretations of selective legal traditions that had been preserved orally since at least the time of Ezra (ca. 450 BCE). The second part of the Oral Torah is the Gemara, which comments on the Mishnah and expands it into law and practice, halakhah. The Mishnah and parts of the Gemara make up the Talmud, which was produced in identical texts both in Jerusalem and in Babylon. The first Talmud, the Jerusalem Talmud, was produced in Jerusalem between 300 and 350 CE. The second Talmud, the Babylonian Talmud, is more extensive and is considered to be more authoritative than the Jerusalem Talmud. It was compiled in Babylonia and published between 450 and 500 CE. I will refer repeatedly to these canonical texts and earlier canonical biblical texts.

For readers not familiar with Jewish texts, Avi Sagi and Zvi Zohar's discussion of halakhic texts may be helpful:

---

[1] Hereafter the title Rabbi will be abbreviated R. when appearing before a name.

Halakhic texts have an internal history: while written in a specific time and place, their meaning is not defined by that time and place. We hold the hermeneutical principle that the meaning of texts is not reducible to their sociological genesis. Rather, it derives from the *weltanshaung* [*sic*] that they embody, their internal argumentation and rhetoric, and the fact that they are read by successive generations whose close reading leads to the attribution of immanent meanings to the text. While some texts may be significantly conditioned by their historical context, historical contextualization of their meaning should be guided first and foremost by clear indications within the text itself. . . .

The diachronic aspect of our project therefore primarily reflects the internal dynamic of halakhic discourse over the centuries. . . .

The synchronic aspect of our project is reflected in our view that the continuity of halakhic dialogue over the generations generates an arena of discourse characterized by the persistence of basic similarities and structures that transcend time and place.[2]

R. Mark Washofsky, the Solomon B. Freehof Professor of Jewish Law and Practice at the Hebrew Union College–Jewish Institute of Religion (HUC-JIR) in Cincinnati, a leading Reform scholar of halakhah, offers another helpful commentary on reading halakhah as a dialogical discourse. In the following passage quoted by Sagi and Zohar, he refers to the 1,300 opinions issued by the Responsa Committee of the Central Conference of American Rabbis (CCAR)[3] as Reform's engagement in the ongoing conversation about Judaism:

> To call halachah a "language" is to say it is more than simply a collection of rules and directives, of thou-shalts and thou-shalt-nots imposed upon the Jew. Halachah is better understood as a discourse, a way of speaking, a conversation carried on through history by the students of Jewish tradition. It is the medium of communication through which Jews for more than fifteen centuries have analyzed and explored, discussed and debated how they should answer the myriad manifestations of the central question of Jewish life: what is it that God wants us to do? We might summarize the nature of this discourse in the words "interpretation" and "argument." By "interpretation" I mean a claim of meaning that a reader or readers make upon a text, which serves as the object

[2] Sagi and Zohar, *Transforming Identity*, 3.
[3] The CCAR is the governing body of American Reform rabbis.

of interpretation. . . . [And] since one cannot *deduce* the answer to a question of Jewish practice as though it were a problem in mathematics, one must *argue* that a suggested answer is correct or, at least, it is better than the other answers that might be reasonably be adopted. . . . The argument succeeds to the extent that a consensus forms around it, a consensus that takes shape when the halachist persuades the intended audience, the particular community of interpretation to which he or she addresses the argument, that *this* answer represents the best reading of the texts and sources of Torah as they relate to the question in hand.

The responsa literature [a responsum (pl.: responsa) is a rabbi's response to a question about the application of halachah in a specific situation], by far the largest body of rabbinical legal writing, occupies a central position in this culture of halachic argument.[4]

Exegesis of Jewish texts often follows the concepts of *peshat, remez, derash*, and *sod*. In interpreting texts, we will favor peshat, the plain meaning of the text. A plain reading usually provides sufficient information for a meaningful understanding. These four types of reading (exegesis) of biblical stories and Talmudic texts are collectively called PaRDeS, an acronym composed of the first letter of each type of reading:

Peshat, "surface," is the literal meaning.
Remez, "hints," is the allegoric meaning.
Derash, "inquire," is the comparative meaning between texts.
Sod, "secret" or mystical meaning, comes from inspiration or revelation.

Michael Fishbane, in *Sacred Attunement: A Jewish Theology*, explored with profound spiritual sensibility the exegesis of religious texts. His work is a richly nuanced introduction to reading and understanding the texts I will present. According to Fishbane:

Jewish thought has developed four principle modes of scriptural reading, which variously train the mind and heart for a life of spiritual alertness in the world. These hermeneutical activities cultivate different types of religious perception and consciousness, even diverse theological orientations and ways of living with God in mind. Separately, these modalities of interpretation have been designated by the following terms: *peshat*

---

[4] Washofsky, "M'nuchah and M'lachah."

(he so-called plain or contextual meaning of scripture; the direct and ungarnished sense, so to say, insofar as we can know it); *derash* (the far-ranging theological and legal reformulations of scripture; providing more indirect and mediated meanings of the text, in response to ongoing challenges of religious life and belief); *remez* (the assorted hints or allusions of scripture, insofar as its words and phrases may be decoded to reveal moral or philosophical or psychological allegories); and *sod* (the intuited spiritual or mystical dimensions of scripture, inseparable from the cosmic and supernal truths of divine Being). Taken together, this exegetical quaternary has been denominated by the acronym PaRDeS (a term that connotes the "paradise" or "garden" of scriptural senses). This designation also points to the multifaceted truth of Jewish tradition, which can sponsor diverse meanings and truths simultaneously.[5]

Peshat. One of the great sages of medieval Ashkenaz (in Northern Europe), Rabbi Solomon ben Isaac (known familiarly as Rashi), once referred to his sense of the *peshat* as the concern to interpret the words of scripture as they fittingly unfold within their own contents, and as the teachings of tradition fit sensibly into this same literary frame. In formulating this (dual) understanding, Rashi utilized a phrase from an old biblical proverb, "Like apples of gold in a filigree of silver *is a word fitly spoken*" (*devar davur al ofonav* Prov. 25:11, my emphasis)...

Reading for the *peshat* sense involves a subjugation of the self in the words of the text as they appear, both singly and in syntactic combinations.... For all their apparent similarity to the language of everyday speech, the words of a text, such as scripture, are semblances of life-acts and speech.... They are mute signs on a page and remain dormant until filled with human phrasing and emphasis. They thus rise into actuality through the role of a reader, who calls them forth in the process of reading.... The words do not answer back... The text never indicates that it is being misread.[6]

Such an attuned responsiveness to a text may be called the ethics of the *peshat*. It is a distinct shaping of consciousness through the act of scriptural interpretation — for the sake of life and theology.[7]

---

[5] Fishbane, *Sacred Attunement*, 65–66.
[6] Ibid., 67.
[7] Ibid., 71–72.

Derash. A reading of scripture oriented toward the *derash* turns away from the discursive contexts of the text, and the concern to disclose its meaning as a document of antiquity. The new turn is toward the contemporaneous meanings of scripture as a document that speaks to ongoing receivers, who believe it to be ever meaningful and renewed for post-Sinai generations. This type of reading is less a subjection of the self to a given scriptural sense than an active engagement with its inner eros—that is to say, the attraction of the words of scripture to one another, beyond their immediate context, and the meanings that may be discerned from such intertextual activations of the components of scriptural language. The reader is thus involved in new conjugations of the old words of the text in order to reveal through the human self the ongoing voice of Sinai. . . .

Such a mode of reading restores the textual inscription to a living voice.[8] Interpretive acts of *derash* lock on to specific terms in a text, and then interpret scripture by means of scripture, for the sake of expanding religious life and thought. Any textual point can serve as a matrix, drawing other passages to it and yielding new clusters of insight.[9]

Remez. Another great medieval sage (of Spain and Egypt), Rabbi Moses ben Maimon (known familiarly as the Rambam or Maimonides), was a master of textual insight: for he was able to perceive in the language of scripture stylistic significations of more hidden truths of pure thought (philosophical and spiritual). He spoke of these verbal signs as as providing a *remez*, or hint, of these supersensual ideas, and found just the biblical phrase to make his point:[10] the first clause of the same proverb used by Rashi to promote the *peshat* sense. For the Rambam, the image, "*Like apples of gold in a filigree of silver* . . . is a word fitly spoken," conveyed just that art of concealment that he discerned in the composition of scripture. The fitly wrought word or image, he taught, was a double communication: it conveyed a surface sense and a deeper one, the first being like a stylistic trellis which covered a figure set within or behind it. The deeper understanding was like an apple of gold, perceivable to the discerning eye without disturbing the field of vision. As sight

---

[8] Ibid., 74–75.
[9] Ibid., 80.
[10] Maimonides is said to have been able to recall the entire Talmud. Other sages were said to have had the same ability.

is to insight, so is *peshat* to *remez*. One simply has to know what to look for and how.[11]

Sod. The [words of the] proverb we have been pondering . . . ("Like apples of gold in a filigree of silver is a word fitly spoken") put us in mind of the truth that language both reveals and conceals, and often does so at one and the same time. . . . From a mystical point of view (derived from esoteric tradition), scripture is regarded as the earthly manifestation of the most supernal truths of God. Indeed, according to classic kabbalistic lore, the creative emanations of divine Being, and their transcendent interactions and modalities, are believed to be refracted and encoded in the language of scripture. . . . The inner soul of this language and the depictions of scripture embody dimensions of Divinity, since the external manifestations are verbal symbols of the supernal realities and pulse with their esoteric energies. Hence from the perspective of *sod*, there is no gap between the hidden mysteries and revealed scripture; they are complex variations of one another. . . .

For the human being to read scripture properly as *sod*, it is necessary to seek a spiritual alignment with its language and the energy of its images. As one does so, the divine structures and dimensions of the self may reciprocally penetrate the structure and dimensions of the text, which, as noted, constitutes an aspect of God's supernal reality; and then these divine aspects of the self will be activated, and one may ascend into the higher realms in deepest contemplation, or embody this wisdom in worldly acts. The *sod* of scripture is thus not so much a level of reading as a mode of reality and being. Reading is a spiritual rite of passage into this truth so that it may be enacted for God's sake, in the most ultimate sense.[12]

I will illustrate these different ways to read a text later when exploring a rabbinic text named The Oven of Aknai, a text considered arguably to be the prooftext for rabbinic Judaism.

The texts we will examine are texts from the Bible, called the Written Torah, *torah she-bekhtav*, and from the Talmud, called the Oral Torah, *she-be'al peh*. There is a third Torah, *torah kelulah*, that is thought of as a Torah from heaven, *torah min he-shamayim*. It is the primordial Torah, God's

---

[11] Fishbane, *Sacred Attunement*, 86–87.
[12] Ibid., 94–95.

essence and his manifestation of his loving-kindness, by which he created the world and man. The Written and Oral Torahs are thought to be created from the *torah kelulah*. According to Fishbane, "The *torah kelulah* denotes absolute reality, and comprises the totality of existence and world-being."[13]

Both God, who is called the *ein sof*, the Infinite, and the torah kelulah are beyond man's ability to know and understand. The torah kelulah is thought to include God's blueprint for creation, in which God's overflowing loving-kindness created the world and man and woman. Moshe Halbertal, Paul Mendes-Flohr, and Elaine Pagels, all of whom will be cited later, view this universal creation as the foundation for the inherent human dignity of man and woman. It is incumbent on all human beings to emulate God's creativity and to value each human being by valuing human dignity, acting with dignity and respecting the dignity of the other.

In the Image of God: Genesis 1 and Genesis 2

This book proposes that human dignity is the metavalue in Reform Judaism and a metavalue in the Jewish tradition overall. I will demonstrate this to the satisfaction of Reform Jews who are familiar with the Jewish tradition, although I may not demonstrate it to the satisfaction of Jews who have conservative beliefs such as Orthodox Jews. I do not assert that human dignity is the fundamental Jewish value. Moshe Idel, a distinguished Israeli scholar of mysticism, said that whenever one makes a definitive statement about Judaism, it is not true. Another distinguished scholar and educator, Jonathan Cohen, argues that it is impossible to make definitive statements about Jewish values because values are implicit, not explicit, in the tradition and the tradition is multivalent and multivocal.

Nevertheless, an affirmation of human dignity resonates with the values of most contemporary American Jews. It offers a reason to embrace Reform Judaism. It is the lens through which a Reform Jew is expected to view and to act toward those who are interested in converting to Judaism and those who have converted. It relies on the Bible and the Five Books of Moses and is instructed by the haggadah, the nonhalakhic (nonlegal) texts in the Talmud. An exploration of the different stories of the creation of man and woman in Genesis 1 and Genesis 2 in the Bible will illuminate these different views of human dignity.

[13] Ibid., 158.

In Genesis 1 God creates both man and women in his image. Human beings have inherent value and are assigned the dignified task of ruling the world. In Genesis 2 God creates man from the dust of the earth and creates woman from man's rib. He expels both of them from the garden of Eden and commands them to till the soil. A Reform perspective suggests that man and woman, who are created equal by God, have majestic, inherent dignity. Man, who is created from dust, and woman, who is created from man's rib, do not have the same majestic dignity, but they share the supreme dignity of being created by God in his image.

Human dignity is thus embedded in the Jewish tradition, beginning with the stories of the creation of man and woman in the Bible in Genesis 1:26–28, 31:

> And God said, "Let us make man in our image, after our likeness. They shall rule the fish of the sea, the birds of the sky, the cattle, the whole earth, and all the creeping things that creep upon the earth." And God created man in his image, in the image of God he created him: male and female he created them. God blessed them and God said to them, "Be fertile and increase, fill the earth and master it; and rule the fish of the sea, the birds of the sky, and all the living things that creep on earth. . ."
> . . . And God saw all that he had made, and found it very good.

Nothing could be more dignified than being created by God and in his image. Nothing could be more dignified than for man and woman to be created equally, in the same manner at the same time. However, as is true in much of the Jewish tradition, there is a second opinion. In the second story of creation, Adam, the first man, is not created to rule but is assigned to till the fields, and woman, Eve, who is created from the rib of Adam, is assigned to be Adam's helper. This second story of creation, beginning at Genesis 2:7, follows soon after the first:

> The LORD God formed man from the dust of the earth. He blew into his nostrils the breath of life, and man became a living being. . . . The LORD God took the man and placed him in the garden of Eden, to till it and to tend it. . . . For Adam no fitting helper was found. So the LORD God cast a deep sleep upon the man; and, while he slept, he took one of his ribs and closed up the flesh at that spot. And the LORD God fashioned the rib that he had taken from the man into a woman: and he brought her to the man. (Genesis 2:7, 15, 20b–22)

Although in this story man and woman are both created by God, women are not accorded in Genesis 2 the same of human dignity and human agency that is found in Genesis 1. According to Genesis 2, man is placed by God in the garden of Eden to till it and to tend it. In the first story man and woman are created equal and at the same time. God blessed them and said to them: "Be fertile and increase, fill the earth and master it. . . . And God saw all that he had made, and found it very good." There is no similar statement of satisfaction after the creation in Genesis 2:7. Woman is not created at the same time. She is not created equal; she is created from man's rib. She is deceived by the snake and induces Adam to disobey God's command not to eat the forbidden fruit. God expels both from the garden of Eden. Even so, God is concerned about them and their dignity: "Even so, the LORD God made garments of skins for Adam and his wife, and clothed them" (Genesis 3:21). Adam and Eve were ashamed of their nakedness, and God had compassion on them. He clothed them so they would not feel ashamed and devoid of dignity.

MORAL BEHAVIOR: GENESIS 18

Our discussion of human dignity in the Bible continues with Genesis 18, in which God planned to wipe out all the inhabitants of Sodom and Gomorrah, good and bad, because of the iniquity of the society. Abraham felt empowered to speak with God and to argue on behalf of the good people in Sodom, because Abraham assumed that God had the same moral values as he. And God accepted Abraham as a partner in discussion and as one whose moral values should be honored:

> The men went on from there to Sodom, while Abraham remained standing before the LORD. Abraham came forward and said, "Will you sweep away the innocent along with the guilty? What if there should be fifty innocent within the city? Will you then wipe out the place and not forgive it for the sake of the innocent fifty who are in it? Far be it from you to do such a thing, to bring death upon the innocent as well as the guilty, so that innocent and guilty fare alike. Far be it from you! Shall not the judge of all the earth deal justly?" And the LORD answered, "If I find within the city of Sodom fifty innocent ones, I will forgive the whole place for their sake." (Genesis 18:22–26)

Abraham acts as a responsible, moral human being who is following God's command in Genesis 1. He confronts God on behalf of other human beings. God confirms Abraham's dignity by negotiating with him about the lives of the good inhabitants of an immoral community. Abraham expresses moral and spiritual values that were imbedded in him prior to God's revelation of the law to Moses.

These statements in Genesis 18 in support of universal human dignity are seminal. Abraham has a moral compass that precedes God's revelation at Sinai. He is willing to assert it before God and assumes that God, as the Creator of the universe, has the same moral compass. God accepts Abraham's challenge and negotiates with him. Abraham holds God accountable to the same moral standards that God holds for others when he asks God, "Shall not the judge of all the earth deal justly?" (Genesis 18:25). God agrees with Abraham and changes his intent in accordance with his commitment to Abraham. However, the culture of Sodom and Gomorrah fails to affirm human dignity; in those cities public sodomy and the debasing of women play out so strongly that God destroys the entire community, saving only Lot (who protected the visiting angels) and Lot's two daughters. It is interesting that God destroys Sodom and Gomorrah because the community practices consensual and forced sodomy. Even then, he creates a situation in which two of those he saved, Lot's two daughters, feel they must engage in incest with their father to produce children because no other men are available to them.

Some Talmudic scholars criticize God for destroying Sodom and Gomorrah. They argue that God promised Noah that he would never again wipe out humankind and that the flood of fire and brimstone that engulfed Sodom and Gomorrah was equivalent to the flood of water that wiped out all the inhabitants of the earth except Noah and his family. But the Bible nowhere indicates that Sodom and Gomorrah contained all of mankind. Their flood, fire and brimstone, wiped out a malevolent society. Fire and brimstone wiped out a malevolent community. Lot survived with God's help, as Noah survived with God's help. The story continues: "There being no men available, Lot's daughters made him drunk. Each slept with him and conceived a child." Human dignity proceeds in mysterious ways.

History also proceeds in mysterious ways. Ruth descended from Lot. King David descended from Ruth. The Messiah will descend from King David.

Moral Behavior: Job

The story of Job illustrates the importance to God of human dignity and honesty. Job refuses to compromise his own dignity in spite of many injustices that are inflicted on him by the devil with God's permission. God's purpose in testing Job is inscrutable. The plain reading of the text is that God wishes to prove to the devil, and perhaps to himself, that it is not Job's good fortune that causes him to honor God and to live an "upright" life. The devil causes Job to suffer serious personal misfortunes. Job's companions tell him that his misfortunes are punishment from God because Job has acted improperly. Job's wife tells him to blaspheme God and die. Job does not believe that he has acted improperly. He refuses to confess that he has acted improperly. And he refuses to blaspheme God. Job maintains his dignity and his personal integrity. Job prevails.

God agrees with Job that he has been punished unfairly, and God chastises Job's companions for telling Job that he is the cause of his own misfortunes. God asks Job to forgive his friends and to pray to God on their behalf. Job does this; God restores Job's fortunes and doubles them. *Job died old and contented.*

On Yom Kippur, the Day of Repentance, God forgives man for transgressions against him but not for transgressions against another. One must ask forgiveness from the person directly. In the book of Job, God instructs Job to pray for his friends who have wrongly accused him of acting improperly. In effect, God is forgiving them. Many Jews today during the ten days between Rosh Hashanah and Yom Kippur ask forgiveness of others for harm they might have committed against them. The story of Job[14] is uplifting. God's behavior is unfathomable.

> Job . . . was whole-hearted and upright, and one that feared God, and shunned evil. And there were born unto him seven sons and three daughters. His possessions also were seven thousand sheep, and three thousand camels, and five hundred yoke of oxen, and five hundred she-asses, and a very great household; so that this man was the greatest of all the children of the east. And his sons used to go and hold a feast in the house of each one upon his day; and they would send and invite their three sisters to eat and to drink with them. And it was so, when the days of their feasting were gone about, that Job sent and sanctified them, and

---

[14] *JPS Hebrew-English Tanakh.*

rose up early in the morning, and offered burnt-offerings according to the number of them all; for Job said: "It may be that my sons have sinned, and blasphemed God in their hearts." Thus did Job continually.

Now it fell upon a day, that the sons of God came to present themselves before the Lord, and Satan came also among them. And the Lord said unto Satan: "Whence comest thou?" Then Satan answered the Lord, and said: "From going to and fro in the earth, and from walking up and down in it." And the Lord said unto Satan: "Hast thou considered My servant Job, that there is none like him in the earth, a whole-hearted and an upright man, one that feareth God, and shunneth evil?" Then Satan answered the Lord, and said: "Doth Job fear God for nought? Hast not Thou made a hedge about him, and about his house, and about all that he hath, on every side? Thou hast blessed the work of his hands, and his possessions are increased in the land. But put forth Thy hand now, and touch all that he hath, surely he will blaspheme Thee to Thy face." And the Lord said unto Satan: "Behold, all that he hath is in thy power; only upon himself put not forth thy hand." So Satan went forth from the presence of the Lord. (Job 1:1–12)

So Satan went forth from the presence of the Lord, and smote Job with sore boils from the sole of his foot even unto his crown. And he took him a potsherd to scrape himself therewith; and he sat among the ashes. Then said his wife unto him: "Dost thou still hold fast thine integrity? blaspheme God, and die." But he said unto her: "Thou speakest as one of the impious women speaketh. What? shall we receive good at the hand of God, and shall we not receive evil?" For all this did not Job sin with his lips. (Job 2:7–10)

And it was so, that after the Lord had spoken these words unto Job, the Lord said to Eliphaz the Temanite: "My wrath is kindled against thee, and against thy two friends; for ye have not spoken of Me the thing that is right, as My servant Job hath. Now therefore, take unto you seven bullocks and seven rams, and go to My servant Job, and offer up for yourselves a burnt-offering; and My servant Job shall pray for you; for him will I accept, that I do not unto you aught unseemly; for ye have not spoken of Me the thing that is right, as my servant Job hath." So Eliphaz the Temanite and Bildad the Shuhite and Zophar the Naamathite went, and did according as the Lord commanded them; and the Lord accepted Job. And the Lord changed the fortune of Job, when he prayed for his friends; and the LORD gave Job twice as much as he had before. (Job 42:7–10)

IMMORAL BEHAVIOR: GENESIS 22

Genesis 22:1–19, the Akedah, in which Abraham follows God's request but not command to sacrifice Isaac, depicts Abraham with a different moral compass than in Genesis 18. In Genesis 22 Abraham is subservient to God and, consequently, through the lens of a Reform Jew, relinquishes his human dignity and moral responsibility. Traditional rabbinic and contemporary Orthodox Judaism regard an unwavering obedience to God's commandment as the ultimate ground of human dignity and moral responsibility.

Genesis 18, in which Abraham negotiates with God over saving the good inhabitants of Sodom, and Genesis 22, the Akedah, in which Abraham accepts without question God's request to sacrifice Isaac, express opposing paradigmatic religious-cum-ethical sensibilities in Judaism. Yet both are *the words of the living God.*

The Akedah, the sacrifice of Isaac, is one of the most compelling and most studied stories in the Bible. God speaks and Abraham gets up early in the morning to obey. Isaac does not speak in the story except in verse 7, nor does the Genesis narrative quote him speaking to his father after this episode. For many Orthodox Jews the Akedah is the paradigm of the proper relationship to God. For a Reform Jew, it is an aberration from the tradition's valorization of human life and human dignity.

HUMAN DIGNITY: HILLEL AND SHAMMAI

Hillel the Elder (ca. 110 BCE–10 CE), the founder of the House or School of Hillel, and Shammai (50 BCE – 30 CE), the founder of the House or School of Shammai, were direct opponents in the interpretation of the tradition. A plain reading of the text indicates that Hillel interpreted the text through a Reform frame of reference and with concern for human dignity. A plain reading of the texts indicates that Shammai had a frame of reference that was diametrically opposed to Hillel. He interpreted the texts through a conservative lens and without concern for the dignity of the prospective convert. A process for conversion to Judaism became essential after Ezra (480–440 BCE) declared that all men must divorce their wives if the wives were not born Jewish (Ezra 9–10). At that time, Jewish descent was patrilineal. The change from patrilineal to matrilineal descent developed during the period from Ezra to Hillel and Shammai. It became accepted practice during their time. The development of a process for conversion to Judaism also developed during this time. This practice became legal in the Second Temple period. It had become accepted practice prior to the time of Hillel and Shammai. Acceptance of the commandments was not stated as a condition for membership. Membership was assumed to carry with it acceptance of the practices and beliefs that were incumbent on all Jews.

The differing practices for conversion were illustrated by the renowned disputes between Hillel and Shammai. The major differences between them concerned acceptance of the Oral Law (i.e., the Talmud) and motivation.

Hillel the Elder is the paradigmatic example of a Jewish sage who privileges human dignity over other values. The most well known of the stories about him is one in which Hillel accepts a proselyte who is dismissive of the need to study and to understand Judaism much less to practice it. The prospective proselyte is dismissive of the process itself. In this story Hillel states his famous adage, "What is hateful to you, do not to your neighbor: that is the whole Torah, while the rest is the commentary thereof; go and learn it."[15] Hillel respects the dignity of the gentile, whereas Shammai, who often takes a more strict interpretation of the tradition, offends the gentile.

Two other well-known stories follow. In the second story Hillel converts a proselyte who does not believe in the foundation of halakhah, the Oral Law. In the third, Hillel converts a proselyte who openly states that his motivation is power and riches. In each case, Shammai, who is more conservative than Hillel, humiliates the proselyte by repulsing him, whereas Hillel maintains the dignity of the proselyte even while being provoked by him.

It is interesting to note that in the second story Shammai repulsed the proselyte "with the builder's cubit that was in his hand." At that time, Rabbis were not paid. They needed to work to provide for themselves and their families if they did not marry rich women. Maimonides (1135–1204)

---

[15] Jerusalem Talmud, Shabbat 31a. [Editor's note: At various points throughout the book, the author has quoted English translations of passages from the Jerusalem or the Babylonian Talmud found in various secondary sources. For a complete translation of the Jerusalem Talmud, readers are referred to *Schottenstein Edition Talmud Yerushalmi* (Rahway, NJ: Artscroll Mesorah Publications, 2005). For a translation of the Babylonian, see *Schottenstein Edition Talmud Bavli* (Rahway, NJ: Artscroll Mesorah Publications, 2007).]

worked as court physician to King Ferdinand II of Aragon and Queen Isabella of Spain. R. Akiva (50–135 CE) married a rich woman. It was an honor to the family if a daughter was married to a rabbi.

The second story involves the question of the authority of the Oral Torah, halakhah.

> Our rabbis taught: A certain heathen once came before Shammai and asked him, "How many Torahs have you?" "Two," he replied, "the Written Torah and the Oral Torah." "I believe you with respect to the Written, but not with respect to the Oral Torah: make me a proselyte on condition that you teach me the Written Torah [only]." [But] he scolded and repulsed him in anger. When he went before Hillel, he converted him. On the first day, he taught him, Aleph, Beth, Gimmel, Daleth [the first four letters of the Hebrew alphabet]; the following day he reversed [the order] to him. "But yesterday you did not teach them to me thus," he protested. "Must you then not rely upon me? Then rely upon me with respect to the Oral [Torah] too."[16]

The third story concerns a proselyte who intended to become rich by converting and then becoming the high priest.

> On another occasion it happened that a certain heathen was passing behind a House of Learning, when he heard the voice of a teacher reciting, "And these are the garments which they shall make; a breastplate, and an ephod." Said he, "For whom are these?" "For the High Priest," he was told. Then said that heathen to himself, "I will go and become a proselyte, that I may be appointed a High Priest." So he went before Shammai and said to him, "Make me a proselyte on condition that you appoint me a High Priest." But he repulsed him with the builder's cubit which was in his hand. He then went before Hillel, who converted him.[17]

The Sages said: Always should the disposition of man be pleasant with people.[18]

Hillel and Shammai react differently to the same request. Hillel's view

---

[16] Ibid.
[17] Ibid.
[18] Babylonian Talmud, Ketubbot 17a:30.

is followed in most cases described in the Talmud, but not in all cases. Both views are retained. Although Hillel and Shammai often interpret the Talmud differently, they discuss each other's views. Their children marry one another.

In many of the texts we have discussed there are two opposing viewpoints, sometimes more. Often in the tradition there are two opposing viewpoints, such as those of the Sadducees and the Pharisees or the paradigmatic texts concerning conversion *Yevamot* and *Demai*, which we will analyze later. It is likely that these viewpoints in their time were less clear, more nuanced, and heatedly debated within their constituencies. These viewpoints and the stories about them were selected and edited by redactors who lived in different times from ours with different cultures, experiences, and historical conditions. Yet the value of human dignity and of God's dignity is expressed clearly in all of them. In what follows, I will cite the Talmud and other canonical texts.

Rabbinic Responsibility for Human Dignity

In the following three stories about rabbis, the purpose of study and the responsibility to honor and dignify one's wife are primary issues in the first, and leadership and human dignity are primary issues in the second and third.

Obligation to a Wife
R. Rechumel constantly studies Torah on the roof of the yeshiva while his wife remains at home. One year he does not return home for Yom Kippur. His wife, despairing of him returning, begins to cry. As her tears fall, so does the roof upon which he studies. He falls to his death.[19]

Obligation to Intervene Personally
Kamza and Bar Kamza is a famous story of an event in Jerusalem that is said to have occurred during the Roman siege of the city. While Jerusalem was under siege, opposing Jewish sects were engaged in vicious internecine conflict. It is reported that each sect burned the other's stores of wheat. The rabbis were criticized for being compliant instead of exercising leadership to stop the destructive behavior. During this time, the rabbis in this text are portrayed as remaining indifferent to the other quarrel in the community.

[19] Babylonian Talmud, Ketubbot 17.

The following story illustrates their indifference to a clear affront to the dignity of Bar Kamza and their irresponsible deference to scruples about minor violations of halakhah. Criticism of their indifference and of their privileging a concern about minor violations of halakhah over concern for the welfare of the community is emphasized by an accusation that they were responsible for the fall of Jerusalem to the Romans in 80 CE, which led to the destruction of the Second Temple. The story of Kamza and Bar Kamza follows:

> The destruction of Jerusalem came through a Kamza and a Bar Kamza in this way. A certain man had a friend Kamza and an enemy Bar Kamza. He once made a party and said to his servant, Go and bring Kamza. The man went and brought Bar Kamza. When the man [who gave the party] found him there he said, See, you tell tales about me; what are you doing here? Get out. Said the other: Since I am here, let me stay, and I will pay you for whatever I eat and drink. He said, I won't. Then let me give you half the cost of the party. No, said the other. Then let me pay for the whole party. He still said, No, and he took him by the hand and put him out. Said the other, Since the Rabbis were sitting there and did not stop him, this shows that they agreed with him. I will go and inform against them, to the Government. He went and said to the Emperor, The Jews are rebelling against you. He said, How can I tell? He said to him: Send them an offering and see whether they will offer it [on the altar]. So he sent with him a fine calf. While on the way he made a blemish on its upper lip, or as some say on the white of its eye, in a place where we [Jews] count it a blemish but they do not. The Rabbis were inclined to offer it in order not to offend the Government. Said R. Zechariah b. Abkulas to them: People will say that blemished animals are offered on the altar. They then proposed to kill Bar Kamza so that he should not go and inform against them, but R. Zechariah b. Abkulas said to them, Is one who makes a blemish on consecrated animals to be put to death? R. Johanan thereupon remarked: Through the scrupulousness of R. Zechariah b. Abkulas our House has been destroyed, our Temple burnt and we ourselves exiled from our land.[20]

---

[20] Babylonian Talmud, Gittin 55b.

Obligation to Intervene Politically

In the preceding story, the rabbis remained silent while Bar Kamza was humiliated, and they privileged a concern about minor violations of halakhah over a concern for the welfare of the community. In this story, Vespasian, the future Roman emperor, criticized R. Yochanan ben Zakkai, the leading rabbi in Israel, for not intervening to stop the internecine warfare during the Roman siege of Jerusalem. R. Yochanan said that he could not control the *biryoni* (bandits). The Second Temple fell. Jerusalem fell.

This interchange is a strong criticism of the rabbis from both outside the tradition and within it. Vespasian, soon to become the Roman emperor, criticized the rabbis for their lacks of leadership in quelling the internal fighting. The story of Kamza and Bar Kamza criticizes them for their lack of concern for human dignity and for their strict interpretation of halakhah, which led to the fall of the temple and the fall of Jerusalem. A current Orthodox website disputes this story and states that R. ben Zakkai did all he could to stop the fighting.

CHAPTER 2

The Prooftext for the Rabbinic Conception of Human Dignity

The Oven of Aknai: A Plain Reading

The tensions between revelation and reason, between God's word and man's interpretation of his word, and between human dignity and rabbinic authority, are illustrated in The Oven of Aknai (Babylonian Talmud, Bava Metzi'a 59a–b). It is cited as the prooftext for Rabbinic Judaism's claim that *Torah is not in Heaven* and as the basis for this tradition's determination that henceforth halakhic[1] decisions will be decided by the majority (of rabbinic sages), not by God.

This narrative can be read not as a prooftext for rabbinic authority but as a warning against the excesses of rabbinic judicial power. Justice and mercy, two attributes of God, must be values that instruct rabbinic deliberation. The narrative can also be read to support the value of human dignity in the tradition and its application to halakhah. The mishnah, or section,[2] that contains this story begins by commenting on the previous section, which concerns proper conduct in commerce by both seller and buyer. Then it relates "overreaching in buying and selling" to "wrong done by words." It comments specifically on the proper conduct toward the son of a proselyte to Judaism. The gemara[3] that follows expands the plain

---

[1] In Judaism, *halakhah* (also spelled "halachah" or "halakah"; Hebrew: "the Way") refers the totality of laws and ordinances that have evolved since biblical times to regulate religious observances and the daily life and conduct of the Jewish people. Quite distinct from the law of the Pentateuch (the first five books of the Bible), halakhah purports to preserve and represent oral traditions stemming from the revelation on Mount Sinai or evolved on the basis of it. The legalistic nature of halakhah also sets it apart from those parts of rabbinic, or Talmudic, literature that include history, fables, and ethical teachings (haggadah). That halakhah existed from ancient times is confirmed from nonpentateuchal passages of the Bible, where, for example, servitude is mentioned as a legitimate penalty for unpaid debts (2 Kings 4:1).

[2] The Mishnah is a collection of writings. Within this collection, a single paragraph or section is called a mishnah (lowercase).

[3] The Gemara incorporates the analysis and commentary on the Mishnah. Within this collection, a single paragraph or section is called a gemara (lowercase).

meaning of the Mishnah through stories and through discussion between rabbinic sages. The Oven of Aknai is one of these stories.

Because The Oven of Aknai is considered by many to be the prooftext of Rabbinic Judaism and because halakha is the law and practices of Rabbinic Judaism, we will discuss this story at length, presenting different exegeses of the text viewed from within and from without the tradition. The frequent references to proselytes in the text prior to and after The Oven of Aknai make it reasonable to interpret the story as emphasizing the importance of respecting the dignity of proselytes. The consequences to R. Gamaliel of his undignified treatment of R. Eliezer make it reasonable to read the story as an admonition against hurting the dignity of the other. This admonition may be extended to the undignified treatment of God's word, even to the undignified treatment of God himself in the story. The text may be read in support of liberal Judaism, which values justice and mercy and prioritizes human dignity.

The Oven of Aknai begins with a reference to one who repents and one who is a proselyte. In both cases each has changed his previous condition and must learn to act differently in accordance with his new position, be it a repentant or a proselyte. The rabbis know that a change in behavior is difficult. Others may continue to act toward you as they did prior to the change. Others may resist the change because it requires them to act differently toward you.

> If a man was a repentant [sinner] one must not say to him, "Remember your former deeds." If he was a son of proselytes one must not taunt him, "Remember the deeds of your ancestors" because it is written, Thou shalt neither wrong a stranger nor oppress him.[4]
>
> Our Rabbis taught: He who wounds the feelings of a proselyte transgresses three negative injunctions, and he who oppresses him infringes two. Wherein does wronging differ? Because three negative injunctions are stated: Viz., Thou shalt not wrong a stranger [i.e., a proselyte], And if a stranger sojourn with thee in your land, ye shall not wrong him, and ye shall not therefore wrong each his fellowman, a proselyte being included in "fellowman." But for "oppression" also three are written, viz., and thou shalt not oppress him, Also thou shalt not oppress a stranger, and [If thou lend money to any of my people that is poor by thee,] thou shalt not be to him as a usurer which includes a proselyte! — But [say] both

---

[4] Babylonian Talmud, Bava Metz'ia 59a–b, quoting Exodus 22:21.

[are forbidden] by three [injunctions].[5]

It has been taught: R. Eliezer the Great said: Why did the Torah warn against [the wronging of] a proselyte in thirty-six, or as others say, in forty-six, places? Because he has a strong inclination to evil.[6] What is the meaning of the verse, Thou shalt neither wrong a stranger, nor oppress him; for ye were strangers in the land of Egypt? It has been taught: R. Nathan said: Do not taunt your neighbor with the blemish you yourself have. And thus the proverb runs: If there is a case of hanging in a man's family record, say not to him, "Hang this fish up for me."[7]

The Oven of Aknai is a weak prooftext for what is perhaps the most important authentication of Rabbinic Judaism. It can be read to indicate that God was displeased when, as reported by Elijah, he smiled and said, "My children have defeated me." It can be read to indicate that God was displeased with the decision of the Sages to "distance themselves" (ban, a form of excommunication) from R. Eliezer, the most learned of the sages. It was he, not R. Gamaliel, who, according to God, interpreted God's meaning correctly. The story concludes with the death of R. Gamaliel, the head of the sages, when R. Eliezer prayed to God about his suffering because of the ban imposed by R. Gamaliel. Although God permitted the sages to overrule his opinion, he did not permit them to humiliate and cause suffering to another human being with impunity.

The Full Text of The Oven of Aknai

The oven of Aknai was not constructed in a solid piece of clay. It was built by layers of clay that were separated by sand. R. Eliezer posited that because the oven was made of separate layers, it could not be unclean. The Sages declared that it was unclean because it was unified by the outer coating. God supported R. Eliezer's interpretation that the oven was clean. Both God and R. Eliezer were overruled by the sages.

We learnt elsewhere: If he cut it into separate tiles, placing sand between

---

[5] Ibid.
[6] Ambivalence toward proselytes is expressed throughout the Talmud. Welcoming proselytes predominates in most historical periods from 500 CE to the present.
[7] Babylonian Talmud, Bava Metzi'a 59a–b.

each tile: R. Eliezer declared it clean, and the Sages declared it unclean; and this was the oven of 'Aknai. Why [the oven of] 'Aknai? — Said Rab Judah in Samuel's name: [It means] that they encompassed it with arguments as a snake, and proved it unclean. It has been taught: On that day R. Eliezer brought forward every imaginable argument, but they did not accept them. Said he to them: "If the halachah agrees with me, let this carob-tree prove it!" Thereupon the carob-tree was torn a hundred cubits out of its place — others affirm, four hundred cubits. "No proof can be brought from a carob-tree," they retorted. Again he said to them: "If the halachah agrees with me, let the stream of water prove it!" Whereupon the stream of water flowed backwards — "No proof can be brought from a stream of water," they rejoined. Again he urged: "If the halachah agrees with me, let the walls of the schoolhouse prove it," whereupon the walls inclined to fall. But R. Joshua rebuked them, saying: "When scholars are engaged in a halachic dispute, what have ye to interfere?" Hence they did not fall, in honour of R. Joshua, nor did they resume the upright, in honour of R. Eliezer; and they are still standing thus inclined. Again he said to them: "If the halachah agrees with me, let it be proved from Heaven!" Whereupon a Heavenly Voice cried out: "Why do ye dispute with R. Eliezer, seeing that in all matters the halachah agrees with him!" But R. Joshua arose and exclaimed: "It is not in heaven." What did he mean by this? — Said R. Jeremiah: That the Torah had already been given at Mount Sinai; we pay no attention to a Heavenly Voice, because Thou hast long since written in the Torah at Mount Sinai, "After the majority must one incline."[8]

The prooftext for the determination that halakhah is decided by the majority ends here. However, the story does not. It continues:

R. Nathan met Elijah and asked him: What did the Holy One, Blessed be He, do in that hour? — He laughed [with joy], he replied, saying, "My sons have defeated Me, My sons have defeated Me." It was said: On that day all objects which R. Eliezer had declared clean were brought and burnt in fire. Then they took a vote and excommunicated him. Said they, "Who shall go and inform him?" "I will go," answered R. Akiba, "lest an unsuitable person go and inform him, and thus destroy

---

[8] Ibid.

the whole world."⁹ What did R. Akiba do? He donned black garments and wrapped himself in black and sat at a distance of four cubits from him. "Akiba," said R. Eliezer to him, "what has particularly happened to-day?" "Master," he replied, "it appears to me that thy companions hold aloof from thee." Thereupon he too rent his garments, put off his shoes, removed [his seat] and sat on the earth, whilst tears streamed from his eyes.¹⁰ The world was then smitten: a third of the olive crop, a third of the wheat, and a third of the barley crop. Some say, the dough in women's hands swelled up.

A Tanna taught: Great was the calamity that befell that day, for everything at which R. Eliezer cast his eyes was burned up. R. Gamaliel too was traveling in a ship, when a huge wave arose to drown him.¹¹ "It appears to me," he reflected, "that this is on account of none other but R. Eliezer b. Hyrcanus." Thereupon he arose and exclaimed, "Sovereign of the Universe! Thou knowest full well that I have not acted for my honour, nor for the honour of my paternal house, but for Thine, so that strife may not multiply in Israel!" At that the raging sea subsided.¹²

R. Gamaliel's statement seems to be a partial truth. His exercise of personal power to prevail over R. Eliezer is clear. As nasi, head of the Sanhedrin, the highest Jewish court of law, he may have thought it necessary to call upon the power of the Sanhedrin. However, it seems unnecessary for him to use his personal power to humiliate R. Eliezer and to destroy his life. His explanation of his action is accepted by for God for the moment. Perhaps God expects that his warning from the storm will induce R. Gamaliel to cancel the ban on R. Eliezer. Gamaliel, as nasi, is responsible for both justice and mercy in Israel. He is a role model for the community.

The story ends in tragedy. R. Eliezer's wife finally fails in her long efforts to prevent him from expressing his grief to God. R. Gamaliel, her brother and the brother-in-law of R. Eliezer, dies. The story can mean that R.

---

⁹ R. Akiba volunteers to inform R. Eliezer that he is excommunicated because he, R. Akiba, fears that the ban will result in the destruction of the world. R. Akiba thus implicitly respects R. Eliezer's dignity and has compassion for him, knowing the pain the ban will cause him. R. Akiba fears that an unsuitable person might seek to inform R. Eliezer of the ban. He seems to have thought that other members of the court were unsuitable persons. The excommunication of R. Eliezer and the destroying of all the items he declared clean support this interpretation.

¹⁰ The *derash*, the metaphorical reading, is that the tears in R. Eliezer's eyes stand for the waves that nearly engulf R. Gamaliel.

¹¹ This is a clear indication of God's displeasure.

¹² Babylonian Talmud, Bava Metzi'a 59a–b.

Gamaliel is punished for humiliating another human being. Human dignity is a metavalue in the story that is considered to be the prooftext for rabbinic authority, halakhah.

> Ima Shalom was R. Eliezer's wife, and sister to R. Gamaliel. From the time of this incident onwards she did not permit him to fall upon his face.[1] Now a certain day happened to be New Moon, but she mistook a full month for a defective one. Others say, a poor man came and stood at the door, and she took out some bread to him.[2] [On her return] she found him fallen on his face.[3] "Arise," she cried out to him, "thou hast slain my brother." In the meanwhile an announcement was made from the house of Rabban Gamaliel that he had died. "Whence dost thou know it?" he questioned her. "I have this tradition from my father's house: All gates are locked, excepting the gates of wounded feelings."[4]

Rabbinic Disputes and Their Resolution

R. Gamaliel,[5] who appears to be egotistic and ruthless, uses his power as head of the Sanhedrin to disgrace R. Eliezer, who, in turn, appears to be arrogant and stubborn.[6] The story describes a struggle between two rabbis, Gamaliel ostensibly struggling for power, Eliezer ostensibly for truth and

---

[1] The morning prayer of the Eighteen Benedictions is followed by time for a private prayer to God in which one prostrates oneself. R. Eliezer's wife feared that in his private prayer he would ask God for help and that God would punish her brother R. Gamaliel for causing grief to her husband, R. Eliezer.

[2] Consequentially, she did not prevent her husband from supplicating God.

[3] R. Eliezer had fallen on his face and was praying to God for relief from his suffering.

[4] Babylonian Talmud, Bava Metzi'a 59a–b. Ima Shalom knew from a tradition in her family that her brother would be punished if her husband asked God for help.

[5] R. Gamaliel, Ima Shalom's brother, was the nasi, the head of the Sanhedrin, the principal rabbinic court and the promulgator of the ban against R. Eliezer.

[6] The character of R. Eliezer is debated. He is thought to be stubborn and conceited because he refused to agree to the view of the majority. He is thought to be humble because he did not fight against the decision of the Sanhedrin. Perhaps he was both stubborn and conceited at times, humble at other times. The character of R. Gamaliel is also debated. He forced Joshua b. Hananiah to wear traveling clothes on the day that Hananiah thought to be Yom Kippur when Gamaliel declared another day to be Yom Kippur. However, when Hananiah came in traveler's clothes, Gamaliel greeted him warmly and thanked him for submitting to his, Gamaliel's, demand (Babylonian Talmud, Rosh Hashanah 25a–b; Sifre to Deuteronomy 38; Kiddushin 32b).

possibly prestige. It describes a rejection of the intent of God in the text (Exodus 22:21), perhaps even of the authority of God. R. Gamaliel humiliates R. Eliezer after defeating him in the Sanhedrin. R. Gamaliel's sister protects him for many years by ensuring that her husband, R. Eliezer, does not supplicate God and express the pain his ban is causing him. When R. Eliezer finally prays to God, R. Gamaliel dies.

The *Jewish Encyclopedia*'s entry (1906) on R. Gamaliel II expresses a favorable opinion of him and his conduct.

> The guiding principle in all of Gamaliel's actions is set forth in the words which he spoke on the occasion of his quarrel with Eliezer b. Hyrcanus (B. M. 59b): "Lord of the world, it is manifest and known to Thee that I have not done it for my own honor nor for that of my house, but for Thy honor, that factions may not increase in Israel." The ends which Gamaliel had in view were the abolition of old dissensions, the prevention of new quarrels, and the restoration of unity within Judaism. To attain these objects he consistently labored to strengthen the authority of the assembly at Jabneh as well as his own, and thus brought upon himself the suspicion of seeking his own glory. His greatest achievement was the termination of the opposition between the schools of Hillel and Shammai, which had survived even the destruction of the Temple.
>
> In Jabneh, says tradition (Jerusalem Talmud, Berkot. 3b; 'Eruvin. 13b), a voice from heaven (*"bat kol"*) was heard, which declared that, although the views of both schools were justifiable in principle (as "words of the living God"), in practice only the views of Hillel's school should be authoritative.[7]

R. Gamaliel is reported to have been proud that he was able to mediate successfully the disputes between the schools of Hillel and Shammai. He ignored the *bat kol*, the voice from heaven that announced that the decision of Eliezer was to be followed.

Disputes in the Jewish tradition are common. God's *bat kol* is common. Hillel welcomed the prospective proselytes. Shammai repulsed and humiliated them. The Talmud is in accordance with Hillel because he was humble and cited the opposing opinion before expressing his own. Hillel recognized the human dignity of the other and gave it precedence over the strict interpretation of the law.

[7] Bacher, "Gamaliel II."

Tension between Halakhah and Morality

The Oven of Aknai was aptly named The Oven of Snakes. Man and woman first encountered a snake in the garden of Eden. Eve and the snake conversed with one another. The snake employed specious reasoning to induce her and Adam to disobey God. Adam and Eve's punishment was expulsion from the garden of Eden. R. Gamaliel ignored God's *bat kol* and the dignity of God's creation, a human being. His punishment was death. The rabbis and the redactor are telling us that God and God's attributes must guide us as we humans attempt to interpret God's word and to follow God's word in our lives.

Arthur Cohen and Paul Mendes-Flohr point out the tension in halakhah between pure ethical principles and their use to guide action. "A living morality is not assessed as a system of values but, as Martin Buber has observed, in the way it determines an ought, and an ought not only in the here and now. Accordingly, the tension between halakhah and ethics does not originate in an extra-halakhic category but is prominent within the halakhah itself. This tension comes to the fore when concrete halakhot are formulated."[8] Many of the texts we will explore in this book attest to the tension within halakhah between morality and halakhah. This tension becomes more pronounced when the tradition encounters the metavalue of human dignity in the outside world, as it has since the Enlightenment and the emancipation of Jews in Europe. We will discuss this tension when we examine the history of conversion.

A Criticism of Rabbi Eliezer

One creative interpretation of The Oven of Aknai is in the form of *derash*, a sermon, that likens the oven, which is constructed from shattered pieces of pottery, to a life that has been shattered and needs to be rebuilt. The exegesis of R. Amichai Lau-Lavie of New York is an example of the use of associative thought in interpretation. It is not intended to be a legal argument, but instead a lesson in human conduct. It is also an apology for the rabbis and a forceful ad hominem attack on R. Eliezer. The author substitutes rhetoric for logic, using an interpretation by Maimonides that is congruent with that of the Sages. Maimonides' logic is no more convincing

---

[8] Cohen and Mendes-Flohr, *20th Century Jewish Religious Thought*, 202.

than theirs, but that is because in this interpretation, R. Lau-Lavie uses the text as the basis for a *derash*, a sermon. He does not analyze Eliezer's claim that the oven of Aknai is not impure. Instead, he criticizes R. Eliezer's character as the basis for a lesson on repairing a broken life.[9]

The Miracles as Metaphors for Great Sages

Marcus Lehmann, in his book *Akiva*, interprets two of the miracles that R. Eliezer produces as metaphors for the decisions of two great rabbis who both were pupils of R. Yochanai ben Zakkai, himself a pupil of Hillel the Elder.[10] The third miracle of the walls of the schoolhouse is a metaphor for the pupils themselves. The miracles are described as allegories in an exegesis in the form of *remez* (hints).

> There was a certain oven — called Achnai's oven — that these Sages differed about. Rabbi Eliezer considered that oven to be like a building, and held the halachic opinion that it was not susceptible to impurity. His colleagues however, considered it to be like an earthenware vessel, and thus they believed that it could become impure. It was a heated discussion, and although Rabbi Eliezer supported his view with a wealth of arguments and proofs, the other Rabbis refused to change their minds. At this point Rabbi Eliezer said, "If my authority is not enough for you, then let 'the Charuv' ('the Carob Tree') decide!"
>
> "The Charuv" was a name which people used for Rabbi Chanina ben Dosa, who was one of the most renowned men of his time. He was so poor that he lived solely off the fruit of his carob tree (carob trees were quite common in Eretz Yisrael). He too had been a disciple of Rabban Yochanan ben Zakkai. He was a great tzaddik, and God had often answered his prayers in a miraculous manner. So highly esteemed was

---

[9] Lau-Lavie, "'Like a Broken Potsherd'"; see also *Doroth* 1, no. 5 (n.d.): 374.

[10] R. ben Zakkai escaped from Jerusalem during its fall and the fall of the Second Temple in 70 CE and asked the soon-to-be Roman emperor Titus for permission to found a rabbinic school in Yavneh, Israel. Titus criticized him and his fellow rabbis for failing to quell the internecine warfare among the Jews. Titus did not accept ben Zakkai's excuse that he did all he could to stop the warfare.

The school of Hillel was more lenient in its decisions and more concerned with human dignity than the school of Shammai. Those who studied under Hillel would be likely to emphasize human dignity. These rabbis, including R. Akiva, supported R. Eliezer in his more lenient decision on the purity of the oven of Aknai.

he that even his teacher, Rabban Yochanan ben Zakkai, once asked him to pray for his son, who was very ill at the time. And God answered his prayer and Rabban Yochanan ben Zakkai's son recovered.

Now Rabbi Eliezer called for him, so that he should voice his opinion on the disputed matter. And the result was that the great and celebrated Rabbi Chanina ben Dosa agreed with Rabbi Eliezer! But Rabbi Eliezer's colleagues still held firmly to their view.

So Rabbi Eliezer said, "If our authority is insufficient, then let 'the Brook' decide!"

"The Brook" was the nickname of Rabbi Elazar ben Arach, one of the most distinguished Sages of his time. His teacher, Rabban Yochanan ben Zakkai, had compared him to a powerful spring that gathers force and turns into a strong, flowing brook. He favored his sayings over those of all his other students. He also said of him, "If all of Israel's Sages were measured in greatness against Elazar ben Arach (even if Rabbi Eliezer ben Hurkanos would be counted among them), he would take first place over all of them."

When Rabban Yochanan ben Zakkai died, Rabbi Elazar had moved to Emmaus. He expected all his companions to follow him there, but they did not. Then he thought of moving to Yavneh, but his wife, who was very proud of him, felt that it was beneath his dignity to do so if the other scholars had not followed him to Emmaus. Because they remained in Emmaus Rabbi Elazar hadn't participated in the study sessions in Yavneh for many years. Now Rabbi Eliezer called for him, and he too decided like Rabbi Eliezer. But the Sages still refused to accept Rabbi Eliezer's decision.

Rabbi Eliezer then proposed the following challenge: "If you really insist on the rule of the majority, then let 'the walls of the beit midrash' decide!"

What are "the walls of the beit midrash"? They are the pupils (the future teachers), who lend purpose and structure to the house of learning. So the pupils who were present stood up and they too confirmed Rabbi Eliezer's view. In reaction to this, Rabbi Yehoshua told them sharply, "My dear pupils, you are still too young and immature to join this debate!" So they remained silent. They no longer dared to take part in their elders' controversy.

Rabbi Eliezer now stood up and said, "So let it be decided from Above!"

And God accepted his appeal. Without delay He sent the Prophet

Eliyahu, who said to the Sages: "Why are you fighting against Rabbi Eliezer? He is always right in his rulings!"

Rabbi Yehoshua stood up and replied, "It says in the Torah: 'The Torah is not in Heaven.' The Torah was given to us by God at Mount Sinai, and in it we find the precept that decisions shall be made according to majority rule!"[11]

R. Eliezer's ruling that the oven is pure because it is similar to a building and that a building cannot become impure is supported by the great scholars he enlists. Although these scholars were pious, they did not represent the political mainstream. Consequently their rulings are unlikely to be affected by ulterior motives. In order to protect the assets of an owner and of Israel, they will likely relate positively to rulings such as that a building cannot become impure.

"Rabbi Chanina ben Dosa, The Charuv, was thought to have miraculous power. 'God had often answered his prayers in a miraculous manner.' His sustenance was a carob tree. The carob tree near the deliberations about the Oven of Aknai flew '100 or 400 cubits' in support of Rabbi Eliezer." Some commentators say that the uncertainty about the distance indicates the faultiness of memory, and therefore they question the validity of the event. I lean toward the view that the flight of the carob tree indicates the support of nature, perhaps through heavenly intervention. R. Elazar ben Arach's history illustrates the importance of dignity to the rabbis and is an example of how they were willing to pay a high price to maintain their personal sense of dignity.

The students, a metaphor for the walls of the *beit midrash*, are unlikely to have a political motivation that influences their interpretation. They may wish to support their teacher. They may wish to express what they have been taught. The leaning walls reflect the uncertain motivations and the different interpretations of the tradition. There are many truths in Judaism. Humans are not infallible in interpreting God's word and are incapable of knowing his intent. A *bat kol*, voice from heaven, is thought to express his intent.

[11] Babylonian Talmud, Baba Metzi'a 59b:4.

Through the Lens of American Jurisprudence

American jurisprudence provides an illuminating lens for analyzing Talmudic texts. David Luban, a professor at the Georgetown University Law Center, provides such a lens. He published in 2004 in the *Chicago-Kent Law Review* a thoughtful analysis of The Oven of Aknai. It was republished in 2010 by the Georgetown University Law Center.

Luban's concern with his ability to understand Talmudic texts is worth noting. In the article he expresses reservations about his ability to understand Talmudic texts because he is not a part of the Orthodox community that lives them. He quotes Wittgenstein: "To imagine a language is to imagine a form of life."[12] Luban explains this to mean that "those within the tradition understand that the story's real meaning is for members only. It does not disclose itself to modernist readers who privilege their own one-on-one relationship to the printed text over the many-on-many relationships between texts and readers that makes up the form of life the text itself celebrates."[13] Contrary to Luban, one need not privilege the leading rabbinic voices of halakhah as the only ones who are in the position to express the most accurate or authoritative analysis of the tradition. Their lens is restricted; and, like all human beings, they have a viewpoint that influences the topics they choose to examine, the texts they select, and the conclusions they reach.

Luban's review of the text leads him to a conclusion that is congruent with the argument in this thesis: "Viewed through the lens of its Talmudic content, the focal point of the Oven of Aknai fable in not the nature of legal authority, but rather the humiliation of Eliezer." Humiliation is the denial of human dignity. "Oral Law cannot really understand the basic texts of Judaism, any more than someone who has studied every line of the U.S. Constitution but knows nothing of Supreme Court cases can really understand constitutional law. Unable to trace the lineage of my reading back in an unbroken chain to Moses, I am not really a reader in the only sense the tradition takes seriously."[14]

A fascinating story about Moses and God indicates that the line of belief that Luban postulates to be a straight line may not be that straight because the interpretation of the law changes with each generation. After several generations, the law may be unrecognizable to those in later generations. The

---

[12] Wittgenstein, *Philosophical Investigations*, 198E.
[13] Luban, "Coiled Serpent of Argument," 1287.
[14] Ibid., 1282.

following story of Moses, who is seated in the last row of a *beit midrash*, a school in which the Talmud is studied, illustrates the differences in interpretation in succeeding generations.

> Rabbi Yehudah said, "Rav said, 'When Moshe ascended to the heavens, he found the Holy One, Blessed be He, sitting and attaching crowns to the letters. He said before Him, "Master of the Universe! Who is staying your hand?"
>
> He said to him, "There is one man who will exist after many generations, and Akiva the son of Yosef is his name, who will in the future expound on every crown and crown piles and piles of laws."
>
> He said before Him, "Master of the Universe! Show him to me."
>
> He said to him, "Turn backwards."
>
> He went and sat at the end of eight rows [of students in Rabbi Akiva's Beit Midrash], and he did not know what they were talking [about]. He got upset. As soon as he got to one [other] thing, his students said to him, "Our teacher, from where do you learn this?"
>
> He said to them, "It is a law [that was taught] to Moshe at Sinai."
>
> He calmed down. He returned and came before the Holy One, Blessed be He, and said before Him, "Master of the Universe! You have a man like this, and You are giving the Torah through me?"
>
> He said to Him, "Be silent. This is what I have decided."
>
> He said before Him, "Master of the Universe! You have shown me his Torah; show me his reward."
>
> He said to him, "Turn backwards." He turned backwards, and saw that they were tearing his skin with iron combs.
>
> He said before Him, "Master of the Universe! Such Torah, and such reward!"
>
> He said to him, "Be silent. This is what I have decided."'"[15]

---

[15] Babylonian Talmud, Menahot 29b.

CHAPTER 3

Social Mitzvot and Human Dignity Prevail

Daniel Sperber,[1] an Orthodox rabbi and professor at Bar-Ilan University, argues in his book *On the Relationship of Mitzvot between Man and His Neighbor and Man and His Maker* (2014), that in halakhah, social mitzvot, in which human dignity is embedded, take precedence over ritual mitzvot. This book follows two earlier books by Sperber. He writes that he sought in the earlier books,

> among other things to demonstrate that there are very basic ethical values that for what we might call a conceptual bedrock upon which our halachah is based, values, such as the dignity of the individual, the sanctity of life, the positive nature of mitzvot, and the foundational notion of moral rectitude. In a sense, this volume continues this theme, examining the relationship between the two major categories of mitzvot: social ones, or perhaps we should call them interpersonal ones; and ritual ones—otherwise formulated as mitzvot between man and his neighbor, and mitzvot between man and his Maker. I would seek to prove that there is a hierarchic distinction between them, in which the social mitzvot have a degree of superiority over the ritual ones.[2] And although classical rabbinic literature does not have a clear and systematic theology, or even a philosophy of halachah, there is sufficient evidence in the sources to enable us to reconstruct, or perhaps more correctly to uncover, such key principles.[3]

This book by a distinguished Orthodox scholar is written from within the Orthodox tradition and the halakic system even though it supports universal over particular values and is critical of current Orthodox thought. It supports the precedence of human dignity inherent in what Sperber calls

---

[1] R. Sperber is the Milan Roven Professor of Talmud at Bar-Ilan University in Israel, where he is also the president of the Ludwig and Erica Jesselson Institute for Advanced Torah Studies. He also serves as rabbi of Menachem Zion Synagogue in the Old City of Jerusalem. In 2010, Rabbi Sperber accepted an appointment as honorary chancellor of the Canadian Yeshiva & Rabbinical School in Toronto.
[2] Sperber, *On the Relationship of Mitzvot*, 9.
[3] Ibid.

social or interpersonal mitzvot — obligations between man and man — over ritual mitzvot.[4]

Sperber regards human dignity as a metavalue in halakhah. He begins and ends the book with quotations that support his basic premise that social mitzvot, those that concern one's fellow human beings, take precedence over ritual mitzvot, those appertain directly to one's relation to God.

R. Sperber prefaces his book with several quotations that emphasize the priority of dealing faithfully with one's fellow. Here are two.

> When man appears before the throne of Judgment, the first question he is asked is not "Did you believe in God?" or "Did you pray and observe the rituals?" He is asked: "Have you dealt honorably and faithfully in all your dealings with your fellow man? (BT Shabbat 31a)

> The Besht (the Bal Shem Tov [1700–1760], Master of the Good Name, who founded Hasidic Judaism) was the first to proclaim for all to hear: The way to heaven leads through the world; the way to divine reward leads through human commitment; the way to God leads through your fellow man.[5]

Eugene Korn's review of Sperber's book concludes with a reflection on contemporary orthodoxy in Israel: "Orthodoxy's current pan-halakhism [deemed as primarily concerned with ritual] seems to have lost interest in the human condition per se, and is rapidly losing the language to discuss universal human concerns like ethics, justice, spirituality and human purpose."[6] This observation is exemplified in the first text cited in the book. It a chilling story (Babylonian Talmud, Yoma 23a) in which mitzvot between God and man take precedence over mitzvot between man and man. The characters are blind to universal moral values. In this enactment of halakic values, a father exhibits no concern over the impending death of his son. He is concerned only with the ritual purity of the knife that entered his son's heart. The father tells his son's assassin that there is still time for him to atone for the murder of his son by making the knife ritually pure.

Sperber writes that this shocking story reflects a scale of priorities that

---

[4] Ibid.
[5] Wiesel, *Somewhere a Master*, 150, quoted in Sperber, *On the Relationship of Mitzvot*, 6.
[6] Korn, review of *On the Relationship of Mitzvot*, 3, quoted in Sperber, *On the Relationship of Mitzvot*, 192.

is not uncommon in certain sectors of Jewish religious society. Here is the story.

> It once happened that there were two Cohanim [priests] who had equal rights [rights to carry out a sacrifice], and they were running up the gangway [to the altar]. One of them got ahead of his fellow by within four cubits, and he took a knife and stabbed it into his fellow-Cohen's heart. . . .
> The father of the young Cohen came and found his son convulsing. He said: May he be your atonement, for my son is still convulsing (i.e. still alive), and the knife has not been made ritually pure. To teach you that the purity of [Temple] vessels was more serious for them than bloodshed.[7]

The Bible and Natural Law

Sperber begins his argument in the first section of his study, "Halachic Theory," in which he supports social mitzvot over halachic mitzvot, citing a famous *sugya* (an elaboration of a mishnaic text) at the end of Babylonian Talmud, Masechet Makkot 2:4a in which the 613 commandments, mitzvot, were limited progressively because there were progressively fewer righteous people who could manage the "yoke of many mitzvot." He points out that when the Talmud enumerates these mitzvot of highest priority, it does so based on biblical verses. This is significant to Sperber's argument, because biblical verses take priority over rabbinic laws. In other words, he moves from an internal discussion within halakhah to a discussion within the tradition in which halakhah, with its particular values, is one component and the Bible, with its universal values, is another component that takes precedence over halakhah.

Sperber concludes his argument in the final chapter of "Halachic Theory," entitled "On the Primal Nature of '*Derech Eretz*,'" in which he quotes the Maharal of Prague (R. Judah Loew, 1520–1609: "Derech eretz (natural law) came before Torah, and it is impossible to read a Torah situation without derech eretz."[8] In this statement, the Maharal of Prague moves beyond the particular values in halakhah to the universal values of natural law. We

---

[7] Sperber, *On the Relationship of Mitzvot*, 13.
[8] Ibid., 142.

will elaborate on this after following Sperber's argument.

After citing the story of the young Cohan who kills another to be the first to reach the altar to worship God, Sperber writes about the progressive reduction of the original 613 commandments to one. He notes the following:

> The Talmud selects the *mitzvot of highest priority, it does so basing itself on biblical verses.*
> Thus King David's list is to be found in Psalms 15:
> Lord, who shall abide in Thy tabernacle? Who shall dwell in Thy holy hill?
> 2. (1) He that walketh uprightly, and (2) worketh righteousness, and (3) speaketh the truth in his heart.
> 3. (4) He that backbiteth not with his tongue, nor (5) doeth evil to his neighbor, nor (6) taketh up reproach against his neighbor.
> The Talmud then gives examples of individuals who in their behavior characterize each of these principles. When he states Isaiah's six principles, he is quoting Isaiah 33:15.
> 15. (1) He that walketh righteously, (2) and speaketh uprightly; (3) he that despiseth the gain of oppressions, (4) that shaketh his hands from holding of bribes, (5) that stoppeth his ears from hearing of blood; (6) and shutteth his eyes from evil . . . [16. He shall dwell on high . . .]

[Sperber writes,] And when we come to Micah, we are referred to Micah 6:8: He hath shewed thee, O man, what is good, and what doth the Lord require of thee, but (1) to do justly, (2) and to love mercy, (3) and to walk humbly with thy God.

[Sperber writes,] And returning again to Isaiah, we are referred to Isaiah 56:1: Thus saith the Lord, (1) keep ye judgment, (2) and do justice, [for thy salvation is near to come, and My righteousness to be revealed].

[Sperber writes,] And finally Habakuk came and reduced it to one single commandment, as is said in Habakuk 2:4: . . . but the just shall live by his faith.[9]

Sperber interprets walking humbly with God as being humble before hu-

---

[9] Ibid., 15.

man beings. The final statement,

> "the just shall live by his faith" [Habakkuk 2:4], is best understood in the context of that whole chapter, in which the prophet rails against the evils that men do.
> 5. Yea also, because he trangresseth by wine.
> 9. Woe to him that coveteth an evil covetousness to his house.[10]

Sperber points out that the mitzvot listed are of primal importance, yet no mitzvot of a ritual nature, or those between man and God, are listed. He then points out that in most situations if one is engaged in performing a mitzvah, one is exempt from performing another. However, one who is engaged in a mitzvah between man and God is not exempt from performing a mitzvah with another person. Moral action toward a fellow man takes precedence over moral action toward God. Sperber reminds us that this principle does not apply to mitzvot that are of biblical authority, because these mitzvot always take precedence over those mitzvot that are of rabbinic authority.

Sperber concludes the first chapter, "Two Categories of Mitzvot," with a quotation from R. Shimon bar Yohai in Jerusalem Talmud, Pe'ah 1:1:

> R. Shimon bar Yohai said, "Honoring one's father and mother is of such great importance that the Holy One blessed be He preferred it over his own honor. It said, "Honor thy father and thy mother" (Exodus 20:12), and it is said, "Honor the Lord with thy substance" (Proverbs 3:9). With what do you honor Him? With that with which He graced you. You separate gleanings, the corner of the field, the various tithes . . . , you make a sukkah, [take] a lulav, a shofar, tefillin and tzitzit,[11] and feed the poor and the hungry and give drink to the thirsty. [All this] if

---

[10] Ibid.

[11] A *sukkah* is a temporary, hut-like structure partly roofed with branches, used as a ritual dwelling space by Jews in celebrating Sukkot, the gathering of the harvest. A *lulav* is a bundle containing a palm frond, two willow branches, and three myrtle branches that is ceremonially waved during the celebration of Sukkot. A *shofar* is ram's horn that has been hollowed out and is blown like a trumpet during Rosh Hashanah services and at the end of Yom Kippur. Tefillin, or phylacteries, are a set of small black leather boxes containing scrolls of parchment inscribed with verses from the Torah. They are worn by observant adult Jews during weekday morning prayers; historically and traditionally, this is a male obligation, and thus, only males within Orthodox Judaism perform this mitzvah, or commandment. *Tzitzit* are tassels that hang down from the four corners of a rectangular garment, especially from a talit, a prayer shawl.

you have [the wherewithal] you are obligated to do. But if you do not have the means, you are not obligated to any one of them. But when it comes to honoring one's father and mother, whether you have the means or no, you [are obligated] to honor your parent, even if you have to go begging at the doors.[12]

... One's duty toward one's parents overrides many *mitzvot* of a ritual nature, i.e. those which are God directed.[13]

CHARITY: SHARING GOD'S PROVIDENCE

Another example of social *mitzvot*'s preeminence over ritual *mitzvot* appears in Maimonides' interpretation of Leviticus 23:10–16, in which he overrules Rashi (1040–1105) and states that the mitzvah of the *omer*—in which a sheaf of new wheat, a symbol of the firstfruits of the harvest, is placed on the altar as a gift for God—does not supersede obligations to the poor as stated in Leviticus 23:22: "And when ye reap the harvest of your land, thou shalt not make clean riddance of the corners of thy fields when thou reapest, neither shalt thou gather the gleanings of thy harvest; thou shalt leave them unto the poor and to the stranger: I am the Lord your God."[14] This succinct command in Leviticus is the basis for the development in the Jewish tradition of elaborate systems of caring for the poor and at the same time protecting their dignity. The corners of the field, the *pe'ah*,[15] of the landowners, and the rich are not harvested, so that the poor, without asking, may enter the field and take the produce that remains. The field is not harvested a second time, so that the produce remaining after the first harvest is available for the poor. Even the *mitzvah* of gathering the *omer*,[16] the sheaves from the firstfruits of the harvest that are presented to God, does not supersede this prohibition. Maimonides wrote about Leviticus 23:22:

"The Ramban [Maimonides] states that 'you should not reap the corner

---

[12] Sperber, *On the Relationship of Mitzvot*, 18.
[13] Ibid.
[14] Ibid., 27.
[15] *Pe'ah* also means the sideburns that Orthodox men wear and do not cut.
[16] *Omer* also refers to counting each day from the second day of Passover to the first day of Shavuot. Shavuot is the festival that celebrates the gathering of the harvest and the giving of the Torah by God to Israel at Mount Sinai.

of your field for the omer, nor glean the gleanings,' meaning that the mitzvah [of the omer] does not supersede those prohibitions."[17] Fruit trees and other agricultural products are assumed to be included in the same commandment and are fulfilled in a similar manner.

It is said in Deuteronomy 15:11, "For the poor shall never leave out of the land: therefore I command thee, saying 'Thou shalt open thine hand wide unto thy brother, to the poor, and to thy needy, in thy land.'" Poverty is considered to be a condition that will befall some Jews. There will always be those who will need assistance, some temporarily, some permanently. This is not considered an abnormal condition in society. The dignity of the poor is not diminished because they are poor. They are entitled to share in God's sustenance along with all humans. The fruit of the land comes from God, who created all mankind and whose loving-kindness extends to all the earth.

There will be those who choose to beg even if help is available from the community. They are entitled to support themselves through begging. Recall that in the story The Oven of Aknai one of the explanations for Rabbi Eliezer finally being able to supplicate God is that his wife, who previously had prevented him for doing so, was distracted by a beggar at the door.

In Judaism, charity must be given in accordance with the dignity of the recipient. A person accustomed to a rich table is given richer food than one who is unaccustomed to rich fare. Hillel is said to have pulled for two miles the vehicle of a previously distinguished person who had become poor.

Ethical Mitzvot Have Precedence over Ritual Mitzvot

A person is not exempt from performing a mitzvah for another person even when he is engaged in performing a ritual mitzvah; when engaged in a mitzvah between man and his Maker, one is not exempt from a mitzvah between oneself and one's fellow human being.[18] In support of this position, Sperber points to the difference between mitzvah of biblical authority and

---

[17] Sperber, *On the Relationship of Mitzvot*, 27.
[18] Plotzky, in his classic *Kli Hemdah*, commenting on Deuteronomy 25:26 (section 5, subsection 4), cited in Sperber, *On the Relationship of Mitzvot*, 17.

those of rabbinic authority. Among the former, as previously noted, are honoring one's father and mother and providing for the poor; these mitzvot must be performed before the gathering of the omer — the offering to God of the firstfruits — and also take precedence over rabbinic mitzvah. Throughout this book my support for the precedence of human dignity and my focus on the dignity of the convert are of biblical authority, not halakic authority, even though I posit that human dignity is a metavalue in halakhah. The absence of human dignity often causes human suffering, as in The Oven of Aknai.

Communal Affairs Have Priority over Ritual Obligations

Work on communal affairs, those concerning people, takes precedence over liturgical prayer:

> Said R. Yehudah: Once I was walking after R. Akiva and R. Elazar ben Azaria, and it was time to say the Shema, and I thought they had given up on saying it. But [then I realized] that they had been involved in communal affairs.[19]

> Said R. Elazar be-R. Tzadok: When Rabban Gamliel and his court at Yavneh were involved in communal affairs, he would not interrupt [for prayer], so as not to confuse his thoughts.[20]

Sperber writes about a complicated halakic situation in which he concludes that "God only requires of a person that which he can carry out. But when dealing with a mitzvah relating to one's fellow human, such as paying a debt, or building a protective fence (*maakeh*) on the roof, etc., who would suggest that one who was unable to do so at a given time is exempt in the future! Clearly he has to find another opportunity to fulfill his social obligations."[21] Ritual obligations may be postponed or omitted. Obligations to human beings may be delayed, but they must be fulfilled at some time.

---

[19] Tosefta Berakhot 1:2 (ed. Lieberman, p. 2), cited in Sperber, *On the Relationship of Mitzvot*, 28.
[20] Cf. Babylonian Talmud, Berakhot 11a, cited in Sperber, *On the Relationship of Mitzvot*, 28.
[21] Sperber, *On the Relationship of Mitzvot*, 29.

Sins against God and Sins against One's Fellow

Sperber discusses Yom Kippur, in which sins against God are forgiven but sins against others are not forgiven. Sins against others must be forgiven by those against whom the sin was committed. Maimonides states that one must ask for forgiveness three times and that if the person against whom one sinned will not grant forgiveness, then the person who refuses to forgive has sinned and the initial perpetrator of the sin is forgiven: "Sins between man and his Maker Yom ha-Kippurim atones; sins between man and his fellow Yom ha-Kippurim does not atone until he appeases his fellow."[22]

Deeds Are More Important than Wisdom

Sperber quotes a well-known pronouncement by R. Haninah ben Dosa (Mishnah Avot 3:12)[23] asserting that deeds are more important than wisdom. In this quotation, Sperber relates deeds to social mitzvot and relates *hochmah* (learning or wisdom) to Torah: "He [Rabbi Haninah] used to say: He whose deeds exceed his wisdom, his wisdom endures; but he whose wisdom exceeds his deeds, his wisdom does not endure."[24] Sperber elaborates on this thought through an interpretation by R. Yitzhak Abohab in his commentary to Avot: "The explanation: He whose deeds exceed his wisdom—meaning: when a person's moral behavior and the honesty of his relationship with others, such as in business transactions, come first, his wisdom will endure. But if a person studies but is not honest in his business transactions, . . . then his wisdom (i.e., his study [of Torah]) will not endure."[25] Sperber further mentions a comment by his grandfather, a distinguished rabbinic scholar, on a verse in Avot 3:11 that expresses the same thought about the importance of one's actions toward other human beings. "He in whom the spirit of mankind finds pleasure, in him the spirit of God finds pleasure; but he in whom the spirit of mankind finds no pleasure, in him the spirit of God finds no pleasure."[26]

---

[22] Ibid., 32.
[23] Avot is commonly known as The Ethics of the Fathers.
[24] Sperber, *On the Relationship of Mitzvot*, 36.
[25] Spiegel, *Magen Elohim*, 168 (2014 ed.), cited in Sperber, *On the Relationship of Mitzvot*, 36.
[26] Sperber, *On the Relationship of Mitzvot*, 36.

Strict and Lenient Rulings in Halakhah

Sperber relates a fascinating story about a controversy over declaring meat kosher or nonkosher that took place in Poland before the High Holidays (Rosh Hashanah and Yom Kippur). If the meat—in this case the lungs—was declared nonkosher, a poor slaughterer would lose a large sum of money and poor Jews could not afford to buy meat for the holiday because the better cuts were too expensive for them. The Rema[27] and members of the Beit Din (rabbinic court) decided to rule that the meat was not kosher. R. Avraham Abush searched for a way to argue against the Rema and the highest Jewish authorities in Poland so that he could declare that the meat was kosher. His argument is intriguing:

> I prefer at the end of my days when I come [before the Heavenly Court] to argue my case with the Rema and his colleagues, rather than with this poor slaughterer. The slaughterer is a simple man, and it will be very difficult for me to argue my case with him before the Heavenly Court if he brings me to court claiming that I declared his animal *treif* [not kosher], and that in doing so I caused him great monetary loss,[7] and that I damaged his business on the eve of the festival. But I am sure that when I lay out my arguments before the Rema and his colleagues, we will reach an agreement.[28]

R. Sperber in 2010 asked an esteemed rabbinic colleague to interpret this text. He responded,

> Both the slaughterer and the Rabbi were caring for the poor, they were concerned about *Mitzvot she-Bein Adam le-Havero* [mitzvot between a person and fellow human beings] as well as the *Mitzvot Bein Adam la-Makom* [mitzvot between a person and God]. The lung is one of the least desirable organs for a butcher, generally sold to the poor. The strict rendition of *treif*, the slaughterer argued, would make all the poor who rely on this meat not to have the ability to celebrate the holiday with a little meat, making the poor unnecessary anguish, before *Yom Tov* [a holiday]. Therefore, the Rabbi who recognized the potential anguish

---

[27] R. Moses Isserles (1530–72), celebrated for his learning; he was appointed chief rabbi of Krakow, Poland, at age nineteen.
[28] Sperber, *On the Relationship of Mitzvot*, 42.

of the poor not having cheap meat for *Yom Tov* as well as the greater monetary loss required of them to purchase cleaner portions of the meat, rendered a lenient *psak* (rabbinic decision) predicated on the *shitah* [ritual slaughter as prescribed by halachah]. There is a double consideration of *Kevod Ha Beriyot* [human dignity].[29]

Sperber adds that there is a misconception about ruling stringently in order to avoid permitting what is halakically forbidden. In contradistinction to this, he quotes the Rosh Rabbi Asher ben Jahiel (1250–1328): "And he who rules forbidding something must bring clear and strong evidence, for the Torah was concerned for the property of Israel."[30] An incorrect ruling is, according to halakhah, a sin against God. The rabbi can atone for his sin on Yom Kippur, and he will be forgiven. However, if he rules against the slaughterer and causes himself and his clients monetary loss and the loss of the dignity of eating meat on a holiday, he is not forgiven by God. He must ask forgiveness of the slaughterer and even the slaughterer's clients. It is unlikely that they will understand as easily as God and unlikely that he will be forgiven by them.

Sperber cites other cases in which rabbinic rulings are lenient. One involves suspicion of leprosy in a house. Rabbis are instructed to delay inspection of the house until the contents are removed, because of concern for the property of Israel. In the case of a bridegroom whose house is suspected of being impure, the rabbis are instructed to wait seven days before inspecting the house.

Good Deeds Come before Study

Next Sperber discusses the mitzvah of learning Torah and other mitzvot that can or cannot be performed by another person. If a mitzvah can be performed by someone else, then the scholar continues studying Torah. If it cannot be performed by another, then the person who is responsible for the performance of the mitzvah must interrupt his or her Torah study and perform the mitzvah himself. However, if the mitzvah is to give charity, that takes precedence over Torah study in all cases:[31] "If there came before him

---

[29] Ibid.
[30] Rule 2, section 17 to the end, cited in Sperber, *On the Relationship of Mitzvot*, 42.
[31] Maimonides, *Hilchot Talmud Torah* 3:4, followed by the *Shulchan Aruch*, Yoreh Deah

[the choice of performing] a mitzvah and (i.e., or continuing) learning Torah, if that mitzvah could be carried out by another, he should not interrupt his learning; but if not, he should carry out that mitzvah and then return to his study. And when it comes to giving charity, one should always give charity first."[32] The Talmud continues that it was already decided at Beit Nitzeh in Lod that "study is greater; for it leads to deeds." However, the rabbis of Caesarea qualified this by saying: "This is the case when there is someone else to carry out the deeds. But if there is not anyone else to carry them out, the deed comes before [the study] (i.e., has precedence)."[33]

Sperber explains that although the Talmud states that study is greater than deeds, the rabbis later qualify this to mean that study leads to the proper interpretation of Talmud and, consequently, to the proper performance of the deed. If there is no one else to perform the deed, it must be performed by the individual who is able to do so.

Sperber emphasizes this with quotations from the Hafetz Hayyim, who wrote in 1886, and R. David ha-Nagid, Maimonides' grandson, who in 1222 quoted Shammai. The Hafetz Hayyim (1839–1933) wrote, "You occasionally see a Jew who [in a praiseworthy way] learns Torah [as much as possible] and values his time [not wasting a minute]. But if he does not set aside part of the day to do deeds of kindness, what a lack of intelligence."[34] He cites Shammai: "Make thy [study of the Torah] a fixed habit... And receive all men by its cheerful countenance."[35] This means that even during one's fixed period of Torah study, one should receive people cheerfully. You are not wasting time that was assigned to the study of Torah.[36]

Welcoming Guests Is Welcoming the Shekinah

Sperber further discusses hospitality to guests as hospitality to the Shekinah, the nearest to earth of God's emanations. The Bible states that Abraham's tent was open on all four sides so that he could welcome guests from wherever they came. "R. Yehudah in the name of Rav said: Greater is the hosting of guests than the hosting of the Shechinah, as it is said (Genesis 18:3), 'And

---

246:8; cited in Sperber, *On the Relationship of Mitzvot*, 46.
[32] Sperber, *On the Relationship of Mitzvot*, 46.
[33] Ibid.
[34] Ibid., 53.
[35] Ibid.
[36] Ibid.

he [Abraham] said: My Lord, if now I have found favor in Thy sight, pass not away, I pray thee, from Thy servant.'"[37]

Sperber elaborates on this theme by quoting several passages from *Tikunei ha-Zohar.*

> He who welcomes a guest . . . with a joyful countenance [cf. Avot 3:15] and with true pleasure in this world, when the soul and spirit leave the body from this world, they will be welcomed in the world-to-come.[38]

> And he who receives guests in full friendship it is as though he has received the countenance of the Shekinah, for in that measure that a person acts, so [heaven] acts towards him. R. Eleazar [the son of R. Shimon bar Yohai] came and kissed his hand. And all the members of the group (*haverim*) bowed down before him saying: "Had we to come to this world only to hear these words, it would have sufficed."[39]

In a footnote, Sperber interprets a quote by R. Yosef Yaavetz to mean that welcoming the poor is the perfect way to express *devekut*, cleaving to God, because God is with the poor. The Maharal of Prague believes that guests are the image of God and that one welcomes God himself when one welcomes one who is in His image.[40]

Welcoming Guests in Violation of the Sabbath

Sperber also notes that one is to welcome guests, even when it is necessary to violate the Sabbath to do so. Maimonides characterizes the welcoming of guests and accompanying them to the door or to the gates of the house as an act of loving-kindness. Acts of loving-kindness posit the dignity of the individual. The mishnah in Shabbat 18:1 states: "One may clear away [on the Sabbath] as much as four or five baskets of straw or grain to make room for guest, or [to avoid] hindrance in the House of Study."[41] Rashi comments

---

[37] Babylonian Talmud, Shabbat 127a; Babylonian Talmud, Yevamot 65b; both cited in Sperber, *On the Relationship of Mitzvot,* 82.
[38] Tikunei ha-Zohar 6 (ed. Margaliot, p. 46), cited in Sperber, *On the Relationship of Mitzvot,* 82.
[39] Sperber, *On the Relationship of Mitzvot,* 82.
[40] Ibid., 83.
[41] Ibid., 92.

that one can move bails of straw — that is, work on the Sabbath — in order to make room for seating guests.

An earlier comment on this mishnah in the Babylonian Talmud (Shabbat 127a) states that the hosting of guests takes precedence over rising early to attend the House of Study. "Said R. Yohanan: Great is the hosting of guests as rising up early to the House of Study [of Torah, of course], as we have learned 'to make room for guests or [to avoid] hindrance in the House of Study.' But Rav Dimi of Nehardea said: It is greater than rising up early to the House of Study. For we have learned: 'for guests,' and only afterwards 'to avoid hindrance in the House of Study.'"[42]

Pikuach Nefesh

The principle of *Pikuach Nefesh* (saving a life) overrides virtually all halakic rulings. Sperber quotes Maimonides.

> When we do these things (i.e., desecrating the Sabbath for a sick person), we do them not through the agency of a non-Jew, or a child, neither by slaves nor women, in order that the Sabbath be not light in their eyes. But one does so by the great ones of Israel and their Sages. And one may not hesitate (or: delay) in desecrating the Sabbath for a sick person, as it is stated, "[Ye shall therefore keep My statutes and My judgments:] which if a man do he shall live in them" (Leviticus 18:5) — and not die by them (referring to BT Yoma 85ab).[43]

Acknowledging the Dignity of the Poor

An orphan girl who had no relatives was to be married on a Friday. The parents of the bridegroom were not satisfied with the size of the dowry, and, consequently, the groom asked to withdraw from his commitment to marry the orphan. By the time the continuing negotiations concluded between the parents of the groom and the elders of the community, Sabbath had begun. The great authority R. Moses Isserles ruled that the wedding could proceed

---
[42] Ibid.
[43] Ibid.

on the Sabbath. He overruled a clear mishnaic ruling in order to maintain the dignity of the orphan girl and to provide for her future: "'[So] great is [the need] to respect the dignity of individuals that it has precedence over a negative commandment.' And indeed this ruling is to be found in the Rema's annotations to the *Shulhan Aruch*."[44]

The amount of charity that the community gives to the poor depends upon the previous lifestyle of the one who is now poor. The intent is to maintain their dignity. We mentioned earlier the case of an impoverished rich man who was given rich food by the community and the case of Hillel pulling for several miles the chariot of another impoverished rich man. However, an individual is prohibited from giving more than 20 percent of his income to charity lest he become poor and become liable to lose his dignity. The community is instructed that the rescue of hostages is the first priority for the use of its resources. The community is also instructed not to impoverish itself while doing so.

Do Not Embarrass Another

The requirement to avoid embarrassing someone when he is mistaken or even sinful is the subject of a short story about the father of the Baal Shem Tov. It appears in Martin Buber's *Tales of the Hasidim: The Early Masters*.[45] The Baal Shem Tov ("master of the good name"; 1700–1760), founder of Hasidic Judaism, stressed a direct relationship between God and man without intermediary. This is the story:

> Rabbi Eliezer, the Baal Shem's father, lived in a village. He was so hospitable that he placed guards at the outskirts of the village and had them stop poor wayfarers and bring them to his house for food and shelter. Those in Heaven rejoiced at his doing, and once they decided to try him. Satan offered to do this, but the prophet Elijah begged to be sent in his stead. In the shape of a poor wayfarer, with knapsack and staff, he came to Rabbi Eliezer's house on a Sabbath afternoon, and said the greeting. Rabbi Eliezer ignored the desecration of the Sabbath, for he did not want to mortify the man. He invited him to the meal and kept him in his house. Nor did he utter a word of reproof the next morning,

---

[44] Ibid., 103.
[45] Buber, *Tales of the Hasidim* (1947). See Sperber, *On the Relationship of Mitzvot*, 92.

when his guest took leave of him. Then the prophet revealed himself and promised him a son who would make the eyes of the people of Israel see the light.[46]

Sperber points out that the Sages were concerned to secure human dignity and thus avoid the humiliation of one's fellow. It was, for them, a serious offense to inflict indignity on anyone, free or slave. Humiliating someone in public was akin to shedding blood: "'The red disappears and the white comes,' making the infliction of indignity akin to an act of murder" (Babylonian Talmud, Neziqin, Bava Metzi'a 58b). In the Ethics of the Fathers we are told that "Rabbi Eleazer of Modin included those who humiliate a fellow man in public among those who have no share in the world to come (Mishnah Avot 3:11)."[47]

Dignity Is Inherent in Each Person

R. Akiva expressed the importance of respecting the dignity of each person in his decision that a woman had not violated her dignity when she loosened her hair in the street and washed it in oil that was spilled. He ruled that dignity inheres in the person and that one cannot violate his or her own dignity. Another person can, however. R. Akiva had previously ruled that the man who intentionally spilled oil on a woman had violated her dignity. Akiva duly imposed a heavy fine upon him.

R. Akiva argued that when the woman loosened her hair in the street she had done nothing of consequence. One may demean oneself. But one may not demean another person. He further taught that human rights do not depend on the wealth of the individual. As it is stated in the Mishnah:

> This is the general rule: All is in accordance with the person's honor. Rabbi Akiba said: Even the poorest in Israel are looked upon as free men who have lost their possessions for they are the sons of Abraham, Isaac and Jacob. It once happened that a man unloosed a woman's hair in the street and she came before Rabbi Akiba and he made him liable for four hundred zuz. Said the culprit, Rabbi, extend for me the time, and Rabbi Akiba extended him the time [for payment]. He [the culprit]

---

[46] Sperber, *On the Relationship of Mitzvot*, 106.
[47] Ibid., 109.

watched her standing at the entry of her courtyard and he broke before her a cruse that held an issar worth of oil. She then unloosed her hair and scooped up the oil in her hand and laid her hand on her head. He set up witnesses against her and came before Rabbi Akiba and said to him: Rabbi, should I give to such a one [who has no regard for her own dignity] four hundred zuz? Rabbi Akiba answered: Thou hast said naught at all. For he who inflicts wounds on himself, even though he is not permitted to do so, is not culpable; but if others wound him they are culpable (M. Baba Kama 8:6).[48]

Sperber explains the important lessons that Rabbi Akiva taught in this story. Human dignity is not determined by relative standards; surely it is not determined by a person's wealth or stature in the community.

The Overarching Importance of Charity

Sperber avers that his thesis that social mitzvot supersede ritual mitzvot is supported by the preeminent significance of charity (*tzedakah*) for the rabbis:

The house of Israel is obligated to give charity from their monies to whosoever is in need thereof. And he who shows pity for the impoverished is likened by the Holy One blessed be He as if he did good deeds to God himself, as it is stated (Exodus 25:2), "that they should bring to Me an offering" (i.e., if they give charity to the poor, it is as though they are giving it to God himself).[49]

And in BT Baba Batra 10a we read in the name of R. Yohanan:
What is the meaning of the verse in Proverbs 19:17, "He who hath pity upon the poor lendeth unto the Lord"? If it were not written, it would be impossible to say it, namely that "the borrower is servant to the lender" (22:7).[50]

Rashi explains that he who has pity for the poor it is as though he is lending to God, and "the borrower," God, becomes, as it were, "servant

---

[48] Quoted in Sperber, *On the Relationship of Mitzvot*, 109.
[49] Sperber, *On the Relationship of Mitzvot*, 115.
[50] Ibid.

to the lender."[51]

Sperber continues his discussion of charity by citing Babylonian Talmud, Sanhedrin 103b, in what he believes may be the most remarkable testimony to the superior status of charity.

> Why was Michah not listed [among the evil kings]? Because his fare was available for wayfarers. . . . R. Natan taught us: From Gereb [Michah's temple] to Shiloh is three miles, and the smoke of the altar [at the Temple of Shiloh] and the smoke from the idol of Michah would intermingle with one another. The angels wished to harm him (i.e., Michah). But the Holy One blessed be He said to them: "Leave him alone for his fare is available for wayfarers."[52]

Maimonides states that the second-highest form of charity occurs when you give without knowing to whom you give and the recipient does not know who gave (Hilchot Talmud Torah 10:11): "One who gives charity to the poor and does not know to whom he has given it, and the poor man does not know from whom he has received it . . . For pious people would give secretly and poor people from a wealthy family would receive it covertly. And close to this is placing charity in an alms box."[53] Respect for the integrity of the poor is implicit in this text; and one who acts with integrity acts with dignity.

In the appendix to his monograph, Sperber again indicates the ethical priority of a person's relationship to his fellow human being over his relationship to his Creator.

> The giving of charity prior to beginning one's morning prayer again underscores the moral priority of relationship towards one's fellow human even before one turns to one's Creator. This is clearly mirrored in the tradition attributed to the great Kabbalist R. Hayyim Vital, that, when one rises in the morning, even before one goes to prayer, one should remind himself of the mitzvah "to love one's neighbor as oneself" (Leviticus 19:18). Surely,

---

[51] Ibid.
[52] Quoted in ibid., 123.
[53] *Hilchot Matnot Aniyim* 10:7 et seq., cited in Sperber, *On the Relationship of Mitzvot*, 122.

this would be a clear expression of one's hierarchic scale of ethical values.[54]

Sperber cites a statement written in 2003 by R. Yosef Hayyim Sofer on the importance of interpersonal behavior that enhances the dignity of the other.

> It is very clear that the Tanna of [Mishnah] Peah 1:1, in listing "those [mitzvot] that one eats of their fruits in this world . . . ," only notes those acts which serve well both to God and to man, where human beings also have real material benefit therefrom, such as honoring one's parents, righteous deeds to one's fellows; but those which are only good towards heaven, such as sending away the mother bird [Deuteronomy 22:7],[55] are not listed.[56]

Righteous but Not Necessarily Good Persons

Rabbinic tradition makes a striking distinction between individuals who are righteous and good and those who are righteous but not necessarily good. Although they were *tzaddikim* and *hasidim* who were righteous and virtuous, they lacked ethical integrity: "There were *tzaddikim* and *hasidim*, righteous and virtuous men, who toiled in the learning of Torah, but who had no integrity in the ways of the world. . . . And the Holy One blessed be He, who is integrity personified, cannot bear righteous people of this nature, but only those who walk the paths of integrity in the ways of the world: and not in a distorted manner."[57]

Natural Law: *Derech Eretz*

Sperber concludes the first section of the book with citations of three texts that give strong support to universal moral ethical values and to claims that *derech eretz*—natural law—is at the heart of the Torah and that in

---

[54] Sperber, *On the Relationship of Mitzvot*, 211.
[55] An allusion to a famous passage about the removal of eggs from a bird's nest. It is commanded that one should let the mother go before removing the eggs.
[56] Zarka, *Menuhat Shalom*, 2:22, cited in Sperber, *On the Relationship of Mitzvot*, 124.
[57] Netziv's introduction (petiha) to Genesis, cited in Sperber, *On the Relationship of Mitzvot*, 133.

its absence the Torah is null and void. Sperber quotes three authorities. The first is from the Maharal of Prague (ca. 1512–1609), the second is a well-known statement by Maimonides, and the third is a recent text by Menachem Kellner of the University of Haifa, written in 2006. The statement by the Maharal of Prague is as follows:

> Therefore, a person should not view lightly those matters which are *derech eretz*, for *derech eretz* [natural morality or common decency] came before Torah . . . and it is impossible to read a Torah situation without *derech eretz*, as they said, "If there is no *derech eretz* there is no Torah" (Avot 3:17), for "*derech eretz* is the basis of Torah which is the way of the Tree of Life."[58]

The text from Maimonides reads:

> The bad things to which the philosophers referred when they said that someone who does not desire them is more virtuous than someone who does desire them and restrains himself, these are the things generally accepted by all people as bad, such as murder, theft, robbery, fraud, harming an innocent man, repaying a benefactor with evil, degrading parents, and things like these. They are the laws about which the Sages, peace be upon them said, "If they were not written down, they would deserve to be written down" (BT Yoma 67b).[59]

Menachem Kellner comments on Maimonides:

> In other words, these kinds of practices belong to a category of "natural morality," i.e., *derech eretz*. This homiletically suggests yet another meaning for *derech eretz* in Maimonides. *Derech eretz* preceded Torah, namely that rules and customs of *derech eretz*, i.e., morality, preceded the giving of the Torah at Sinai.[60]

---

[58] Maharal of Prague, in his *Netivot Olam, Netiv Derech Eretz*, cited in Sperber, *On the Relationship of Mitzvot*, 142.

[59] Commentary to Mishnah Avot (Ethics of the Fathers), sixth of the "Eight Chapters," cited in Sperber, *On the Relationship of Mitzvot*, 145.

[60] Kellner, *Maimonides' Confrontation with Mysticism*, 146, cited in Sperber, *On the Relationship of Mitzvot*, 142.

Sperber concludes his book by reiterating that piety cannot be limited to ritual behavior alone. It is constituted by life with our fellow human beings. Accordingly, he cites an essay of 2010 by Eugene Korn, a leading modern Orthodox scholar: "Orthodoxy's current pan-halakhism [which I see as primarily concerned with ritual, D.S.] seems to have lost interest in the human condition per se, and is rapidly losing the language to discuss universal human concerns like ethics, justice, spirituality and human purpose."[61] In a nutshell, human dignity is the metavalue in Judaism.

---

[61] Korn, review of *On the Relationship of Mitzvot*, 3, cited in Sperber, *On the Relationship of Mitzvot*, 193.

CHAPTER 4

Two Rabbinic Paradigms of Conversion

During the rabbinic period, 500–1550 CE, two paradigms for conversion were prominent. Each is named after the rabbinic text in which it first appeared. The *Yevamot* paradigm dominated until challenged by the ultra-Orthodox paradigm, *Demai*, in the middle of the eighteenth century. The *Demai* paradigm, a minor voice in the tradition for over a thousand years, has become the most powerful voice today because of the political influence of the Orthodox in Israel and their control over the Orthodox in America. There is little precedence in halakhah for this radical change of paradigm. The Demai paradigm has come to hold that conversion is an internal spiritual transformation that is more characteristic of a confessional faith than of Judaism. It is dependent on a rabbi's personal assessment of the internal and external commitment of the proselyte and on the proselyte's commitment to live an Orthodox lifestyle. Conversion is no longer permanent. It can be nullified by the rabbinate at any time. Human dignity is insignificant in the decisions of both the rabbi and the convert.

Reform Judaism, on the other hand, follows the Yevamot paradigm, which values human dignity and human agency. This will be clear in the following analysis, for which I am indebted to Avi Sagi and Zvi Zohar for personal conversations that began in 1984 shortly after the publication of the first edition of their seminal study of conversion, *Transforming Identity: The Ritual Transformation from Gentile to Jew; Structure and Meaning*.

Sagi and Zohar's concepts for the interpretation of texts offer an important foundation for reading the texts that follow:

> Halakhic texts have an internal history: while written in a specific time and place, their meaning is not defined by that time and place. We hold the hermeneutical principle that the meaning of texts is not reducible to their sociological genesis. Rather, it derives from the *weltanshaung* [*sic*] that they embody, their internal argumentation and rhetoric, and the fact that they are read by successive generations whose close reading leads to the attribution of immanent meanings to the text. While

some texts may be significantly conditioned by their historical context, historical contextualization of their meaning should be guided first and foremost by clear indications within the text itself. . . .

The diachronic aspect of our project therefore primarily reflects the internal dynamic of halakhic discourse over the centuries. . . .

The synchronic aspect of our project is reflected in our view that the continuity of halakhic dialogue over the generations generates an arena of discourse characterized by the persistence of basic similarities and structures that transcend time and place. A clear manifestation of this . . . is the presence of two paradigms of *giyyur* [conversion] from earliest times to the present.[1]

Sagi and Zohar state their conclusions in the following excerpts from their book, in which they trace the historical trajectory of the two major paradigms for conversion and the historical trajectory of motivation in conversion, all three of which culminate in the current radical innovations in conversion by the Orthodox in Israel. These excerpts will be followed by a detailed discussion of Sagi and Zohar's analysis of conversion from 500 CE to the present. The Demai paradigm stresses the normative cognitive aspect of *giyyur* (denoting that procedure whereby the stranger, *ger*, becomes a Jew—i.e., conversion), while the Yevamot paradigm emphasizes bodily ritual.[2]

Sagi and Zohar employ the Hebrew word *giyyur*; I use the term "conversion," because it is more accessible to a reader who is not familiar with the Jewish tradition. They explain that the term "conversion" in Christian theology is associated with an internal psychological manifestation that accompanies belief in Christ as Savior. The dominant view of conversion in Judaism until the modern time, the Yevamot paradigm, does not entail an internal psychological transformation or commitment.[3] "The *Demai* paradigm views the meaning of conversion as a transition from a previous religion to the Jewish religion and, correspondingly, perceives the commitment to observance as the very core of conversion although after conversion the proselyte will remain a Jew however she behaves."[4]

---

[1] Sagi and Zohar, *Transforming Identity*, 3.
[2] Ibid., 2.
[3] Ibid., 3.
[4] Ibid., 289.

Observance of halakhah defines the ideal member of the Jewish collective. It is required of the proselyte as a condition for conversion but is not required of a born Jew. The Yevamot paradigm views conversion as a transition from a gentile identity to a Jewish spiritual "kinship" identity, and, correspondingly, circumcision and immersion are perceived as the core of conversion. The obligation to observe the commandments is a consequence of the Jewish kinship identity that the proselyte has acquired. The Torah was given by God at Mount Sinai to Moses for all the people who were present and to all their descendants. A proselyte is considered to be a descendant of those present at Sinai. In this paradigm, "the *giyyur* process is one in which a former Gentile joins the Jewish kinship collective; *halakhah* regards the Jewish collective as a 'natural-primordial' entity, constituted by kinship."[5] The convert joins the Jewish kinship spiritually.

In the Demai paradigm, "the meaning of that process is joining the Jewish religion in the sense of a commitment to observe the Torah and the commandments . . . [, and] the Torah and the commandments are regarded as the constitutive elements of the collective. On this view, the identity of the Jewish people is thus determined by commitment to Torah."[6] While both options exist, it is clear that mainstream halakhic tradition over the millennia identifies circumcision and immersion as constitutive of giyyur. Furthermore, most of the halakhists who also require acceptance of the commandments as a condition of giyyur do not interpret this demand as a performative commitment. Thus, most halakhists from earliest times to the present regard giyyur as a transition from one kinship identity to another—and both the Yevamot and the Demai paradigms explicitly state that giyyur is as irrevocable as birth to a Jewish mother.[7]

These different views and practices of conversion reflect different views about Jewish identity and the nature of the Jewish collective. These differences manifest themselves strongly in the post-Enlightenment world, in which Jews were emancipated under Napoleon and became citizens of the countries in which they lived. The differences were sharply drawn in the middle of the nineteenth century in Germany, when Orthodoxy separated itself from the reformers, who did not intend to create a separate denomination. The beginning of Reform is credited to Israel Jacobson, who, in 1810, in Seesen, Germany, changed the design of a synagogue and introduced

---

[5] Ibid.
[6] Ibid.
[7] Ibid., 290.

music and German in the services. His objective was to make the synagogue and the services more like those of their Christian neighbors and more accessible and interesting to the Jewish laity.

The Orthodox reacted angrily and vehemently opposed these reforms, which were adopted by other synagogues in Germany. Unsuccessful in inducing the government to intervene, they withdrew from interaction with the reformers, thus creating a separate Jewish denomination for the first time in Jewish history. In Orthodoxy, everything new was forbidden. The Orthodox became insular. German Reform engaged with society and developed religious beliefs and practices that dealt with the challenges of the Enlightenment, emancipation, intermarriage, and the increasing number of conversions to Christianity. This is the background in which the two paradigms for conversion have become a divisive issue in the Jewish world today.

In the following pages we will review, from 500 CE to the present, the positions of the most renowned halakhists on these issues. We will analyze the two major paradigms of conversion, Yevamot and Demai, which are named after the tractates in which they first appear. We will explore the different interpretations of concepts such as "for the sake of heaven," "for the sake of peace," "acceptance of the commandments," and "better to eat gravy," which are used to support each position. Following this analysis, we will review responsa, rabbinic analysis and decisions, on conversion by Rabbi David Ellenson, past and current president of HUC-JIR,[8] the college in which Reform Rabbis are trained. David is one of many brilliant Reform rabbis and scholars who engage with the tradition and with halakhah.

The Canonical Text for Conversion: Yevamot

The canonical text for conversion appears in the baraita Yevamot 47a–b, which is reproduced below in the translation by Sagi and Zohar. We will undertake a plain reading of the text and then relate this to the two major paradigms of conversion, Yevamot and Demai.

Our Rabbis taught: If a prospective proselyte comes to undergo *giyyur* in

---

[8] HUC-JIR, Hebrew Union College–Jewish Institute of Religion, is the rabbinic school that trains Reform Rabbis in the United States on its campuses in Cincinnati, New York, Los Angeles, and Jerusalem. Hebrew Union College was founded in Cincinnati in 1875. The Jewish Institute of Religion was founded in New York in 1922. They merged in 1950.

the present era, we say to him: "What did you see that made you come to seek *giyyur*? Do you not know that nowadays the Jewish people are afflicted, oppressed, downtrodden and harassed and that hardships come upon them?" If he responds: "I know, and I am unworthy [of joining them]," we accept him immediately. And we inform him of some minor commandments and some major commandments. And we inform him of the sin [of the neglect of the commandments] of Gleanings, of the Forgotten Sheaf, of the Corner, and of the Poor Man's Tithe. And we inform him of the punishment for the transgression of the commandments. We say to him: "Be aware, that before you reached this situation, if you ate [forbidden] suet you were not punishable by *Karet* [extinction by Heaven]; if you profaned the Sabbath, you were not punishable by stoning; but now [after *giyyur*], if you eat suet, you will be punished by *Karet*, and if you profane the Sabbath, you will be punished by stoning." Just as we inform him of the punishments for [transgressing] the commandments, we inform him of the rewards [for observance]. We say to him: "Know, that the world to come is not made except for the righteous. And, in the present era the Jewish people cannot receive an abundance of good or an abundance of calamity." We do not overwhelm him, nor are we strict with him. Once he received [the meaning of the Hebrew word is ambiguous], we circumcise him immediately. If shreds that impede a valid circumcision remain, we circumcise him again. Once he has healed, we immerse him immediately. And two rabbinic scholars stand over him, and inform him of some minor commandments and some major commandments. Once he has immersed and come up, he is like a Jew in every respect.[9]

The text is a guideline for those who perform the process of conversion. It is not addressed to the proselyte, who, throughout the procedure, need only agree to the statement that he or she is unworthy to join the Jewish people. Continuing the process is considered to be agreement. He or she can withdraw at any time prior to immersion, the final step in the process. After immersion, proselytes, both men and women, are said to reborn as Jews, and their conversion is irrevocable.

In discussions prior to the ritual immersion, the rabbinic authorities question the prospective converts' understanding of the current condition of the Jewish people. They make clear to them that they are affiliating with

[9] Sagi and Zohar, *Transforming Identity*, 141–42.

the Jewish people [not with the Jewish religion alone] and that they will be joining a people under duress who are "afflicted, oppressed, downtrodden and harassed" and who find themselves afflicted by hardships. If the prospective proselytes indicate that they understand this and if they declare that they nevertheless are unworthy of becoming a part of the Jewish people, they are immediately accepted as candidates for conversion. The rabbis are instructed that they are not to question the prospective proselytes any further. At this point, the candidates are told about some minor and some major commandments. The nonspecific nature of this instruction and the limitation to some commandments indicate that this is a perfunctory procedure and that the commandments per se do not define the essential nature of conversion and the adoption of a Jewish identity.

Observing the Commandments as a Jew

After informing the proselyte of the specific requirements to aid the poor, the text tells the proselytes that once they become Jews they are liable to punishment if they do not observe the commandments. Observing the commandments is not stated as a requirement for conversion. It is a requirement that is incumbent on all Jews. Reborn on conversion as Jews, they become responsible for the commandments, as any other Jew.

The Requirement of Circumcision and Immersion

There is a difference of opinion about the necessity or relative importance and sequence of circumcision and immersion. Some authorities ruled that circumcision for men was sufficient because Abraham was circumcised and did not immerse. Later authorities agreed that both circumcision and immersion were necessary and that circumcision should precede immersion because immersion was the crucial and final step in the process of conversion. If a man was born circumcised or had been circumcised as an adult, a symbolic circumcision called *hatafat dam brit* (drawing a drop of blood from the site of the circumcision) was performed. In a normal circumcision, the foreskin surrounding the penis was removed by a *mohel* (circumciser), a man who was trained to perform circumcisions on Jewish male babies, who were required to be circumcised on the eighth day after birth.

The following discussion will help one understand the Tannaitic texts on conversion, which present the differences between the school of Hillel and the school of Shammai, the two dominant schools of thought at the time the texts were written. You will recall that in the three cases of men presenting themselves for conversion, each with an inappropriate request, Shammai rejected them and Hillel accepted them:[10] "Rabbi Shimon ben Elazar said: The school of Shammai and the school of Hillel did not disagree that a [Jewish] child who was born circumcised should undergo covenantal blood-letting. For it is a suppressed foreskin. With regard to what did they disagree? With regard to a circumcised Gentile who seeks *giyyur*. The school of Shammai say: It is required that he undergo covenantal blood-letting. And the school of Hillel say: It is unnecessary that he undergo covenantal blood-letting."[11] Immersion following circumcision indicates that the essential element in conversion is immersion, not circumcision. Men circumcise and immerse. Women only immerse. Immersion symbolizes coming under the wings of the Shekinah. The Shekinah is the female manifestation of God that is between the other higher manifestations of God and human beings. In the most significant Jewish mystical text, the *Zohar*, the Shekinah is the lowest of the ten spheres that emanate from God. It is the sphere that connects God to the world.

In early texts, a millennia prior to Saint Paul's negation of the need for circumcision, circumcision was considered essential for joining the Jewish people. Abraham was commanded by God to circumcise as the bond of the covenant. At that time contracts were sealed through the exchange of blood. Each party to the contract cut himself on the arm and drank a drop of blood from the other's arm. They became "blood brothers."

Circumcision as the critical act of conversion was superseded by immersion when patrilineal descent was replaced by matrilineal descent. The transition was characterized by the debate in the Jerusalem Talmud between R. Eliezer and R. Joshua. R. Eliezer claims that "we learn from our fathers." R. Joshua claims that "we learn from our mothers." R. Eliezer supports traditional, patrilineal descent. R. Joshua supports a transition to matrilineal descent. Matrilineal descent was unknown before the destruction of the Second Temple and the emergence of rabbinic Judaism.[12]

---

[10] See chapter 1, under "Human Dignity: Hillel and Shammai."
[11] Shabbat 135a, cited in Sagi and Zohar, *Transforming Identity*, 119.
[12] Sagi and Zohar, *Transforming Identity*, 127.

A Convert Is like a Newborn Child

Matrilineal descent is embodied in the symbolic meaning of immersion as expressed by Mircea Eliade: "Immersion in water symbolizes a return to the pre-formal, a total regeneration, a new birth, for immersion means a dissolution of forms, a reintegration into the formlessness of pre-existence; and emerging from the water is a repetition of the act of creation in which form it was first expressed."[13] In Jewish understanding, the act of immersion is like the act of birth. The proselyte is transformed. She is a new creation. When she emerges from the *mikveh*, the ritual bath, she emerges as a Jewess. The Talmud states that "a proselyte is like a new-born child."[14]

The proselyte becomes a Jew through a symbolic process that emulates birth to a Jewish mother. Immersion remained the essential act for conversion. However, in early Jewish history beginning with Abraham, circumcision was the ritual through which a male became a Jew. When both circumcision and immersion became essential for conversion in Amoraic times (200–500 CE), circumcision was required prior to immersion, and the two procedures, in that order, continue to be required today.

The positive description of the proselyte in this text as a Jew in every respect is eroded in subsequent texts. During the periods when Jews were being persecuted, the proselyte was said to be a like a scab on the Jewish people. When conversion to Judaism was punishable by death in Europe, Jews themselves discouraged proselytization.

The Need to Accept the Commandments

Sagi and Zohar and David Ellenson, whom we will subsequently discuss, cite from the Babylonian Talmud tractate Gerim an obscure baraita. The baraita states that the central act of conversion is acceptance of the commandments. Religious belief and action are defined as the essence of Judaism. The proselyte's relationship to God, not to the Jewish people, is paramount. The tractate Gerim stresses the proselyte's relationship to God through joining

---

[13] Eliade, Patterns in *Comparative Religion*, 188, quoted in Sagi and Zohar, *Transforming Identity*, 127. Mircea Eliade (1907–86), a professor at the University of Chicago, was one of the most influential scholars of religion of the twentieth century and one of the world's foremost interpreters of religious symbolism and myth.

[14] Yevamot 22a, 48b, 47b, cited in Sagi and Zohar, *Transforming Identity*, 127.

the Jewish people. Being a member of the Jewish people is not inherently significant. It is a means to create a relationship with God.

The ritual described earlier, which is presented in the classic tractate on conversion, Yevamot 49a–b, predominated during the rabbinic era and continued to do so until recently. A different paradigm, Demai, was a minor voice that gradually became the dominant paradigm within the Orthodox world. It has been transformed radically, perhaps without precedent, into a text that the Orthodox rabbinate in Israel uses to strictly limit all conversions in Israel and in Orthodox communities throughout the diaspora. The process has been altered, and the meaning of becoming a Jew has changed under the Demai paradigm. Sagi and Zohar describe conversion according to the Yevamot paradigm as "a ritual process by which one acquires membership in a society defined primarily by kinship.["][15] In the Demai paradigm conversion is "a voluntaristic normative commitment by which one acquires membership in a society defined primarily by normative praxis."[16]

Havura: Similarities with Conversion

The second chapter of tractate Demai contains a baraita that relates conversion to joining a *havura*, a community, which commits itself to strict practices for purity in eating, drinking, and observance of Jewish law. One must follow all of the norms without exception. Continuing membership is contingent on following these norms. After discussing this, the redactor of the text inserts a comment on conversion: "A proselyte who took upon himself all matters of Torah, excepting one thing, they don't accept him. Rabbi Jose son of Rabbi Judah says: even [excepting] a small matter enacted by the scribes."[17] This statement regarding a proselyte mirrors the requirement that a member of the havura must adhere to all the norms of the community to be accepted as a member. However, the redactor notes that once someone converts to Judaism, like other Jews a convert remains a Jew regardless of her or his observance: "A proselyte who took upon himself all matters of Torah and is suspected [of non-observance] with regard to one matter, even with regard to the entire Torah behold, he is like an Israelite apostate."[18] The

---

[15] Sagi and Zohar, *Transforming Identity*, 107.
[16] Ibid.
[17] Tosefta Demai 2:6–7, cited in Sagi and Zohar, *Transforming Identity*, 109.
[18] Tosefta Demai 2:5, cited in Sagi and Zohar, *Transforming Identity*, 109.

Demai paradigm, which is expressed in these texts, requires acceptance of the Torah unequivocally for a proselyte to be accepted. The critical requirement is commitment to the Torah, not commitment to the Jewish people. However, once the proselyte is converted, he or she remains a Jew, and if a woman, her children are born as Jews.

The Yevamot paradigm of conversion was prevalent from the Geonic period, 550–1050 CE, in Babylon. Conversion did not focus on faith or commitment during this period. It focused on the covenantal practice of circumcision and the practice of ritual immersion in the *mikveh*, ritual bath, in which a gentile is reborn as a Jew. There are no theoretical barriers to marriage with previous members of one's non-Jewish family, although subsequent rabbinic strictures prohibit this. The convert can serve as a witness for or against members of her previous family, a practice that is forbidden in Jewish law.

Motivation was not a significant concern in the Yevamot paradigm, whereas it was essential in the Demai paradigm. Motivation is also essential for conversion in contemporary Orthodoxy.

Ruth: A Moabite Who Joined the Jewish People

Ruth married one of the two sons of Naomi, a Hebrew. When Ruth's husband and her brother-in-law, Naomi's second son, died, there was no one to support Ruth, Naomi, or Naomi's other daughter-in-law. Naomi planned to return to her home in Bethlehem and told both daughters-in-laws to return to their homes. Ruth, a Moabite, insisted on remaining with Naomi, even though Naomi had no means to support them: "Entreat me not to leave thee, or to return from following after thee: For wherever thou goest I will go; and where thou lodgest I will lodge; thy people shall be my people and thy God my God. Where thou diest I will die, and there I will be buried" (Ruth 1:16–17). Ruth's statement "wherever thou goest I will go" is reminiscent of Abraham's journey from his home to a land that God will show him. Her statement "Thy people will be my people," followed by "and thy God my God," follows the Yevamot paradigm, in which the proselyte undertakes a religious process to become born again as a Jew. In Ruth Jewish identity is primarily ethnic or territorial, not religious. It does not support the Demai paradigm, in which identity is primarily a religious identity.

In Bethlehem, Ruth gathered the remnants of the harvest from the fields, the practice prescribed by the laws of pe'ah,[19] to support the poor such as Naomi and herself. According to the tradition, Naomi's loyalty and care for Ruth were noticed by a wealthy landlord, Boaz, who married Ruth after she followed Naomi's instructions to lie down beside him on the floor of a threshing room and to ask him to place his robe over her. This act of covering with the robe is symbolic both religiously and sexually. Religiously, it signifies being covered by the wings of the Shekinah. Sexually, it is a request for the consummation of a marriage: "The Lord recompense thy deed, and may a full reward be given thee by the Lord God of Israel, under whose wings thou art come to take refuge" (Ruth 2:11–12).[20] The concept of entering under the wings of Shekinah first appears in the rabbinic tradition in the book of Ruth. The Shekinah is the female manifestation of God, which hovers over the earth. In the kabbalistic or mystical tradition it is the tenth sphere of the attributes of God, the one that is closest to earth and that mediates between God and man.

It is noteworthy that Ruth gathered the remnants of the crops for Naomi. Naomi was spared the labor and whatever negative feelings she might have experienced while gathering the crops. Ruth acted with respect and loyalty to her mother-in-law, protecting Naomi's dignity.

Motivation for Conversion: Maimonides

The subject of motivation for conversion as it appears in Talmudic sources generated during the Geonic period (ca. 550 to ca. 1040 CE) and the period of the *Rishonim* (leading rabbinic authorities; 1040–1550 CE) is discussed in depth by Sagi and Zohar. Two of the most authoritative scholars of Jewish law were Maimonides (1135–1204), who wrote during the period of the Rishonim, and Joseph Caro (1488–1575), who wrote at the end of the same period. Sagi and Zohar clarify the positions of Maimonides and Caro in their analysis of three different positions on the motivation of a proselyte. First they outline the three basic positions:

---

[19] Pe'ah (Hebrew, literally, "corner") is the second tractate of Seder Zeraim (Order of Seeds) of the Mishnah and of the Talmud. This tractate begins the discussion of topics related to agriculture, which is the main focus of this seder (order) of the Mishnah. The tractate discusses the laws of gifts to the poor when a person harvests their field, vineyards, or trees, based on commandments in the Torah. See also chapter 3 of this volume, under "Charity: Sharing God's Providence."

[20] Sagi and Zohar, *Transforming Identity*, 123.

1. Improper motivation disqualifies an otherwise valid *giyyur* ritual.
2. Motivation is inconsequential as far as the validity of a *giyyur* is concerned, but should influence the court's decision on whether to perform it.
3. The proselyte's motivation is altogether irrelevant to the *giyyur* procedure, even a priori.[21]

They note that "Talmudic literature offers two sources stating that the validity of *giyyur* is contingent on the proselyte's motivation. According to the 'strong' version, which appears in Tractate Gerim, the validity of a *giyyur* is contingent on the presence of a positive religious motivation. According to the 'weaker' version, stated by Rabbi Nehemia in Yevamot, the validity of *giyyur* is contingent on the absence of negative motivations."[22] This latter position is used to characterize a prospective proselyte as worthy of conversion if he or she is motivated for the sake of heaven. However, there is no explicit Talmudic discussion of the meaning of the phrase "contingent on the absence of negative motivation," either in the context of conversion or elsewhere.[23] This lack of clarity permitted the phrase to become a major source of contention, and it has continued to be so to this day. We will examine this later in several exegeses of Jewish law in this regard.

Maimonides adopts the first approach delineated by Sagi and Zohar when he declares that the motivations of the proselyte should be investigated carefully before the process of conversion is begun. The court is instructed to ascertain that the proselyte has no ulterior motive and that she or he comes because of love of the Torah:

> The proper procedure, when a man or a woman comes forth with the intention of becoming a proselyte, is to investigate: perchance he comes to enter the religion in order to gain money, or to qualify for a position of authority, or out of fear. In the case of a man, they check if perchance, he has cast his eyes upon an Israelite woman. In the case of a woman, they check if she has cast her eyes upon one of the youths of Israel. If no such motive is found in them, they should be informed of the heavy weight of the yoke of the Torah, and how burdensome it is for vulgar

---
[21] Sagi and Zohar, *Transforming Identity*, 9.
[22] Ibid., 10.
[23] Ibid., 9.

folk to observe its precepts, in order to induce them to withdraw. If they accept and do not withdraw, and it is evident that they come out of love, they should be accepted.[24]

However, Maimonides adopts the second approach in subsequent texts. In the following text, a proselyte whose motives were not investigated or was not instructed properly but who was circumcised and immersed remains a Jew, regardless of subsequent behavior or belief. The process is essential. But proper motives or knowledge about the Jewish people are not essential. Once the proselyte has immersed her- or himself, she or he is irreversibly a Jew. Although they are now fully Jews, the converts' subsequent behavior should be observed to make certain that they are suited to marry a Jew. The question about the complete integration of the convert into the Jewish community arises in different contexts. In his *Mishneh Torah*, Maimonides expresses his love for the convert who believes in the principles of faith that Maimonides finds essential, and he expresses his resolute rejection of those who do not:

> And when a person has all these elements [namely: the principles of faith], and truly believes in them, then he has joined the community of Israel, and it is our duty to love him and be compassionate towards him, and to manifest towards him all norms of love and brotherhood that God has commanded each of us towards his fellow . . . but when a man doubts any one of these elements, he has removed himself from the community . . . and we are obliged to hate him and destroy him.[25]

In a later section of the *Mishneh Torah* entitled *The Laws of Forbidden Intercourse*, Maimonides adopts a more lenient position that is contrary to his earlier positions.

> A proselyte whose motives were not investigated, or was not informed of the commandments and the punishment for transgressing them, but was circumcised and immersed in the presence of three laymen, is a proselyte. Even if it becomes known that he became a proselyte for some

---

[24] Maimonides, *Laws of Forbidden Intercourse* 13.14, cited in Sagi and Zohar, *Transforming Identity*, 23.
[25] Maimonides, *Mishneh Torah* [Review of Torah], vol. NN, *Nezikin* (ed. Kafih, pp. 144–45), trans. in Sagi and Zohar, *Transforming Identity*, 24.

ulterior motive, he has exited from the Gentile collective, because he was circumcised and immersed. However, he should be regarded with reservation until his righteousness becomes apparent. Even if he once again worships idols, he is as an apostate Israelite, whose betrothal is valid. And we are commanded to return his lost property to him. Because he immersed, he is an Israelite.[26]

In a responsum, Maimonides adopts a position that is inconsistent with his *Mishneh Torah*, a code of Jewish law, and that differs from a Talmudic ruling. A community brought him a case that involved a man suspected of having intercourse with his female slave, a practice that was forbidden. Maimonides said that the relationship must not continue and offered two options: sell the slave or free her and marry her. He recommended the second option because it was less harmful to the couple:

> In light of this negative rumor, the court should force him to sell her. Alternatively, they may force him to free her and marry her, even if an apparent offence is thereby entailed, for if a man was suspected [of intercourse] with a bondwoman, *ab initio* he may not marry her. For we have already ruled several times, in such cases, that he should free her and marry her. And the reason we did this is because of the enactment for the encouragement of penitents, and we said: "He should rather eat gravy than the fat itself." And we relied on the words of the rabbis, may their memory be blessed: "It is time to act for the Lord: they have made void thy Torah" (Ps. 119.126). And he is to be helped to marry her, kindly and gently, and a date should be set for the marriage or the release.[27]

Maimonides made it clear that this lenient ruling was consistent with many of his other rulings. He supported it with concepts such as "encouragement of penitents," "he should rather eat gravy," and "It is time to act for the Lord." The first, "encouragement of penitents" to repent and reform, is in accordance with the Talmud. The second, "rather eat gravy," is in accordance with a Talmudic ruling that changed the prohibition against eating nonkosher food. The Talmud adopts a lenient stance toward a pregnant woman who has a craving for nonkosher food. The rabbis are concerned that she

---

[26] Maimonides, *Laws of Forbidden Intercourse* 13.17, cited in Sagi and Zohar, *Transforming Identity*, 25.
[27] Sagi and Zohar, *Transforming Identity*, 27.

and the fetus may be endangered if she does not have nonkosher food. The preservation of life takes precedence over halakhah. The third, "It is time to act for the Lord," is a reading that is directly opposite to the meaning of the full verse in Psalm 119:126. "It is time to act for the Lord: they have made void thy Torah." The full verse means that one must take action against those who void the Torah. However, Maimonides' revised reading means that in situations such as this, it is proper to act contrary to the Torah in order to preserve life. This reversal of the plain meaning of the text illustrates the flexibility of interpretation that is characteristic in Judaism. Reform Judaism in the United States carries forward this posture toward the text.

INCONSISTENT RULINGS: MAIMONIDES

The motivation of the proselyte was immaterial in the Yevamot paradigm and essential in the Demai paradigm. It has become essential in current Orthodox practice. In order to understand the Talmudic background in which such a radical new ruling occurred recently in Israel, we will review motivation in conversion according to two of Judaism's greatest compilers of Jewish law, Maimonides, who was born in 1135 in Cordoba, Spain, and died in 1204 in Fostat, Egypt, and Joseph Caro, who was born in 1488 in Toledo, Spain, and died in 1575 in Safed, Syria. We will not review the third major compilation of Jewish law, the *Arba'ah Turim* (1563), known as *Tor*, which was written by Jacob ben Asher, who was born in 1270 in Cologne, Germany, and died in 1340 in Toledo, Spain, because the current most authoritative compilation, the *Shulchan Aruch*, by Joseph Caro, is based on it.

The complexities of halakhic thought and the lack of consistency both within the body of work of a single halakhist and between the works of different halakhists are evident in these great authorities. Their chronological place in Jewish history is characterized as the period of the Rishonim, the early authorities, from the eleventh to fifteenth centuries. It was during this period, then, that Maimonides wrote his famous philosophical treatise *A Guide for the Perplexed* and the *Mishneh Torah*, the most comprehensive compilation of Jewish law. The *Mishneh Torah* still serves as one of the most important referents for contemporary decisions. Maimonides, like other authorities, held positions that conflicted with one another and in certain cases with the plain reading of the Mishnah. In his earlier interpretations of texts, Maimonides supported the Demai paradigm. In his later interpretations he supported the Yevamot paradigm.

His responsa, in which he ruled on specific cases, did not follow his theory. He considered the implications of his ruling for the individual and for the community. He ruled in favor of the individual and of the community against the tradition, even against the plain meaning of the Mishnah. His rulings enhance the dignity of the individual. A few examples will illustrate this. They will also illustrate the subtlety and flexibility of much great halakhic thinking.

Community and Individual: Maimonides

Although it may appear that Maimonides favored the individual over the community, that was not his intent. He was concerned with both the dignity of the individual and the community. According to David Hartman,

> A careful and sensitive reading of Maimonides' works reveals that commitment to the community is actually a *lietmotiv* of all his works. Even in the Guide [to the Perplexed], Maimonides does not advocate an ivory-tower existence, but instead tries to convince the reader to return to the community.[28]

> Maimonides wanted to show that one could remain anchored in empirical reality and rationality and at the same time be loyal to the God of the Torah.[29]

In his *Mishneh Torah*, Maimonides wrote, "One who separates himself from the community has no position in the world to come [MT Hilkhot Teshuvah 3:20]." According to David Hartman, Maimonides gave his most expressed understanding and concern for the community in his responsum *Epistle to Yemen*:

> In the *Epistle to Yemen* Maimonides confronted the dilemma that the community faced as a result of the triumph of Islam and the consequent policy of forced conversion. Maimonides was addressing an audience

---

[28] Maimonides, *Epistles of Maimonides*, 6 (discussion by David Hartman).
[29] Ibid., 8.

paralyzed by disillusionment and doubt. The approach that he adopted was to enter into the world of the sufferers and restore their dignity despite their inability to act or express themselves freely.[30]

In his treatment of conversion, Maimonides would have been instructed by his concern both for the integrity of the community and for that of individual human beings for whom dignity. He expresses both these universal and particular concerns when he writes: "Do not consider yourself as inferior. While we are the descendants of Abraham, Isaac and Jacob, you derive from Him through whose word the world was created. As is said by Isaiah: 'One shall say, I am the Lord's, and another shall call himself by the name of Jacob' (Is. 44:5)."[31] The full text of the *Epistle to Yemen*, one of the most well-known responsa in Judaism, follows:

> Thus says Moses, the son of Rabbi Maimon, one of the exiles from Jerusalem, who lived in Spain:
>
> I received the question of the master Obadiah, the wise and learned proselyte, may the Lord reward him for his work, may a perfect recompense be bestowed upon him by the Lord of Israel, under whose wings he has sought cover.
>
> You ask me if you, too, are allowed to say in the blessings and prayers you offer alone or in the congregation: "Our God" and "God of our fathers," "You who have sanctified us through Your commandments," "You who have separated us," "You who have chosen us," "You who have inherited us," "You who have brought us out of the land of Egypt," "You who have worked miracles to our fathers," and more of this kind.
>
> Yes, you may say all this in the prescribed order and not change it in the least. In the same way as every Jew by birth says his blessing and prayer, you, too, shall bless and pray alike, whether you are alone or pray in the congregation. The reason for this is, that Abraham our Father taught the people, opened their minds, and revealed to them the true faith and the unity of God; he rejected the idols and abolished their adoration; he brought many children under the wings of the Divine Presence; he gave them counsel and advice, and ordered his sons and the members of his household after him to keep the ways of the Lord forever, as it is written, "For I have known him to the end that he may

---

[30] Ibid., 9.
[31] Twersky, *Maimonides Reader*, 476.

command his children and his household after him, that they may keep the way of the Lord, to do righteousness and justice" (Gen. 18:19). Ever since then, whoever adopts Judaism and confesses the unity of the Divine Name, as it is prescribed in the Torah, is counted among the disciples of Abraham our Father, peace be with him. These men are Abraham's household, and he it is who converted them to righteousness.

In the same way as he converted his contemporaries through his words and teaching, he converts future generations through the testament he left to his children and household after him. Thus Abraham our Father, peace be with him, is the father of his pious posterity who keep his ways, and the father of his disciples and of all proselytes who adopt Judaism.

Therefore you shall pray, "Our God" and "God of our fathers," because Abraham, peace be with him, is your father. And you shall pray, "You who have taken for his own our fathers," for the land has been given to Abraham, as it is said, "Arise, walk through the land in the length of it and in the breadth of it; for I will give to you" (Gen. 13:17). As to the words, "You who have brought us out of the land of Egypt" or "You who have done miracles to our fathers" — these you may change, if you will, and say, "You who have brought Israel out of the land of Egypt" and "You who have done miracles to Israel." If, however, you do not change them, it is no transgression, because since you have come under the wings of the Divine Presence and confessed the Lord, no difference exists between you and us, and all miracles done to us have been done as it were to us and to you. Thus is it said in the Book of Isaiah, "Neither let the son of the stranger, that has joined himself to the Lord, speak, saying, 'The Lord has utterly separated me from His people'" (Is. 56:3). There is no difference whatever between you and us. You shall certainly say the blessing, "Who has chosen us," "Who has given us," "Who have taken us for Your own" and "Who has separated us": for the Creator, may He be extolled, has indeed chosen you and separated you from the nations and given you the Torah. For the Torah has been given to us and to the proselytes, as it is said, "One ordinance shall be both for you of the congregation, and also for the stranger that sojourns with you, an ordinance for ever in your generations; as you are, so shall the stranger be before the Lord" (Num. 15:15). Know that our fathers, when they came out of Egypt, were mostly idolaters; they had mingled with the pagans in Egypt and imitated their way of life, until the Holy One, may He be blessed, sent Moses our Teacher, the master of all prophets, who separated us from the nations and brought us under the wings of the Divine Presence, us and all proselytes, and gave to all of us one Law.

Do not consider your origin as inferior. While we are the descendants of Abraham, Isaac, and Jacob, you derive from Him through whose word the world was created. As is said by Isaiah: "One shall say, I am the Lord's, and another shall call himself by the name of Jacob" (Is. 44:5).[32]

Often there is a difference between an authority's halakhic theory and the theory Maimonides employs in a specific case, as was his practice. Specific cases usually are decided more leniently because they affect an individual human being or the community.

The Court Decides: Rabbi Joseph Caro

Continuing our discussion of the two paradigms, Yevamot and Demai, we will review the views of R. Joseph Caro (1488–1575), who wrote the *Shulchan Aruch*, a summary of an earlier work by R. Jacob ben Asher (1269–1340), which, in turn, summarizes the positions of earlier authorities. Caro's *Shulchan Aruch* (The Set Table) became and remains the canonical text for Orthodox Jews.

R. ben Asher in *Beit Joseph* determines that the proselyte's motivations are halakhically irrelevant: "A man who underwent giyyur for the sake of a woman, as well as a woman who did so for the sake of a man . . . and someone who underwent giyyur for the sake of a royal table, as well as lion proselytes and dream proselytes — all are proselytes."[33] R. Joseph Caro disagrees with R. ben Asher. Caro cites Maimonides, the Tosafists,[34] and *Haggahot Mordekhai* (a compilation of Medieval French and German rabbinic scholars), all of whom held that the rabbinic court should not accept proselytes whose motives are known not to be for the sake of heaven. Caro then expresses his own view that everything is given to the discretion of the court. The court should accept a proselyte whose present views are not for the sake of heaven if he or she is expected to attain that view in the

---

[32] Ibid., 475–76.

[33] Jacob ben Asher, Arba'ah Turim, Yoreh De'ah, #268, 12, cited in Sagi and Zohar, *Transforming Identity*, 36.

[34] The rabbinic scholars in France and Germany from the twelfth to the fifteenth century were the Rishonim, the early leading rabbis, and the *poskim*, the legal scholars.

future. However, Caro later quotes Maimonides' position, which does not grant the court discretion. From the sixteenth century onward the rabbis adopted the position that a proselyte's motivation does not affect her or his conversion afterward but that it should affect the court's decision on whether or not to admit a person to the process of conversion.[35]

It is this position that became the dominant view and the basis for much of the rabbinic debate and innovation that has occurred from that time to the present. It is interesting to note that the pressures on the rabbis from the rapid changes in society led many to radical innovation in the policies and procedures concerning conversion prior to and after the middle of the eighteenth century, when Orthodoxy separated from liberal Jews and created the first separate Jewish denomination. Until that time liberal Jews in Germany, where the changes were initiated, considered themselves to be acting within normative Judaism and did not intend to create a separate denomination. They modified their synagogues and their practices in order to be more compatible with Christian practice and more accessible and inviting to German Jews.

The pressure on Jewish thought and practice initially began with the Enlightenment in Europe, which led to increased individual autonomy and scrutiny of practices and belief. The validity and authority of sacred texts and of rabbis were questioned. Many Jews no longer recognized the authority of either texts or rabbis. The emancipation freed Jews from the authority of the Jewish community in which they lived and from the need to live within a Jewish community. An increasing number of Jews chose to live a secular lifestyle. Interactions between Jews and gentiles became more common. Jews became more acceptable marriage partners. Civil marriages became available to Jews. These sociological changes led to a significant increase in intermarriage. This raised questions about rearing of children and conversion of a non-Jewish spouse.

Rabbis crafted their responses to these pressures on the meaning and practice of conversion by reinterpreting the meanings of the phrase "sake of heaven" and by reconsidering policies. Sagi and Zohar explain this as follows.

> Since the norms of halakhah were formulated in order to achieve certain goals, *prima facie* there is compatibility between following the letter

---

[35] Maimonides, *Laws of Forbidden Intercourse* 13.14, cited in Sagi and Zohar, *Transforming Identity*, 32.

of the law and fulfilling the law's goals. However, in certain circumstances or contexts it is possible for tension to exist, i.e. following the letter of the law may impair the fulfillment of its goals. In such cases, halakhic authorities frequently employ policy considerations, overriding literal performance of the norm in order to ensure better fulfillment of the system's goals. We saw an example of this in the previous chapter: Maimonides encourages the marriage of the young master to the woman with whom he had conducted an illicit relationship when she was his bondwoman, although the Mishnah prohibits such a marriage. His reasons are based on policy.[36]

A VERBAL STATEMENT IS ACCEPTABLE

The Talmud accepts that a person may say one thing and mean something else. That does not invalidate the plain meaning of the verbal declaration: "When Israel stood at Mount Sinai and responded '[All that the Lord has said] we will do, and heed' (Exod. 24.7), that was with their mouth. But their heart was not true, as [king] David said: 'They did flatter him with their mouths, and they lied to him with their tongues. For their heart was not steadfast with him, neither were they faithful in his covenant' (Ps. 78.36–37)."[37] The Talmud also states that the court decides the meaning of a statement made under oath. The intent of the person making the statement is irrelevant. It is the intent of the court that is decisive. Jacob Caro granted the court wide latitude to determine the policies and procedure for conversion. The discretion granted to the court is emphasized by a Tannaitic text on statements made under oath to a court.

> They say to him: "Know, that it is not according to what is in your heart that we adjure you, but in accord with what is in our hearts. And so we find that when Moses adjured the Israelites in the plains of Moab, he said to them: 'Not according to what is in your hearts do I adjure you, but according to what is in my heart.' As it is said: 'Nor is it with you only that I make this sworn covenant, but with him who is not here

---

[36] Sagi and Zohar, *Transforming Identity*, 38.
[37] Midrash halakhah to Exodus, Mekilta of R. Ishmael, Maseket d'Neziqin, Parashah 13, cited in Sagi and Zohar, *Transforming Identity*, 224.

with us this day, as well as with him who stands here with us this day before the Lord our God'" (Deut. 29.13–14).[38]

God Is Faithful: Conversion Is Irrevocable

God told Moses that He expected the Israelites to obey him faithfully and to keep his covenants: "The LORD called to him from the mountain, saying, 'Thus shall you say to the house of Jacob and declare to the children of Israel: You have seen what I did to the Egyptians, how I bore you on eagles' wings and brought you to me. Now, then, if you will obey me faithfully and keep my covenant, you shall be my treasured possession among all the peoples" (Exodus 19:3–6). Nevertheless, God, after telling the Israelites that he was permitting them to possess the land of their enemies not because of Israel's virtues but because of the wickedness of their enemies (Deuteronomy 9:4–5), assured them that he would not abandon them: "Yet even then, when they are in the land of their enemies, I will not reject them or spurn them so as to destroy them, annulling my covenant with them; for I the LORD am their God" (Leviticus 26:44). The paradigmatic rabbinic statement that affirms God's steadfast faithfulness to Israel is this: "'Israel has sinned' (Josh. 7.11). Rabbi Abba son of Zavda said: Even though he has sinned, he is still an Israelite. This is in an accordance with the adage that people say: Even when a myrtle is found among thorns, its name is myrtle and people call it myrtle."[39] Maimonides supports the permanence of membership in the community once it is acquired and questions the permanence of membership for those who doubt certain principles of faith. This ambivalence is characteristic of his rulings on conversion and of his responsa that violate halakhic rulings in favor of respecting the dignity of the individual.

An example of a multivalent statement by Maimonides that both supports and undermines the permanence of election is one that I cited earlier:

> When all these foundations are perfectly understood and believed in by a person, he enters the community of Israel and one is obligated to love and pity him and to act towards him in all ways in which the Creator

---

[38] Babylonian Talmud, Sotah 7:4, in *Tosefta*, trans. Neusner, 1:861, cited in Sagi and Zohar, *Transforming Identity*, 225.
[39] Sanhedrin 44a.

has commanded that one should act towards his brother, with love and fraternity. Even were he to commit every possible transgression, because of lust and because of being overpowered by evil inclination, he will be punished according to his rebelliousness, but he has a portion [of the world to come]; he is one of the sinners of Israel. But if a man doubts any of these foundations, he leaves the community [of Israel], denies the fundamental, and is called a sectarian, apikous, and one who cuts among the plantings.[40] One is required to hate and destroy him.[41]

Conversion was always considered irrevocable until recently, when Orthodox rabbis in Israel determined that it was contingent on sincere belief and on maintaining an Orthodox way of life.

The discretion of rabbis to conduct conversions is strictly limited in Israel. Power is centralized in the chief rabbinate of the state, which has the authority to ensure that rabbinic courts do not accept proselytes whose motives and lifestyle do not absolutely conform to halakhah. These courts can invalidate retroactively the conversion of proselytes who does not maintain an Orthodox way of life. The effect of retroactive annulment of conversion is painful to converts, their children, and their relationships in the community.

The Shift to a Restrictive Conception of Conversion

We will follow the trajectory of these radical innovations in the meaning of conversion and Jewish identity in the controversy over the meaning of the acceptance of the commandments. This is illustrated in the positions of two prominent Eastern European halakhists: R. Shlomo Lipschitz (ca. 1730–1807) and R. Meir Posner (1765–1839), the first chief rabbi of Poland. R. Lipschitz interpreted Caro to mean that conversion was a religious transformation characterized as "a matter of the heart," an internal, spiritual change, in which acceptance of the commandments was a performative and

---

[40] "Cuts among the plantings" refers to R. Aher in a mystical story about four rabbis who went to heaven. One died. One became deranged. Aher became disillusioned, and upon his return to earth Aher argued against traditional beliefs and led young people astray. Only R. Akiva returned unharmed. He alone had reached a sufficiently high spiritual level to permit him to understand all that he saw without it having deleterious effects on his beliefs or his mind.

[41] Maimonides, *Laws of Kings and Wars*, trans. in Sagi and Zohar, *Transforming Identity*, 24.

spiritual transformation. This was an innovative extension of the Demai paradigm, which required an internal spiritual transformation in addition to external observance of the commandments: "The crux of giyyur is, that he [the proselyte] abandoned his people and his gods, and came to take shelter under the wings of the Shekhinah, and accepted the religion of Israel to enter into the congregation of the Lord."[42] R. Lipschitz sent his responsa to R. Posner and asked for his opinion. R. Posner disagreed with R. Lipschitz and, in his response, indicated that he followed the intent of the Yevamot paradigm.

> What proof is this? Perhaps it was by the acceptance of commandments at Sinai [that the mothers entered under the wings of the Shekhinah]? Surely, this [the fact that the Talmud never even suggests that they entered under the wings of the Shekhinah through acceptance of the commandments] is proof that notification about the commandment and their acceptance is not the crux of the giyyur. For it is logically clear to the Talmud that [for giyyur] an act of sanctification must be performed on the proselyte's physis. If so, how is it possible that "judgement" [the required presence of a court] applies specifically to the acceptance of the commandments?[43]

Rabbi Posner accepted the concept that acceptance of the commandments at Sinai was a form of conversion: "All that the Lord has said, we will do and heed."

This was not the opinion of early rabbinic authorities. However, in his responsa, R. Posner demonstrated that the Tosafists, whom R. Lipschitz cited, were not in accord with the Talmud and needed to be reinterpreted because postTalmudic sages were not permitted to disagree with the Talmud. R. Posner wrote that several great medieval scholars had already provided such an interpretation: "It is for this reason that Nahmanides, as well as [Joseph Haviva, author of] *Nimmukei Yosef*, clarified that the contents of 'accepting the commandments' are that he accepts upon himself [to perform] circumcision and immersion; since he accepts upon himself [to perform] an act of sanctification on his *physis*, it is enough if three are present when he declares such acceptance, even if the act [of sanctification] is performed

---

[42] Lipschitz, *Responsa Hemdat Shelomo*, #291, par. 22, cited in Sagi and Zohar, *Transforming Identity*, 208.
[43] Posner, *Responsa Beit Meir*, 69a, cited in Sagi and Zohar, *Transforming Identity*, 212.

later, when he is alone."[44] Posner then applies this view to his reading of the *Shulchan Aruch*, by Joseph Caro. In his responsa cited above and in the following statement, Posner indicates that both the Tosafists and he are in accord with the Yevamot paradigm: "For the Tosafists . . . the crux of accepting the commandments is in that she commits herself, in the presence of the court, to immerse for the purpose of *giyyur*."[45]

The positions of R. Lipschitz and R. Posner illustrate the differing positions of rabbis who preceded them and who followed them. The meaning of acceptance of the commandments became the pivotal issue in the ensuing interpretations of the meaning and process of conversion and in the concepts of Jewish identity that were embedded in them. The validity of a proselyte's conversion became provisional for those who did not live an Orthodox lifestyle.

This radical transformation of the traditional position is embedded in contemporary Orthodox practice, which requires exhaustive investigation of a candidate's lifestyle prior to acceptance for giyyur, continual monitoring of a proselyte's lifestyle after giyyur, and invalidation of the conversion if there is suspicion of deviation from strict Orthodox practice. The Israeli chief rabbis support this position. Under pressure from the Israeli rabbinate, the American Orthodox Rabbinic Board adopted the same position. The prevailing presumption is that those who present themselves for conversion are not worthy candidates and should be rejected.

This view was characterized in the statement of R. Mordecai Jacob Breisch (1896–1976), who knew that in modern times a gentile might sincerely wish to be a Jew and join the Jewish nation or people without intending to live according to halakhah.[46]

> Sinners, who do not want to know anything about Judaism: dietary laws, the Sabbath, family purity, and all the commandments are a burden to them, and they are only Jews by nationality. [The court] knows with certainty that the Gentile woman who is seemingly undergoing *giyyur*, will not at all observe Judaism . . . and it is therefore simple to me, that even ex post facto . . . this is not a *giyyur* at all, since [failing to] assume the yoke of the commandments is a matter that invalidates [*giyyur*] even

---

[44] Posner, *Responsa Beit Meir*, cited in Sagi and Zohar, *Transforming Identity*, 213.
[45] Sagi and Zohar, *Transforming Identity*, 213.
[46] Breisch, *Helkot Ya'akov*, part 1m, #13, i, cited Sagi and Zohar, *Transforming Identity*, 240.

ex post facto . . . and what acceptance of the commandments is there if we know that they mock and despise the Sabbath, family purity, and the dietary laws?! . . . Even if we were to believe that she [the woman proselyte] is genuinely intent on becoming a Jew by nationality, without observing the Sabbath, the laws of family purity and the other commandments, like her husband [the secular Jew]. Such a giyyur is invalid even ex post facto.[47]

Breisch addresses the issue of a Jewish society in Israel that is predominantly secular and nonobservant. He concludes that halakhah does not attribute any significance to a secular Jewish society. He presages a growing alienation between the ultra-Orthodox and secular society.

R. Abraham Duber Cahana Shapira (1870–1943) takes a similar position and generalizes it, whereas R. Breisch addresses a single case.

Regarding what some rabbis have written, that we should not be concerned about what the proselyte thinks in his heart, because matters of the heart are of no consequence—that was so only in earlier times. But now, how can we delude ourselves, when we know that in most cases there exists a confirmed presumption that after the *giyyur* they will not perform the commandments, and their heart is not at all in it? When there exists a confirmed presumption, even matters of the heart are considered of consequence.[48]

R. Isaac HaLevi Herzog (1888–1959), the first Ashkenazi chief rabbi of Israel, outlines in a responsum the religious and sociological differences between traditional and modern Jewish society that have instructed the actions of ultra-Orthodox rabbis since the middle of the nineteenth century. R. Herzog creates a new category for giyyur, an "indeterminate proselyte."

In the days of the Talmudic rabbis and in the days of the great *halakhic* authorities, there was virtually no place within the Jewish community for a deviant Jew. If a Gentile underwent giyyur, even if he did so because of material considerations, we could regard his agreement to perform the commandments as serious, because otherwise [if he would not perform

---

[47] Sagi and Zohar, *Transforming Identity*, 240.
[48] Shapira, *Devar Avaraham*, vol 3. #28 *2 Yevamot 47b, cited in Sagi and Zohar, *Transforming Identity*, 241.

them] his life would be most impossible. But in our times, to our sorrow, the situation is so unruly that Jews who are by law [halakhah] heavy sinners serve as leaders of communities and even of the entire nation. That being the case, what does it matter to the Gentile man or woman to say outwardly that s/he accepts Judaism? And why should they perform the commandments when so many Jews do not do so?

Therefore, there is a presumption that their acceptance [of the commandments] is in doubt, when the reason for their giyyur is ulterior. And therefore, there is reason to rule that they are indeterminate proselytes [*gerei safek*]. If so, the law changes: if such candidates come to us in order to be accepted for *giyyur*, we should refrain. Because . . . [if we accept them] we are enabling the intermingling of the seed of persons who may be Gentiles with Jews.[49]

The scholars we have quoted above agree that acceptance of the commandments is fulfilled by a sincere inner intent to observe them. Their intention to maintain the purity of Jewish seed, however, is deemed impossible to fulfill under prevailing social and ethical realities. They may have forgotten the ethnic consequences of rape, intermarriage, and forced conversions to Christianity.

Sincere Faith and Correct Belief Are Requisite

Toward the middle of the twentieth century, a stronger "Protestant" voice, as Sagi and Zohar describe it, began to permeate ultra-Orthodox discourse. According to this voice, sincere subjective performative intent is not enough. Rather, it is imperative that such performative intent stem from sincere faith and correct belief in the divine source of Torah and of Israel's uniqueness. "To the best our knowledge," Sagi and Zohar state, "the originator of this approach is Rabbi Abraham Isaiah Karelitz [1878–1953], who reasoned" as follows:

It seems that *giyyur* applies only to a person who deeply believes that God, through his prophets, commanded laws and ordinances to the people of Israel and separated them from all nations, and informed them

---

[49] Herzog, *Responsa Heikhal Yitzhak*, Yevamot 47b, cited in Sagi and Zohar, *Transforming Identity*, 243.

that they can accept proselytes from all nations through circumcision, immersion, and acceptance. The proselyte thereby enters the Torah of the Jewish people, including all its past and future generations. But, if he does not believe all this, and undertakes to behave according to the laws of the Torah because he finds that such behavior is beneficial to him or protects him from harm, this is not acceptance of *giyyur*.[50]

"According to Karelitz," Avi and Zohar continue,

> even this is not enough because Israel's separation from all the nations creates an essential difference between them. The question then arises: what are the grounds enabling a person who was not born a Jew to overcome this difference and become a Jew? Karelitz's answer is that giyyur is possible only if the proselyte also believes that the same God that separated Israel from the nations also "informed them that they can accept proselytes from all the nations," and also revealed to them the procedure through which this transformation can be effected: "circumcision, immersion, and acceptance."[51]

Karelitz postulates that a proper candidate who is worthy of joining the Jewish people must have a deep understanding and sincere acceptance of the ultra-Orthodox conception of belief and must not have any ulterior motive. Only an ideal candidate, who has internalized this ideal belief, will be accepted:

> This view was adopted and more fully developed by a hitherto unknown scholar Yitzchak Brand. His book, *Brit Yitzchak*, was approved by leading ultra-orthodox rabbis at the time. He follows Karelitz's view that conversion is entry into the Jewish religion and therefore it can be achieved only through sincere religious belief. In the absence of this belief, conversion is invalid even if the proper procedures were followed.[52]

Now, at the culmination of a century-long transformation within Ultra-Orthodox halakhah, *giyyur* has metamorphosed into conversion, i.e. a

---

[50] Hazon Ish [Abraham Isaiah Karelitz], *Yorea De'ah*, 119.2, Yevamot 47b, cited in Sagi and Zohar, *Transforming Identity*, 244.
[51] Yevamot 47b, cited in Sagi and Zohar, *Transforming Identity*, 246.
[52] Sagi and Zohar, *Transforming Identity*, 246.

dispositional emotional faith experience. Since this experiential event is an internal emotion within the heart of the proselyte, the court's yardstick for the validity of *giyyur* can no longer be legal and objective, but is rather an empathetic emotional feeling generated by that of the proselyte.[53]

RETROACTIVE ANNULMENT OF CONVERSION

A proselyte's inner transformation, an empathetic emotional feeling, is so subjective that it is difficult if not impossible to determine. The rabbis needed a method to satisfy themselves that it had occurred. Several rabbis determined that inner intent could be ascertained by subsequent practice. If the proselyte did not meet their standards of practice, it was clear that she had not transformed herself as they required. Consequently, the conversion was faulty and was annulled retroactively. The first rabbi to articulate this position was R. Yitzchak Brand. Brand stated clearly that a proselyte must observe the commandments as she decides they should be observed, or the conversion is annulled retroactively: "It is obvious . . . that in cases where there is indication that she does not will to accept the commandments, then, due to lack of acceptance, the giyyur is totally annulled. This shall become clear over the course of time: if she subsequently fails to observe the commandments, she is considered an absolute Gentile."[54] Brand's thinking was implemented forty years later, in the early 1980s, when R. Gedalya Axelrod, a member of the rabbinical court in Haifa, used it to mobilize the Israeli rabbinate to support increasingly severe restrictions on admitting proselytes. The support of the Knesset—Israel's Parliament—and prime ministers facilitated his efforts. At the founding of the state, Prime Minister Ben Gurion exempted the Orthodox from military service and gave their rabbis control over marriage, divorce, burial, and conversion—a control that was similar to rabbinic control in Jewish communities prior to the Enlightenment, Haskalah, and the emancipation under Napoleon.

In 1983, R. Axelrod addressed a halakhic question to R. Yosef Shalom Elyashiv, one of the leading Lithuanian authorities in Israel, in which R. Axelrod stated that there were many people who became proselytes without

[53] Ibid.
[54] Yitzchak b.Z. Brand, *Briti Yitzhak* (Jerusalem: Bnei Brak, 1982), 26, quoted in Sagi and Zohar, *Transforming Identity*, 253.

intending to observe halakhah. R. Axelrod proposed enlisting the marriage registrar to ascertain that the conversion court had not converted a proselyte who was not following strict Orthodox practice. It was clear that he thought that many rabbis in Israel were not maintaining proper restrictions on conversion and marriage. R. Elyashiv supported R. Axelrod's suggestion that marriage registrars be required to ascertain the validity of the conversion by determining if the individual was, indeed, living a strict Orthodox lifestyle.

R. Axelrod enlisted two other rabbinical judges to form a committee that on August 31, 1983, sent out copies of his treatise to all marriage registrars in Israel. They were instructed to deny a marriage license to any proselyte they thought was not living according to the strictest orthodox standards: "We the undersigned, rabbis and rabbinical court judges in Israel, request you to examine the lifestyle of hundreds and hundreds of proselytes in the kibbutzim, in the cities and elsewhere, and to ascertain if they observe the commandments — or if they received certificates of *giyyur* through deceit and their *giyyur* is false."[55] R. Axelrod and the two judges intended to transfer the responsibility for giyyur from the special courts that had been established for that sole purpose back to the ordinary courts. The special courts had been established because the regular courts had rejected most applications for giyyur. The special courts were staffed predominantly by moderate Orthodox rabbis, whereas the regular rabbinic courts, which previously had authority for giyyur, were staffed by ultra-Orthodox rabbis who assumed that candidates did not follow their guidelines and, consequently, should be rejected.

R. Axelrod attempted to force the registrars to validate the candidate themselves and to ignore the certificates of giyyur issued by the Chief Orthodox Rabbinate of Israel. "When there is a conflict between [Israeli] law and halakhah, the rabbi acting as marriage registrar is obligated by halakhah and not by law, and he is obligated by halakhah to refer the bearer of the certificate to the [regular] rabbinic court, and not to allow him to marry before clarification of his status."[56] R. Axelrod continued his effort to emasculate the special courts for conversion and to delegitimize the certificates of conversion issued by the chief Orthodox rabbi of Israel. He published a responsum in 1995 in the official publication of the Israeli Rabbinical Courts to accomplish this:

---

[55] *Scandal of the Forged Giyyurim*, 237, cited in Sagi and Zohar, *Transforming Identity*, 256.
[56] Axelrod, *Halachic Value*, 6, cited in Sagi and Zohar, *Transforming Identity*, 259.

> The certificate of *giyyur* is considered by halakhah as a certificate of Jewishness, but only as a certificate affirming that the bearer underwent circumcision and immersion in the presence of a court. But s/he nevertheless falls under the law that she should be regarded with reservation until his righteousness becomes apparent.[57]
>
> All the responsa that we quoted above, and others that we did not cite, indicate that in our times the presumption is that the intention of those seeking to undergo *giyyur* is, to mislead the court when they say that they will observe the commandments, while in their hearts they are far from such intent . . . and the court has no permission to allow those seeking giyyur to fool them.[58]

Sagi and Zohar write that R. Axelrod's novel interpretation of halakhah led him to issue unprecedented guidelines with regard to certificates of conversion. R. Axelrod wrote in his responsum:

> The [halakhic] consequence of our discussion is that the following wording must be added to certificates of *giyyur*:
> a. This certificate is valid only if its bearer observes Torah and its commandments.
> b. The validity of this certificate is limited to [a certain] period of time and must be renewed once a year.[59]

Sagi and Zohar comment: "Thus, only a person who was born to a Jewish mother is irrevocably Jewish. All others are on eternal probation, and their Jewishness is always completely contingent. This new creature—'contingent Jew'—was never even imagined by the authors of the Demai paradigm, let alone the authors of Tractate Yevamot who stress that even if the proselyte reverts to pagan behaviour immediately after immersion 'he is like a Jew in every respect.'"[60]

Although R. Axelrod's responsum on giyyur has not been accepted by the rabbinic authorities in Israel, it is of concern to proselytes who because

---

[57] Axelrod, *Observance of the Commandments*, cited in Sagi and Zohar, *Transforming Identity*, 259.

[58] Axelrod, *Observance of the Commandments*, cited in Sagi and Zohar, *Transforming Identity*, 259.

[59] Sagi and Zohar, *Transforming Identity*, 260.

[60] Sagi and Zohar, *Transforming Identity*, 260.

of the possibility of it being adopted remain in an uncomfortable category of a convert whose conversion may be annulled at any time.

In February 2005 the Knesset Committee on Aliyah and the Diaspora held a hearing in which they were told by the rabbis present that there had not been a case in the past fifteen years in which conversion was annulled retroactively. However, in 2002 a special rabbinic court for conversion annulled the conversion of a woman because of doubt; and the Ashdod Rabbinical Court annulled the conversion of another woman.[61] As Sagi and Zohar note: "A copy of Rabbi Attiyah's decision, dated 22/02/2007, was received by us just before going to press. The majority of sources quoted by Attiyah were composed by Axelrod. *Inter alia*, the document contains a vitriolic attack upon the special courts of *giyyur* operating under the auspices of the Israeli Chief Rabbinate. Arguing that the rabbis serving as those courts are apostates, Attiyah states that in his view they are *ipso facto* halakhically disqualified from serving as judges and therefore all procedures of *giyyur* conducted under their auspices are invalid."[62]

Gentile Impurities

What is there about gentiles that caused the Jewish tradition to be wary of them as candidates for conversion? One constraint is that many authorities, including Rashi and Maimonides, assume that proselytes will not observe the commandments: "Proselytes are as hard for Israel to endure as a sore."[63]

Some of the concern came during periods of pressure or attacks on Jews. Some came when participating in the conversion of a gentile to Judaism was punishable by death. Some came through the notion of holy seed, notably presented in the *Kuzari: In Defense of the Despised Faith*, by Judah ha-Levi (1140). However, the predominant attitude in the tradition was that the gentile should be treated with dignity and that Jewish law applied to those who followed a civilized code of conduct. Even in the *Kuzari*, in which ha-Levi posited a holy seed and the superiority of the Jewish religion over others, there is another voice. The king of the Kuzars says that when Jews had power, they would act like all other people and oppress their enemies.

---

[61] The official decision of the Rabbinical Court was signed on June 27, 2002, and was signed by the head clerk on July 11, 2002; cited in Sagi and Zohar, *Transforming Identity*, 261.
[62] Sagi and Zohar, *Transforming Identity*, 263.
[63] Ibid.

Christine Hayes, the Robert F. and Patricia Ross Weis Professor of Religious Studies in Classical Judaica and former chair of the Department of Religious Studies at Yale University, writes about the meaning in early Judaism of gentile impurities and of holy seed. Immersion in conversion is not considered to be the removal of gentile impurities. She states that although some later authorities speak of the need to retain the purity of Jewish seed, in the postexilic and late antique period, "the types of impurity most consistently applied to Gentiles were moral and genealogical. All ancient Jewish sources — from the Bible to the Talmud — asserted that Gentiles no less than Israelites were capable of generating moral impurity through the commission of heinous deeds of idolatry and immorality."[64]

Moral impurity is avoidable. It can be overcome in a community that observes laws and follows moral codes of conduct: "Thus, to the degree that the distinction between Jew and Gentile was perceived to be a moral distinction, to that degree the boundary between Jew and Gentile could be crossed as Gentiles abandoned idolatry and immorality and adopted the behavioral norms of Jewish culture."[65]

The Jews in exile in Babylonia were freed by the Persian emperor Cyrus the Great in 538 BCE. At that time genealogical purity was required only of the priests. Genealogical purity as the distinguishing characteristic of Israelite identity was introduced by Ezra (480–444 BCE). Ezra applied the requirement for genealogical purity to all Jews. He established a boundary between Jews and gentiles that could not be overcome at that time because a system for conversion had not been created. Ezra required all Jews who had married gentiles to divorce their wives. This was intended to protect the purity of Jewish identity. It also reduced the enticement of other religious practices. Hayes writes, "As two distinct seeds, one holy and the other profane, Gentiles and Jews are permanently and inescapably distinct. Gentiles cannot become Jews."[66]

However, the distinction of holy seed was gradually eroded:

Rabbinic sources retain some dim reflexes of Ezran ideology and terminology, now thoroughly defanged and domesticated. For example, conversion

---

[64] Hayes, *Gentile Impurities and Jewish Identities*, 193.
[65] Ibid.
[66] Ibid. Hayes cites Isaiah 6:13: "But while a tenth part yet remains in it, it shall repent. It shall be ravaged like a terebinth and the oak, of which stumps are left even when they are felled; its stump shall be a holy seed."

is described as a process of sanctification, reflecting the Ezran idea that Israel is holy, but Ezra's intention is entirely undermined by the rabbis' guarantee of foreign access to that sanctified status. Unions with Gentile women are labeled *zenut* . . . [a term that refers] to a union that fails to establish a legally valid marriage, rather than a heinous moral crime that defiles the holy seed of Israel. In addition, although interethnic unions can blemish an offspring's genealogy, this blemish is not a moral stain, transmitted across generations, and does not affect the marriageability of a convert's offspring.[67]

The ideas of pure seed, ritual impurity, and moral impurity eroded gradually. They do not exist in liberal Judaism today. It is unlikely that there is a pure seed, a line of descent that has absorbed no seed from outside a community that has survived for many generations.

---

[67] Hayes, *Gentile Impurities and Jewish Identities*, 195.

CHAPTER 5

A Reform Responsum on Conversion

R. David Ellenson (b. 1942), a Reform rabbi, and R. Daniel Gordis (b. 1959), a Conservative rabbi, coauthored a book on conversion, *Pledges of Jewish Allegiance: Conversion, Law, and Policymaking in Nineteenth- and Twentieth-Century Orthodox Responsa* (2012), twenty-eight years after Sagi and Zohar initially published *Transforming Identity* in Hebrew and five years after they published a revised edition in English. Although the two pairs of authors may not have intended to express a different sensibility, Sagi and Zohar posit that in the Jewish tradition converts were welcomed, whereas Ellenson and Gordis hold that the status of converts was traditionally considered problematic. The predominance of texts that Sagi and Zohar cite reflect a more positive attitude toward conversion and converts than the texts that Ellenson and Gordis cite. Sagi and Zohar posit that during the thousand-year period in Jewish history leading up to the present, converts were welcomed, their motives were not questioned, and conversion was irrevocable. The latter part of their book, in which they discuss contemporary thought and practice after the Enlightenment, is less positive and more in the mood of Ellenson and Gordis, who limited their purview to nineteenth- and twentieth-century rabbinic views on conversion.

Sagi and Zohar in *Transforming Identity* write about the search for halakhic as well as for theological certainty regarding conversion. They quote Joseph Caro, who writes that halakhah follows Beit Hillel (the "house" or school of R. Hillel),[1] because their rulings were always true. The ethical modesty of Beit Hillel causes them to question themselves and to explore the issue more carefully and fully, thus coming closer to the truth. Theological truth is not their objective. They seek human flourishing, which in Greek is called *eudaimonia*. "These and these are the words of the living God, but the Halakhah follows the rulings of Bet Hillel."[2] The legitimacy of a

---

[1] *Beit*, "house," refers to a person and to a school of thought that follows that person's thinking. Quotations ascribed to Hillel may have been made by members of his school who lived during his lifetime and immediately afterward.

[2] Babylonian Talmud, Eruvin 13b.

diversity of focus and of opinion in halakhic discourse is confirmed in this seminal statement. A liberal or pluralistic interpretation of "These and these are the words of the living God" is that both Beit Shammai and Beit Hillel express God's word. Both interpret God's word with equal sincerity. In our era, there are those who follow Beit Shammai and there are those who follow Beit Hillel.

Interpretation and Interpreter Reciprocate

Ellenson and Gordis write that "the personal measure of the interpreter cannot be eliminated." Sagi and Zohar express the same thought:

> The parameters of the law and its holdings are forged in the crucible of life by human beings who bring intense convictions in specific historical contexts to the cases that come before them. Legal decision-making is unavoidably malleable and varied, and a spectrum of positions emerge even when persons devoted to the same canon of law make decisions in difficult cases. There is an inescapable hermeneutical circle that involves, on the one hand, texts containing diverse principles and postures and, on the other, human and therefore finite interpreters who understand and weigh these texts and principles in distinct ways in distinct settings. Rather, it indicates that no judgment that a rabbi offers can fully transcend the limitations that hedge human nature. Every time a rabbi offers an interpretation of law, he necessarily enacts into law parts of his own theological beliefs, his assessment of the particular challenges facing the Jewish people, and his philosophy of *halakhah*. The personal measure of the interpreter cannot be eliminated.[3]

Pledges of Jewish Allegiance exhibits a sympathetic understanding of the basis upon which traditional Orthodox scholars base their decisions. It claims that the Orthodox are seeking to understand God's will and to follow it. Normally this process leads slowly to change. The reforms in Germany in the nineteenth century led to a halt in this process within Orthodoxy that may be considered a reform itself. The spokesperson for this abrupt closing of the tradition was Rabbi Moshe Sofer (1762–1838), who stated that "everything new is forbidden in Torah." In making this

---

[3] Ellenson and Gordis, *Pledges of Jewish Allegiance*, 169.

pronouncement he interpreted imaginatively a text that was unrelated to observance or prayer. It concerned the purity of seed sold in the marketplace. His interpretation forbade the Orthodox from continuing the forward thrust of halakhic discourse, which had enabled that discourse to deal with new existential realities of the Jewish people. The interpretation was diametrically opposed to the trajectory of the tradition that was expressed in the Yevamot paradigm for conversion. It is equally opposed to the current unprecedented changes in the interpretation and practice of the halakhic tradition concerning conversion by the ultra-Orthodox themselves in Israel and in the United States. R. Moshe Feinstein, of New York (1895–1986), the leading Orthodox voice in his time, wrote in 1950 that "it is evident that no conversion performed by a Conservative rabbi has legal standing."[4] He further argued in 1971 that "even if no one witnesses their transgressions of Torah, the name 'Reform' testifies to the fact that they are heretics."[5]

Ellenson and Gordis observe:

> In Orthodox Judaism, the arena in which conversion, law, and politics meet in modern Jewish life is halakhah, or Jewish law. Like all Jewish communities, the world of Orthodoxy grapples with issues of Jewish identity, social policy, and boundary maintenance. But it does so primarily through the halakhic, or Jewish legal, process and by engaging in legal discourse, because Orthodox Judaism in general and the Orthodox rabbinate in particular are theologically committed to the belief that God's will finds expression within the classical texts of the Jewish legal tradition and their ongoing interpretation. And because halakhah (like many other legal systems) is precedent-based, it is impossible to appreciate the subtleties of contemporary arguments without reference to the legal texts and cases to which they allude, whether explicitly or implicitly.[6]

Pledges of Jewish Allegiance discusses the current state of conversion in the Orthodox world, in which converts are not welcomed, their motives are questioned, their sincerity in accepting Judaism is suspect, their future lifestyle is commanded, and their conversion is contingent. This lack of concern for the human dignity of a small and vulnerable group of people

---

[4] Ibid., 104.
[5] Ibid.
[6] Ibid., 15.

who want to become Jewish is uncharacteristic of the Jewish tradition. In New York, a prominent Orthodox named R. Ari Weiss (b. 1944) who heads a yeshiva (an orthodox school of Torah study) performs conversions and ordains male and female rabbis without the approval of the Orthodox rabbinic establishment.[7]

Identity, Status, and Community

Ellenson and Gordis differentiate between identity and status as categories that historically were coterminous but have become separated in the modern world. Others differentiate between identity and membership. I will use the terms "identity," "status," and "membership" as they are used by each source we review. Ellenson and Gordis write early in their book:

> We will preface the analysis of these opinions with a discussion of these modern writings as parts of an ongoing legal tradition draw upon classic Jewish sources. We will employ these works as the lens through which we can understand the overlapping but distinct ways in which traditionalist religious authorities have gone about the task of defining the core of Jewishness—Jewish identity, status, and community—in the modern situation.[8]

> "Status" . . . refers to the condition of a person in the eyes of the law. When employed with regard to a person's relationship to a group, the person's own conception of that relationship may be irrelevant.[9]

> When the term "identity," as opposed to "status," is employed to refer to a person's relationship to a group, it may simply signify the psychological orientation of the individual toward that group. It reflects the individual's autonomous understanding of who he or she is. Individuals

---

[7] R. Dov Haiyun, a leading Conservative rabbi in Israel, was taken for interrogation at 5 a.m. by the Israeli police, according to the United Synagogue of Conservative Judaism (USCJ) umbrella group. Haiyun, who has been officiating at non-Orthodox weddings in Israel for decades, appeared hours after his release at an event at the residence of President Reuven Rivlin to participate in a program in which he taught Torah to Reform, Conservative, Orthodox, and Secular Jewish scholars.

[8] Ellenson and Gordis, *Pledges of Jewish Allegiance*, 2.

[9] Ibid., 2–3.

who participate in the life of a given Jewish community might well identify as Jews despite not having undergone any formal rite of conversion to Judaism.[10]

Rabbis Ellenson and Gordis observe that since in the modern period status and identity are no longer coterminous, Jewish identity and membership have become self-evident.[11]

> Modernity has dissolved the "synonymity" of status and identity and has thrust upon Judaism a number of lasting changes that have redefined the terms under which Jews live. [Historically,] being a member of the Jewish collective was not a matter that was subject to an individual's own beliefs or desires but was dictated by the rules of Jewish law and the communal structures that enforced them. The lines between Jew and non-Jew were clearly drawn.[12]

The diversity of thought in the tradition is illustrated by the texts I have thus far analyzed to this point. We will explore some of the texts in *Pledges of Jewish Allegiance* that illustrate further the diversity of thought in Judaism — in this case, the difference in the valence of interpretation of the same texts by Ellenson and Gordis in *Pledges of Jewish Allegiance* and by Sagi and Zohar in *Transforming Identity*.

The first difference between the two pairs of authors is Ellenson and Gordis's emphasis on the otherness of the convert in traditional rabbinic texts, and the consequent impossibility of the convert ever becoming a full member of the Jewish collective:

> Even after joining the Israelite community, the *geir* is still a stranger, an outsider quintessentially "other" in some sense. That the *geir* remains a foreigner is clear from a variety of passages. Numerous verses in the Torah warn the Israelite not to oppress the stranger. The frequency of such warnings suggests that such oppression must have been a serious issue. The Torah warns: "There shall be one law for the citizen and for the stranger who dwells among you" [Exodus 12:49; cf. Leviticus 24:22]; "You shall not wrong a *geir* or oppress him, for you were strangers in

---

[10] Ibid., 4.
[11] Ibid.
[12] Ibid., 5.

the land of Egypt" [Exodus 22:21]; and "You and the *geir* shall be alike before the Lord" [Numbers 15:15]. Indeed, the classic language of Deuteronomy associates the stranger with those most in need of protection: "You shall not subvert the rights of the *geir* or the fatherless; you shall not take a widow's garment in pawn" [Deuteronomy 24:17]. These warnings against oppressing the *geir* should not be construed to mean that the Torah believes that the stranger can ever be wholly incorporated into Israelite society. These warnings attest to what must have been an abiding sense of "otherness" for people such as these.[13]

Ellenson and Gordis point out that in the Bible, the convert is referred to as *ger*, a word that denotes both stranger and convert.[14] They cite biblical passages that portray the dangers the stranger (*ger*) poses to the citizen. "The *geir* in your midst shall rise above you higher and higher, while you sink lower and lower: he shall be your creditor, but you shall not be his; he shall be the head and you the tail."[15] Rabbinic Judaism was wary of accepting a convert qua stranger. Mishnah Bikkurim 1–4, in a discussion about the firstfruits of the harvest that were to be brought to the temple,[16] asked whether the convert may recite the phrase "which the Lord has sworn to our fathers, to give to us." The Mishnah states that the convert may not recite this phrase.

Ellenson and Gordis's argument that the convert is not a full member of the Jewish collective is well documented. This argument is more salient in *Pledges of Jewish Allegiance* than in *Transforming Identity*, even though the same passages appear in both books. Ellenson and Gordis follow the theme of a convert being an outsider in their discussion of Babylonian Talmud, Yevamot 47a–b. They interpret this text to mean that the essence of Judaism is to an outsider:

> Because the acceptance of the commandments is not as central here as it is in other texts, the essence of Jewishness does not seem to be theological or covenantal. To a degree it is historical, but to be more precise, the Jew here is described as essentially the "other." To be a Jew means

---

[13] Ibid., 17.
[14] Throughout this manuscript I am using the spelling *ger*; Ellenson and Gordis use the spelling *geir* to transliterate the same Hebrew word.
[15] Deuteronomy 28:43–44, cited in Ellenson and Gordis, *Pledges of Jewish Allegiance*, 17.
[16] Deuteronomy 26:1–10, cited in Ellenson and Gordis, *Pledges of Jewish Allegiance*, 23.

to be "persecuted and oppressed, despised, harassed, and overcome by afflictions." A prospective convert has to accept that conception of Jewishness and even deem himself inadequate to it. He is to be "other" among the "others." Note the specific commandments to which the convert is introduced as he is instructed in Judaism. Aside from a rudimentary introduction to the Sabbath and rules of forbidden fat, "he is informed of the sin [of the neglect of the agricultural commandments of] Gleanings, the Forgotten Sheaf, the Corner, and the Poor Man's Tithe." These commandments are those that protect the poor, the disenfranchised, the landless. To become a Jew means to join people at the fringes of humanity and then to dedicate oneself to defending and protecting those who are even more marginalized.[17]

Ambivalence toward proselytes is embedded in an often-repeated axiom about dealing with proselytes: "Let the left hand repel and the right hand draw close."[18]

If the Jew is the outsider who is to be a light among the nations, it is essential for the Jew to understand the world from a universal frame of reference instead of as framed by the Jewish paradigms that are dominant at the time. Converts can provide this outside perspective on Jewish belief and practice and on the meaning of being a Jew.

Motivation in a Minor Tractate

Ellenson and Gordis present another passage from the Talmud—Tractate Gerim—that questions the motivation for conversion: "Anyone who converts [in order to marry] a woman, for love or out of fear, is not a convert. Thus, Rabbi Judah and Rabbi Nehemiah used to say that all those who converted in the days of Mordecai and Esther are not [valid] converts, as it written, 'and many of the populace were converting to Judaism, for the fear of the Jews had fallen upon them.' And anyone who does not convert lesheim shamayim [for the sake of heaven], is not a [legitimate] convert." Here, for the first time, we find mention of the motivations of the convert and the stipulation that the conversion must be free of any ulterior motive.

---

[17] Ellenson and Gordis, *Pledges of Jewish Allegiance*, 23.
[18] Babylonian Talmud, Sotah 47a, cited in Ellenson and Gordis, *Pledges of Jewish Allegiance*, 29.

The Talmudic tractate Gerim goes even further: in addition to listing negative conditions that must be avoided, it specifies that the conversion must be "for the sake of heaven." It does not, however, offer any explanation of what that phrase means.[19]

This minor tractate introduces several notions that became pivotal in traditional and in contemporary halakhic discourse about conversion. It caused a change in halakhic discourse from concern with the dignity of the convert to creating conditions for conversion that submerge the dignity of the convert, to the extent of the possibility of rabbis and laity humiliating the convert.

The convert's heart must be free of ulterior motives such as love or fear. The conversion must be for the sake of heaven. These concepts are not well defined and are subject to the will of the interpreter. Authorities disagree with one another. Some authorities' rulings are stringent. Some rulings are lenient. The delegation of these decisions to a court adds an element of uncertainty. Some rabbis express great concern about the impact of these decisions on actual human beings and on their families. Some do not. The Orthodox establishment in Israel is among the latter. Even the Holocaust did not cause them to adopt a more lenient and inclusive policy. They have taken the position that those who do not follow their practices are not authentic Jews and that the Orthodox community need have no concern for them.

The Formation of Jewish Orthodoxy

Contemporary Judaism with its distinct denominations originated in Germany in the nineteenth century as a reaction against the introduction of changes that were designed to make the practice of Judaism more accessible and compelling to German Jews and more compatible with practices in German Lutheran churches and with their architecture. Some prayers and sermons were in German, not Hebrew. Music was introduced in the services. It was the intent of the early reformers to change some aspects of religious practice, not to create a separate denomination. The Orthodox, however, fought the reformers, rejected all changes, and continued to follow Jewish belief and practice as it existed prior to the midnineteenth century. This led to two separate denominations in Judaism.

The Reform and the Orthodox voices became more confrontational

---

[19] Ellenson and Gordis, *Pledges of Jewish Allegiance*, 22.

and more distinct, presaging the acrimonious confrontation between the two that exists today. The initial failure of the Orthodox to gain support for their positions from the governments in Europe has been followed by their success in gaining hegemony over religious affairs in Israel and, subsequently, over the Orthodox in the United States. One important motivation for this determined effort to maintain control over religious affairs and over the laity was to overcome the decreasing power and relevance of the rabbinate. Another was the growing strength of the Reform movement in Germany:[20]

> In Europe, the problem of intermarriage had erupted. Legislation was enacted by various states in Germany in the late 1840s that facilitated intermarriage between Jews and Gentiles. Isaac Bernays (1792–1849), rabbi of Hamburg and teacher of Rabbi Samson Raphael Hirsch and Rabbi Esriel Hildesheimer [founding voices of Modern Orthodox Judaism], was sufficiently disturbed by the rise of intermarriage in Germany to issue an 1843 responsum in German condemning marriage between Jew and Gentile as unthinkable from the standpoint of Jewish law. In addition, Bernays stated that the children of a marriage between a Jewish man and a non-Jewish woman were unequivocally Gentiles. Finally, he acknowledged that while the community had to recognize that intermarriages enjoyed a civil status, the Jewish community could never accept the religious character of such a union.[21]

> Bernays's harsh tone in his responsum gives support to Moshe Davis's observation that "the basic cause" of the stringent position that the Orthodox initially adopted concerning intermarriage "was the increase of mixed marriage to the point where it alarmed the rabbinical leaders."[22]

The Braunschweig Rabbinical Conference of Reform Jewish rabbis in 1844 decided that Judaism sanctioned marital unions between those who practice monotheism if the state allowed the children to be reared as Jews. The Orthodox reacted vehemently against this. They saw this as an attack on

---

[20] Ellenson and Gordis, *Pledges of Jewish Allegiance*, 38.
[21] Druckesz, *Zur Biographie des Chacham Isaak Bernays*, 322, cited in Ellenson and Gordis, *Pledges of Jewish Allegiance*, 38.
[22] Moshe Davis, "Mixed Marriage in Western Jewry," *Jewish Journal of Social Studies* 10 (December 1968): 181, cited in Ellenson and Gordis, *Pledges of Jewish Allegiance*, 38.

their hegemony over the religious practices of rabbis, congregations, and laity. Prior to this time, many states had strict prohibitions against conversion and imposed severe penalties for those who induced others to convert to Judaism. As these restrictions were relaxed, more people converted and the problem of conversion became more pressing for the Orthodox. Their authority over communities and individuals had been reduced greatly by the Enlightenment and emancipation of the Jews of Europe. Now their authority and their ability to maintain the primacy of Torah in the Jewish community was threatened by the decision of the Braunschweig Conference.

The response of many leading Orthodox rabbis was characterized by R. Zvi Hirsch Chajes (1805–55) in *Minhat Kena'ot*, published in 1845, the year after the Braunschweig Rabbinical Conference of 1844, which had approved interfaith marriages. In *Minhat Kena'ot* R. Chajes "attacked Reform Judaism on multiple grounds, expressing outrage at Reform transgressions of the tradition, including changes in the Jewish prayer book, abandonment of the rite of circumcision by the Frankfurt *Reformverein*, and rejection of the traditional Jewish belief that the Torah was eternal and unchanging."[23]

R. Chajes's attack on Reform Judaism and his stringent rulings on interfaith marriages and conversion were echoed by other leading Orthodox authorities such as R. Jacob Ettlinger (1798–1871), R. Seligman Baer Bamberger (1807–78), and R. Samson Raphael Hirsch (1808–88), who is considered the father of Neo-Orthodoxy. Hirsch and Abraham Geiger, the leading exponent of Reform, studied together at Bonn University. Later they became strident opposing voices that represented Orthodoxy and Reform in Germany. Hirsch refused to cooperate with non-Orthodox Jewish groups. He expressed the rejectionist Orthodox view that "the Law, both Written and Oral, was closed with Moses."[24] Hirsch's view became the authoritative view in Orthodoxy and is followed today. Hirsch supported strict principles for Orthodox conversions and an unyielding opposition to Reform. Proselytes who wanted to convert for ulterior motives were to be rejected. Conversions by Reform rabbis were meaningless.

Hirsch was, however, more open to the outside world than many others among the Orthodox leadership. He interpreted the statement in Pirkei Avot (Ethics of the Fathers) 2:2, "Torah is good together with *derech eretz*, the way of the earth," to mean that Torah study must be combined with

---

[23] Ellenson and Gordis, *Pledges of Jewish Allegiance*, 39.
[24] Hirsch, Horeb, 20, cited in Ellenson and Gordis, Pledges of Jewish Allegiance, 166.

secular study to produce a cultured person, one who can thrive in the modern world: "*Derekh eretz* is used primarily to refer to ways of earning a living [the plain meaning in the text], to the social order that prevails on earth, as well as to the mores and considerations of courtesy and propriety arising from social living and also to things pertinent to good breeding and general education."[25] For Hirsch, *derech eretz* meant that a Jew should act in a dignified manner and treat others with the dignity that is inherent in oneself.

R. Moshe Feinstein followed Hirsch's strict interpretation of halakhah. He wrote in his *Igerot Moshe* that "among the foundational principles of our holy faith [is the belief] that all Torah, whether Written or Oral, was given at Mount Sinai by the Holy One, Blessed be He, Himself to Moses our Rabbi, peace be upon him. *And it is impossible to change even a single jot, either to be lenient or stringent.*"[26]

Lenient Policies for Conversion

Some in the Orthodox community believed that Judaism was best served by a policy of accepting converts and, consequently, by adopting lenient policies and practices for conversion. I will review the positions of three rabbis whose views were characteristic of these lenient policies.

R. Menachem Mendel Kirschenbaum (1894–1942) advanced the view that it was better for Orthodox rabbis to convert those who wished to convert than to reject them and let them be converted by Reform rabbis. He was concerned that those who were converted by Reform rabbis would be considered legitimate Jews and that their children would not be identifiable as the product of a union that was not sanctioned by the Orthodox. In that case, they might marry Orthodox Jews, who would not know that their spouses were not legitimate Jews.[27] Kirschenbaum did not explicitly state as a consequence that in such a case the marriage would not be sanctioned under halakhic law and the children would be considered bastards by the Orthodox.

R. David Hoffman (1842–1921) was another Orthodox rabbi who

---

[25] Hirsch, "Principles."

[26] Feinstein, *Igerot Moshe*, 1, cited in Ellenson and Gordis, *Pledges of Jewish Allegiance*, 166.

[27] Ellenson and Gordis, *Pledges of Jewish Allegiance*, 67.

believed the Jewish people was better served by an inclusive stance on conversion. He was innovative in finding support for his positions. In the case of those who wished to convert for ulterior purposes, he recognized that such a conversion is forbidden in Joseph Caro's *Shulchan Aruch*. However, Hoffman relied on Babylonian Talmud, Shabbat 31, which cited Hillel's acceptance of a proselyte who wished to convert in order to become a high priest, and on Babylonian Talmud, Menahot 44, which cited R. Hiyya, who accepted a female prostitute who wanted to convert in order to marry one of his rabbinic students. Hoffman invoked the ruling that everything depends on the ruling of the court and the court is authorized to convert if it thinks the conversion is for the sake of heaven. Hoffman writes that if the conversion is for the sake of heaven, it is likely that the convert will ultimately become an observant Jew.[28]

The Hungarian rabbi Moses Schreiber (1768–1839; also known as Hatam Sofer) was largely unaffected by the Reform movement in Germany, which began in the latter part of his life. Early in his early career he viewed conversion positively. He even interpreted a Talmudic statement that proselytes cause Israel to suffer evil as a complaint against some converts who were so strict in observing the commandments that few born Jews could follow. In one case, he referred to Shabbat 31a, in which Hillel converted a man who asked to be converted while standing on one foot. Hillel famously said to the proselyte, "That which is hateful to you, do not do unto others. All the rest is commentary. Go and learn."[29] R. Schreiber relied on the rabbinic dictum that when appropriate deeds are performed for the wrong reason, eventually they will be performed for the right reason.

Rabbis who were more contemporary to our time than these three are cited by Zvi Zohar in his paper "A Policy of *Giyyur* for Our Time."[30] Zohar addresses the positions of three rabbis who based their positions on the halakhic possibility of encouraging proselytization based on the interests of the community instead of on the candidates' merit as individuals. These three great twentieth-century rabbis were, according to Zohar, equal in scholarship to R. Moshe Feinstein. Feinstein opposed liberal interpretations of halakhah in all matters, including conversion.

The first rabbi cited in Zohar's article who supported a liberal interpretation

---

[28] Ibid., 58.
[29] Shabbat 31a.
[30] Written in the late 1980s, this paper was never published but did appear for a time on the website of the Shalom Hartman Institute.

of conversion was R. Ben-Zion Uzziel (1880–1953), who was born in Jerusalem, the son of the first chief Sephardic[31] rabbi of Israel. In a case submitted to him by R. Judah Leon Khalfon, head of the rabbinic court of Tetuan, Spanish Morocco, R. Uzziel divided his responsum in two sections. First he addressed the possibility of converting a proselyte who would not be religiously observant. Second, he asked why a rabbi would want to convert such a person. To the first question, as cited by Zohar, R. Uzziel adumbrates what might be characterized as a sober, even a humane realism:

> When a non-Jew comes to convert, [the Shulhan 'Arukh states that] "he is to be informed of the principles of the faith, i.e., God's unity and the prohibition against idolatry, and this is discussed at length." But with regard to acceptance of the commandments "he is informed of some of the light and some of the serious commandments, and of punishments related to some of the commandments." [This indicates that] ... we do not demand from him observance of the commandments, and there is no requirement for the court to know that he will observe them, for if this were the case then no converts would ever be accepted in Israel. For who can guarantee that this non-Jew will be faithful to all of the Torah's commandments? Rather the purpose of him being informed about some of the commandments is to give him a chance to desist from continuing with the conversion, and so that he will not be able to say afterward "Had I known, I would not have converted." And all the above is ex ante. But ex post, if he was not informed (of any commandment at all), it does not impair (the halakhic validity of the conversion . . .). From all of the above we conclude: The condition of observance of the commandments does not hinder the conversion even *ex ante*.[32]

Zohar underscores that R. Uzziel held that no classic halakhic text mentions the need for such a promise. Moreover, Zohar contends that R. Uzziel would surely regard it as absurd to make conversion contingent on an inherently nonverifiable future action.[33]

R. Uzziel, says Zohar, deemed that there are two distinct views in the

---

[31] Sephardim are Jews who originated in areas around the Mediterranean Sea, including Portugal, Spain, the Middle East, and Northern Africa.

[32] Zohar, "A Policy of *Giyyur* for Our Time," 5. The quotations within this quotation are taken from R. Ben-Zion Uzziel, *Mishapati Uzziel*, 2nd ed. (Jerusalem: Mosad HaRav Kook, 1950), 1:250.

[33] Zohar, "A Policy of *Giyyur* for Our Time," 5.

tradition to promote conversion.

> From the words of our sages of blessed memory we learn that it is a positive commandment to accept proselytes and to bring them under the wings of the Shekhina. For The Holy One Blessed Be He loves proselytes and prohibits their mistreatment (see Yevamot 109b, Tosafot s.v. Ra'ah). [Furthermore,] the Holy One, blessed be He, did not exile Israel among the nations except for the sake of having proselytes join them, as it is written (Hosea 2:25): "And I will sow her unto Me in the land"; surely a man sows a quantity of seed only in order to harvest many times more![34]

Rabbi Uzziel adds that over and above the general policy outlined above, there exist in our times special reasons to accept candidates for conversion in cases linked to intermarriage:

> And in our generation we bear special and heavy responsibility, because if we lock the door before converts we are thereby opening wide the gates of exit, pushing Jewish men and women to change their religion and to leave Judaism entirely or to assimilate among the gentiles. And extremely relevant to such a situation is the admonition of our sages of blessed memory: "Always let the left hand thrust away and the right hand draw near" (Sota 47a). And a Jew who assimilates or who is pushed out of Israel becomes an enemy of Israel, as history demonstrates in many cases and in many generations.
>
> And even if we might tend not to take that into concern, and to say "Let the rope follow the bucket"—nevertheless, we must draw them near for the sake of their children. This is obvious if they are the children of a Jewish mother—for then they are totally Jewish. But moreover, even if they are the children of a non-Jew and a Jewish mother—they are Seed of Israel. And they are therefore "lost sheep."[35]

The second rabbi cited by Zohar is R. Joseph Mesas (1892–1974), who was born in Meknes, Morocco, to one of the community's leading rabbis. From 1924 to 1940 he served as rabbi of Tlemcen, Algeria, and he returned to Morocco to serve as a *dayyan*, rabbinic judge, on both the local and the

---

[34] Ibid., 6.
[35] Uzziel, *Mishapati Uzziel*, 1:250, quoted in Zohar, "A Policy of *Giyyur* for Our Time," 7.

national levels. In 1964 he immigrated to Israel, where he was appointed chief rabbi of Haifa. He served as chief rabbi until his death in 1974. Shortly after arriving in Israel, Mesas responded to a question by outlining the position on conversion of the North African rabbis. Similar to R. Uzziel, he argued that in the light of contemporary social realities, conversion should be encouraged:

> Now that the generation is promiscuous, and no one is ashamed of this, and [the Jewish and non-Jewish partners] promenade together hand in hand in the city's streets, and participate in every festive gathering of relatives and friends, and everyone knows that this couple are intimate partners . . . they may convert and marry even ex ante. . . . If he [the Jewish spouse] had wanted to mend what had been crooked, and labored to convince his non-Jewish partner to agree to convert and to enter under the wings of the Shekhina [the Divine Presence], . . . the darkness and everything is forgotten and joy dwells in their home.[36]

> Conversion brings great benefits — including observance of commandments, prevention of many prohibitions, peace and quiet for several families and prevention of assimilation of Jews among the nations; And [sic] since in any case what is at stake is only a Rabbinic prohibition, and even that only *ex ante*; And [sic] since we have seen a number of people whose conversion was not for the sake of heaven who subsequently became truly righteous converts it should be considered a great mitzvah to be lenient on this matter.[37]

The third rabbi Zohar discusses is Hayyim David Halevi (1924–98), who was born in Jerusalem, served in the Haganah[38] during the war of independence in 1948, and was the chief Sephardic rabbi of Tel Aviv from 1973 until his death in 1998. Zohar begins by quoting an Israeli Rabbinic journal, *Ha-Kerem*, which reported how the great rabbi Israel Joshua Trunk (1820–93) of Kutno, Poland, reacted when told that in the early Middle Ages the king of Kiev asked representatives of Christianity, Islam, and Judaism to

---

[36] Zohar, "A Policy of *Giyyur* for Our Time," 8.
[37] Ibid., 10.
[38] The Haganah (lit., "the defense") was the main paramilitary organization of the Jewish population ("Yishuv") in Mandatory Palestine between 1920 and 1948, when it became the core of the Israeli Defense Forces (IDF).

tell him about their faiths so that he could choose one for himself and for his people. The king chose Judaism and asked for leniency in regard to circumcision of the elderly men of the kingdom. He agreed that all other men and future generations would be circumcised. The rabbis refused, and the king of Kiev and his people did not convert to Judaism. R. Trunk criticized them for refusing to add a great nation to "the Lord's estate." R. Trunk, says Zohar, pointed out that Abraham looked for allies:

> "He dwelt by the terebinths of Mamre the Amorite, brother of Eshkol, and brother of 'Aner; and these were confederate with Avram" (Genesis 14:13).
> And the Talmud (Nedarim 32b) says: "Why was our Father Abraham punished and his children doomed to Egyptian servitude for two hundred and ten years? R. Johanan said: Because he prevented people from entering beneath the wings of the Shekhina, as it is written (Genesis 14:21), 'Give me the persons, and take the goods to thyself.'"[39]

Zohar continues:

> Rabbi HaLevy continued his argument in an article on giyyur in the Rabbinic journal *Shvilin* in which he wrote: "In order to deeply understand the significance of the halakhic concept: 'Everything [in conversion] can be in accordance with the judge's view,' and as an introduction to a discussion of the problem of conversion in our own time, we will begin with information relating to conversion in the days of the Second Temple."[40]

Zohar comments,

> An extremely widespread movement of conversion developed towards the end of the Second Temple period. At the time there were about a million Jews in Egypt, about a million and a half in Syria and Asia Minor, about a million in Europe and North Africa, and about a million in Babylonia. These numbers did not stem from emigration, as at the time there were not so many Jews in the land of Israel itself. According to historical experts, these numbers reflect a broad movement of conversion.

---

[39] Zohar, "A Policy of *Giyyur* for Our Time," 11.
[40] Ibid.

It was during this period that the heads of the House of Adiabene, the King Munbaz and the Queen Helena, converted — as described in the Talmud — and doubtless masses of others converted along with them.[41]

Most of the converts at the time were women, who of course did not need to be circumcised to become Jewish. Rabbis and sages disagreed about the need for circumcision for men. They agreed that both men and women required immersion in order to convert. Those who said that circumcision was not necessary relied on the dictum, "Everything can be in accordance with the judge's view." Rabbi HaLevy used this text to support his view that rabbis throughout much of Jewish history had the latitude to decide upon the necessity of conversion in each circumstance and that they should have been lenient when it was in the interest of individuals and in the interest of the Jewish people.

Rabbi Joshua (first century CE) was one of the early rabbis who took a lenient position toward conversion. Zohar explains: "Rabbi Joshua's position was not accepted by most other rabbis at that time. The tidal wave of conversion to Judaism was diverted, and the great masses of non-Jews seeking religious fulfillment in a covenant with the God of Israel chose to do so via Christianity. . . . Had Rabbi Joshua's opinion had been accepted in the *Beit Hamidrash* — the face of history might have looked very different!"[42]

Zohar compares the religions that are competing in the United States now to those that were competing for the allegiance of pagans in ancient times. He emphasizes the opportunity for American Jews to attract proselytes. According to a 2013 report by the Pew Research Center,[43] 28 percent of non-Jews are leaving their religion of birth. Non-Jews make up 98 percent of the population of the United States, and Jews comprise 2 percent. Since born Jews are leaving at a slightly lower rate, 25 percent, it does not require a large percent of non-Jews to choose Judaism for the Jewish population to increase significantly.[44]

Zohar concludes his article by underscoring that the halakhic tradition, as he has argued, allows for a lenient approach to *giyyur*. Moreover,

there are times in which conversion is crucial to Jewish continuity, and

---

[41] Ibid., 12.
[42] Ibid., 15.
[43] I will discuss this report at greater length in chapter 6.
[44] Cooperman et al., *Portrait of Jewish Americans*.

inclusion of non-Jews into God's flock is a strategic imperative. . . .

Ours is such a time. Will future generations look back in regret and say "Had Rabbi Uzziel's, and Rabbi Mesas' and Rabbi HaLevi's opinions been accepted in the *Beit Hamidrash*—the face of history might have looked very different!" Or will they say: "How great were the Torah leaders of those times, who chose the halakhic path most appropriate to the American religious landscape, and led the entire American Jewish community from seemingly inevitable numerical decline to numerical and spiritual growth!"[45]

Strict Interpretation: Moshe Feinstein

R. Moshe Feinstein shared Hirsch's unrelenting opposition to Reform, but not Hirsch's openness to the prevailing culture. Feinstein wrote, "It is necessary to know that among the foundational principles of our holy faith [is the belief] that all Torah, whether Written or Oral, was given at Mount Sinai by the Holy One, Blessed by He, Himself to Moses our Rabbi, peace be upon him. And it is impossible to change even a single jot, either to be lenient or stringent."[46] The reference is to R. Moses Schreiber, whose early positive view toward conversion changed to strong opposition after 1817 when the German Reform movement became active in Hungary. In 1819 in *Eileh divrei haberit*, Schreiber wrote that if secular law permitted it [which it did not], "it would be advisable to push [the reformers] beyond our borders. Our daughters would not be given to their sons, nor our sons to their daughters—they to theirs and ours to ours."[47]

R. Schreiber developed this foundational position of ultra-Orthodox Judaism. He created the emblematic position of the ultra-Orthodox, by taking a statement that related to the purity of seeds out of context and applying it to conversion. The Torah states that the Jews after entering the promised land are not to eat the fruit of the trees they plant until three years after planting. The fruit is said to be uncircumcised before then. R.

---

[45] Zohar, "A Policy of *Giyyur* for Our Time," 16.

[46] Feinstein, *Igerot Moshe*, vol. 4, *Orach Chayim*, sec. 49, cited in Ellenson and Gordis, *Pledges of Jewish Allegiance*, 166.

[47] Moses Sofer, *She'eilot uteshuvot*, *Hoshen Mishpat*, responsum 89, cited in Ellenson and Gordis, *Pledges of Jewish Allegiance*, 73.

Schreiber's dictum that all that is new is forbidden in the Torah is a reinterpretation of this passage.

Much of the early scholarly opinion on conversion in the United States was voiced by rabbis who had emigrated from Europe. R. Feinstein emigrated from Belorussia in 1937 to New York, where he became the head of Mesivtha Tifereth Jerusalem, a well-known yeshiva in New York City. He opposed conversions for the purpose of intermarriage and opposed conversions by ultra-Orthodox rabbis when there were questions about the candidate's motivation or about their intention to accept the yoke of the Torah. Like other Orthodox rabbis, he rejected the validity of conversions performed by non-Orthodox rabbis.[48] He stated his view of Conservative and Reform rabbis clearly in the following excerpts from two of his many responsa. In one place he wrote: "Behold, it is simple that the conversion [performed by Conservative rabbis was] nothing. . . . This rabbinic court of the Conservatives is *pesulin* [unfit] to be a *beit din* [rabbinic court] as [Conservative rabbis] are *loferin* [deniers] of many of the principles of Judaism and deny many negative commandments. . . . Consequently, it is evident that no conversion performed by a conservative rabbi has any legal standing."[49] Feinstein also ruled in regard to the *mikveh*—a ceremonial bath that is used for immersion in conversion and for purification and that was under the control of Orthodox rabbis—that Conservative rabbis were not to be allowed to use the *mikveh* for conversion.[50]

Feinstein has even less respect for Reform rabbis: "Even if no one witnesses the transgressions of Torah, the name 'Reform' testifies to the fact that they are heretics."[51] Consequently, they are unfit to perform conversions.

Feinstein and other ultra-Orthodox rabbis did not communicate with non-Orthodox rabbis. There were Orthodox voices in America that espoused a more open view than Feinstein, and there still are. R. Simcha Levy (d. 1968), the president of the Orthodox Rabbinical Council of America, was one. He chaired its Halakhah Commission for over twenty years. In 1949, in a responsum addressed to a question about a gentile who wished to convert in order to marry a Jew, Levy agreed that it was preferable to convert the

---

[48] Ellenson, *Development of Orthodox Attitudes to Conversion in the Modern Period.*

[49] Feinstein, *Igerot Moshe,* vol. 2, *Yoreh De'ah,* sec. 160, cited in Ellenson and Gordis, *Pledges of Jewish Allegiance,* 104.

[50] Feinstein, *Igerot Moshe,* vol. 2, *Yoreh De'ah,* sec. 125, cited in Ellenson and Gordis, *Pledges of Jewish Allegiance,* 104.

[51] Feinstein, *Igerot Moshe,* vol. 2, *Yoreh De'ah,* sec. 160, cited in Ellenson and Gordis, *Pledges of Jewish Allegiance,* 104.

gentile, "lest the family turn to a Reform rabbi and be lost in its entirety, as would likely be the case if a Reform rabbi conducted the conversion."[52] Levy's identification with the Jewish people, even while excluding them from interacting with the Orthodox, was more pronounced than his colleagues' identification with them. According to Louis Bernstein, another concern of Levy's was that a conversion by a Reform rabbi would not be valid and that the convert would not be accepted by the community as a legitimate Jew.[53]

The consequences, according to halakhah, of a marriage between a born Jew and a spouse who was converted by a Reform rabbi are severe. The children are bastards. Orthodox women and men are not permitted to marry them. There is a risk that the convert and their children may become undifferentiated from authentic Orthodox Jews in Orthodox communities and marry authentic Orthodox Jews when the authorities who check their lineage are lax.

R. Jack Simcha Cohen (1936–2014), rabbi of Congregation Shaari Tefila in Los Angeles, was another Orthodox voice who was more open to halakhic change and more concerned with human feelings. In 1987 he published a responsum in which he said that Jewish men who are married to gentiles and who wish their children to be converted should not be rejected: "Children born to Jewish fathers and Gentile mothers may be converted during infancy by a proper beit din."[54]

Cohen was concerned about more than legal rulings. He was concerned about the human impact of these rulings. He found room within halakhah to incorporate human feelings into his interpretations.

> In a recent case, a Jewish family adopted an infant Gentile girl and after a few years came to rabbis to formally convert the child. The parents were informed that a *beit din* could not properly convert their adopted daughter (aged five) because the parents did not observe the laws of Shabbat. Imagine the trauma attendant upon such an episode.[55]

In one responsum Cohen expressed his understanding that there was a

---

[52] Ellenson and Gordis, *Pledges of Jewish Allegiance*, 110.
[53] Bernstein, *Challenge and Mission*, 43–44, cited in Ellenson and Gordis, *Pledges of Jewish Allegiance*, 110.
[54] Jack Simcha Cohen, "Conversion of Children," cited in Ellenson and Gordis, *Pledges of Jewish Allegiance*, 112.
[55] Jack Simcha Cohen, "Conversion of Children," 7, cited in Ellenson and Gordis, *Pledges of Jewish Allegiance*, 113.

world outside of Orthodoxy: "The principle of insulating the Orthodox community against the sin of intermarriage may necessitate that all who marry out of the faith should be kept at a distance rather than welcomed to the fold. Though we disagree with this orientation, discussion of its halakhic merits is not within the purview of this presentation."[56] Cohen also recognized that the Talmud is not fixed and that interpretation is not uniform: "Though the ideas expressed may appear somewhat bold or innovative, they are grounded in traditional principles of Talmud scholarship. . . . Our concern is not to suggest that the analysis herein is the sole interpretation of the Talmudic text, nor the only reliable theory of the Codes. Such is certainly not the case. Indeed, Torah may be interpreted in numerous ways dependent upon the wisdom and intellectual acuity of scholars and their final decisions."[57]

R. Cohen and R. Levy exhibited courage in expressing opinions that they knew to be contrary to those of most Orthodox rabbis and scholars. The costs could be high. They and their families might be discriminated against religiously by the Orthodox rabbinate and socially by the Orthodox community.

The Denver Initiative on Conversion

Rabbis in Denver resolved to address the issues of conversion in the different denominations. The initiative was instigated in 1977 by lectures in Denver by R. Eliezer Berkovitz (1908–92), professor emeritus of Hebrew Theological College in Chicago, and R. Shlomo Riskin (b. 1933), chief rabbi of Lincoln Square Synagogue in New York City and later chief rabbi of Efrat, Israel. Berkovitz warned the Denver Jewish community that the issue of "who is a Jew" was destroying Jewish unity. Riskin quoted texts from the Talmud and from Maimonides that supported a lenient view of a proselyte's commitment to observe the commandments. The Orthodox rabbi of Denver, Stanley M. Wagner (1932–2013), found that Berkovitz and Riskin had offered theological justification for conversion as an ongoing process, not as a contract signed as a condition of admission.[58] He initiated

---

[56] Ibid.
[57] Jack Simcha Cohen, "Conversion of Children," cited in Ellenson and Gordis, *Pledges of Jewish Allegiance*, 113.
[58] Freedman, *Jew vs. Jew*, cited in Ellenson and Gordis, *Pledges of Jewish Allegiance*, 117.

a meeting of seven rabbis to discuss a single conversion system for the city. These rabbis agreed on a common process for conversion. They converted about 750 people until the Orthodox rabbis announced on June 17, 1983, their withdrawal from the agreement.

The hitherto quiet experiment had become public. Harold Jacobs, president of Orthodoxy's American Council of Young Israel, stated: "We have no choice but to draw the line, clearly, as to who is a Jew and who is not, as to what limits and basic standards of elementary Jewish identity and personal conduct we must insist upon. . . . It is time that Orthodoxy put the rest of the Jewish community on notice: no longer will 'Jewish unity' be bought at the expense of Jewish identity. For *Klal Yisrael* today, that is too high a price."[59] The *Jewish Observer*, an American Jewish journal associated with the Agudath Israel, the international organization of the Orthodox Judaism, wrote: "While compromise for the sake of unity can often make good sense, when dealing with basic principles of faith, 'compromise' is actually a sell-out. . . . It is time that all Orthodox rabbis recognize that Reform and Conservative Judaism are far, far removed from Torah, and *Klal Yisroel* is betrayed, not served, when Orthodoxy enters in religious association with them."[60]

This criticism by the Orthodox of Reform and Conservative Judaism highlights the growing gap between Orthodox and Reform Jews and between Israeli and American Jews. Israeli politics is a significant contributor. The Israeli government supports the control by the Orthodox of conversion, marriage, and burial; and the Orthodox in America have ceded control over their affairs to the Israeli Orthodox. Reform and Conservative rabbis are not permitted to perform these lifestyle events in Israel. The Orthodox control the definition of Jewish identity through their control of these processes. They are becoming increasingly strict in interpreting halakhah.

While leading voices of Orthodox Judaism in our time have expressed opposition to change, some have been innovative. They see the Torah as a living document that God gave to the Jewish people to interpret and to apply in their communities and in their lives. The American Reform community follows this liberal tradition of continual interpretation to meet the needs of contemporary Jews. The Orthodox community claims that the Torah is not subject to change and applies this interpretation to situations in

---

[59] Harold Jacobs, in 1989, quoted in Ellenson and Gordis, *Pledges of Jewish Allegiance*, 119.

[60] *Jewish Observer*, cited in the introduction to Weinberg, *Serdie Eish*.

which it does not want to change, such as the situation of *agunah*, women married to men who refused to grant them a divorce. At the same time, the Orthodox make significant changes in halakhah by restricting conversions, making them dependent on the proselyte's commitment to follow a strictly Orthodox lifestyle, and retroactively annulling conversions.

CHAPTER 6

American Reform Judaism: History and Demographics

A Brief History of Reform Judaism

Changes in beliefs about conversion and in attitudes toward converts in Reform Judaism were a part of broader changes in Reform Judaism itself. These changes resulted initially from pressures within Jewish communities in Germany, such as a desire for better understanding of the language of services, more personal autonomy, and a decrease in the authority of the rabbis. The founders of Reform Judaism were instructed in part by the Haskalah, the Jewish Enlightenment, which mirrored the Enlightenment in Europe, the move from feudalism and religious and institutional authority to science, reason, and the autonomy and value of the individual.

In an overview of the history of Reform Judaism in America, Howard Berman observes:

> Two centuries after the original emergence of Jewish Reform in the Germany, today's movement—the largest organized branch of Judaism in America—embraces a broad spectrum of interpretations, belief, and practice that is so appropriate for a religious community that affirms personal freedom and congregational autonomy. "Mainstream Reform" in contemporary America reflects the widespread re-embrace of traditional Jewish ritual and observance that has characterized the movement's official position, liturgies and approach to observance over the past fifty years.[1]
>
> The conventional analysis of [the adaptation of tradition prayer and ritual practices] generally holds that much of this redirection was a response to the tragedy of the Holocaust and to the new dynamic of Jewish identity engendered by the birth of the State of Israel in 1948. However, there were other social and cultural forces at work as well. The 1960s was a time of major transformation and upheaval in American life. Traditional structures and norms—including the ideal of the "melting

---

[1] Berman, introduction to Plaut, *Growth of American Reform Judaism*, 8.

pot" — were questioned by a counterculture that sought individual freedom of expression, alternative communal and societal structures, and differing personal values based on the assertion of gender, ethnic, racial, and sexual identity. Many of these trends were just beginning to emerge when Plaut's *The Growth of Reform Judaism* was published in 1965.[2]

At his installation in June 2012 as the new president of the Union of Reform Judaism, R. Rick Jacobs affirmed the movement's neo-traditional turn. In his sermon, he observed that

> Reform Judaism is unafraid to change our tradition when it holds us back from growing and deepening our faith. For us, change is not only permitted but obligatory. And sometimes it isn't even fast enough.
> Ours is an inclusive Judaism. Our loving embrace of all who had been excluded has added to our numbers and to our strength.[3]
> Informed choice invariably leads to change. To those who claim "Reform Judaism ain't what it used to be," I say, "Reform Judaism ain't supposed to be what it used to be; it's supposed to be in a constant state of change, adaptation, and growth."
> From the shoulders of our ancestors, we can — and must — see both the past and the promise of the future.[4]

Berman follows this with the following compelling explanation of reform.

> As has often been observed, Reform was a revolution in Jewish life in the nineteenth century, and revolutions often require courageous action that some, in retrospect, might deem "extreme." Perhaps, as we mark the current decade of 2010–20, which encompasses the two hundredth anniversary of Reform Judaism, we can look back and view the innovations of our predecessors not as "groveling assimilation" but as an authentically Jewish response to the intellectual, scientific, social, and political challenges of modernity in nineteenth-century Europe and to the free, open, pluralistic society of American democracy. We can understand their liturgical reforms and new perspectives of Jewish identity not as "aberrations" but as part of the continuous dynamic of Judaism's

[2] Ibid., 11.
[3] Ibid., 13.
[4] Ibid., 14.

history — no more "anomalies" than the equally radical new visions represented by the prophets Isaiah and Micah, Yochanan Ben Zakkai, Maimonides, and even the Baal Shem Tov. In turn, we can understand the early Reformers' rejection of ritualism and legalism as a thoroughly Jewish expression of the principles that have shaped all liberal religious reform throughout the world over the centuries.[5]

In his epilogue to the second edition of *The Growth of Reform Judaism*, Plaut writes of the spiritual needs of American Jews after World War I. These needs, or demands, for a new spiritual understanding were experienced at the same time in the Catholic Church and in Protestant denominations. In response to these needs, American Reform began to reexamine the theology of Reform, which had been developed in 1848 and had remained largely unchanged since then. A contemporary response to these needs occurred in the midfifties when a group of Jewish scholars met in Oconomowoc, Wisconsin, to explore Jewish theology. Plaut writes:

> They found that they shared an acceptance of the covenant as the ineluctable foundation of Jewish existence and they brought to this conviction a deep-felt urge to turn their own religious apprehension and that of the Jewish people more inward. They did not denigrate social justice or political organization, but they were convinced that no Jew could ultimately remain a Jew unless he took his relationship to the God of history seriously.
>
> In 1963 the convention of the Central Conference of American Rabbis gave prominent space to the now commonly recognized need for theology. Its members were reminded, in the words of Martin Buber, that "just as our fathers invented new ways of serving, each a new service according to his own character: one, the service of love; another, of stern justice; a third, of beauty; so each of us in his own way should devise something new in the light of teaching and of service, and do what has not yet been done."[6]

Thanks to Buber and others, religious humanism increasingly appealed to American Jews, as Emil Fackenheim (1916–2003), a member of the Oconomowoc group and a professor at the University of Toronto at the time, noted:

---

[5] Ibid., 15.
[6] Plaut, *Growth of Reform Judaism*, 253.

In search of an answer, the liberal Jew of today must encounter the ancient reflection of the divine incursion which constituted the covenant under which he still stands. He must also encounter the traction of those of his ancestors who sought—and received—answers before him. But if and when he himself receives an answer as a result of this encounter, it will be—if the encounter itself is genuine—the answer heard by him with modern ears, and addressed to him in a modern situation. Heard by him, it will no doubt bear the stamp of his human interpretation, just as did the answers heard by earlier generations. But if it is a genuine answer, genuinely heard, his human interpretation will nevertheless be the result of God's address. For He, the God of Israel, still lives; and the Liberal Jew, son of the Covenant, still stands at Mt. Sinai, as did his fathers.[7]

R. Eugene Borowitz (1916–2003), a professor at HUC-JIR, a member of the group, and later the leading spokesman for Reform Judaism in the United States, held the same view in his widely acclaimed book of 1991, *Renewing the Covenant*. In reflecting on the seminal significance of this work, Plaut wrote:

In this work, he [Borowitz] turned to religious existentialism as expressed in the relational philosophy of Martin Buber as the methodological foundation for his thought. Affirming the Buberian emphasis upon the primacy of dialogue and relationship, Borowitz stated that the ideal of Covenant captured the reality of the relationship between God and Israel.

The Jewish theology he expressed attempted to address the broad swath of American Jewry who, regardless of denominational label, made their Jewish decisions on the basis of personal freedom. At the same time, Borowitz did not celebrate autonomy alone but called upon Jews to take responsibility for the study and practice of tradition: "We need to guide Jews in the difficult art of maintaining an intense loyalty to Jewish tradition, that is, of living by a deeply Jewish faith, while freely assessing the virtues of the various modern ways of interpreting it—and within this continuous dialectic process to find the personal and conceptual integrity of what it means to be a modern Jew." For Borowitz, the modern Jew living within the dialectic tension between the Covenant and the

---

[7] Fackenheim, "Dilemma of Liberal Judaism," 310, in Plaut, *Growth of Reform Judaism*, 354.

modern situation should aspire to be an "autonomous Jewish self."[8]

Plaut clearly articulates the dilemma created by Reform's attachment to the value of autonomy and personal choice and Reform's attachment to Jewish tradition and its metavalues articulated in rabbinic halakhah.

Martin Buber recognized this issue in an article written in 1962 upon the opening of the first Reform synagogue in Israel. Plaut quotes the following paragraphs from the article.

> The religious condition of the people of Israel in its own land is a pathological one. This situation arises essentially out of the historic fact that Judaism in the period of "its call to freedom" (the emancipation) did not bring forth a Reformation but essentially a reduction. Because of this, when the Ingathering of the Exiles began, there did not exist a firm basis for rejuvenating the vitality of the religious faith of Israel.
>
> Secularism, on the one hand, in spite of its slogans of Messianism, has in practice no aim beyond that of self-preservation and survival. Traditionalism, on the other hand, is content with a rigid guarantee that traditional forms will be preserved, without an earnest desire to initiate any improvement in the life of society which is, indeed, the initial step in transforming the contemporary world into "a kingdom of God."
>
> These two forces, the force of secularism and the force of traditionalism, stand opposed to one another, but the presence of a third force is lacking. It may be that the future of the people of Israel depends more on the rise of this third force than it does on external factors.[9]

In 2015 R. David Ellenson wrote an epilogue to the second edition of Plaut's book. The difference between Ellenson's views of Reform Judaism in 2015 and Plaut's views of Reform fifty years earlier illustrates many of the changes in Reform during that half century. Ellenson writes of a narrowing of the differences between Conservative and Reform Jews during those fifty years. The number of members of each denomination changed as well. Whereas fifty years earlier there had been twice as many Conservative Jews

---

[8] Plaut, *Growth of Reform Judaism*, 373, cited in Ellenson, *Jewish Meaning in a World of Choice*, 112.

[9] Buber, Oral greetings on the occasion of the dedication of the Liberal Synagogue in Jerusalem, 12, in Plaut, *Growth of Reform Judaism*, 361. Cf. Heberman, "Martin Buber and Reform Judaism."

as Reform, in 2015 there were twice as many Reform Jews as Conservative. There have been other changes as well. Most of the hundreds of new Jewish initiatives are transdenominational. A growing number of younger people are trying to find Judaism and community in these new initiatives that are outside the synagogue and its historically affiliated institutions such as Sisterhood, Hadassah, and B'nai Brith. An expression of this is the online magazine *Tablet*, which is widely followed by young Jews while the print magazines are struggling to remain solvent.

These changes are reflected in a change in Jewish affiliation. The *National Jewish Identity Report* in 1971 reported that among American Jewish households, 40 percent identified as Conservative, 30 percent as Reform, and 15 percent as nondenominational.[10] Nineteen years later, the 1990 edition of the same report indicated that 41 percent of Jewish households identified themselves as Reform, 40 percent identified themselves Conservative, and 12 percent identified themselves as nondenominational.[11] More than forty years after the *National Jewish Identity Report* of 1971, in 2013 a study by the Pew Research Center reported that 35 percent of those responding identified themselves as Reform, 18 percent identified themselves as Conservative, and 26 percent identified themselves as nondenominational. It is important to note that in 2012, 22 percent of affiliated Jews were Orthodox and 27 percent of all Jews under eighteen years old were Orthodox.[12]

The Pew study of 2013 indicates that Reform has shrunk in the last twenty years, although less than Conservatives, and that the Orthodox are positioned for growth. The Jewish Renewal Movement and the unaffiliated are the fastest-growing groups in American Judaism. In the United States among all groups in society only 24 percent identify with the religious denomination into which they were born. Crossover into different religious denominations and different religions is endemic. Even with these trends, Reform remains the largest Jewish denomination. It is open to all Jews and resonates with liberals, those who believe in gender equality, and those who are searching for a religious experience that is congruent with their personal values.[13]

---

[10] Massarik, *National Jewish Identity Report* (1971), 2, 15–16, in Plaut, *Growth of Reform Judaism*, 366.
[11] Kosmin, *National Jewish Identity Report* (1990), in Plaut, *Growth of Reform Judaism*, 366.
[12] Cooperman et al., *Portrait of Jewish Americans*, chapter 3, cited in Plaut, *Growth of Reform Judaism*, 366.
[13] Plaut, *Growth of Reform Judaism*, 367.

Institutional Positions

Reform instituted radical social reforms during the last half of the twentieth century. In 1974 the Union of American Hebrew Congregations (UAHC) admitted to membership an LGBT congregation in Los Angeles, Beth Chayim Chadashim, The House of New Life. Soon thereafter the college that trains Reform rabbis, HUC-JIR, began admitting openly gay and lesbian students to study for the rabbinate. In 2000 the CCAR passed a resolution that affirmed rabbinic officiation at same-sex marriages.

In 1978 R. Alexander Schindler (1925–2000) became the incoming president of the UAHC, which in 2003 was renamed the Union for Reform Judaism. In his acceptance speech to the board of trustees, Schindler proposed a radical change in Reform, patrilineal descent. Children born to a Jewish father and a gentile mother would be considered Jewish if the parents agreed to rear the child as a Jew. Children born to a Jewish mother and gentile father would be Jewish in accordance with the tradition of several thousand years. In the same speech, R. Schindler announced the establishment of a program of active outreach to intermarried and unaffiliated Jews.[14] Patrilineal descent was affirmed in 1983 by the CCAR.

Although the regulations of the CCAR prohibit Reform rabbis from officiating at a mixed marriage, one in which both parties are not Jewish, today large numbers of Reform rabbis will perform a mixed marriage ceremony if the couple promises that they will maintain a Jewish home and rear their children as Jews. The liberal trends in Reform are accompanied by a return to more traditional practices in observance and belief. Head coverings, prayer shawls, bowing during prayer, and prayers in Hebrew are more common in religious services. Halakhah, though not binding in Reform, is being explored more deeply. David Ellenson, accordingly, in his epilogue to the republication of Plaut's history of American Reform Judaism, avers: "As we move into the twenty-first century, the task that confronts Reform Judaism is how to make Judaism relevant, compelling, joyous, meaningful, welcoming, comforting, and challenging to American Jews and others throughout the world who, to employ the felicitous term of Steven Cohen and Arnold Eisen, are 'sovereign selves.' Reform leaders and laity must creatively and boldly ask how Reform Judaism can succeed in doing this for large numbers of Jews."[15]

---

[14] R. Alexander Schindler, speech to the Board of Trustees of the Union of Reform Judaism, Houston, Texas, December 2, 1978.
[15] David Ellenson, epilogue to Plaut, *Growth of American Reform Judaism*, 384.

In his introduction to the 2015 edition of Plaut's *The Growth of American Judaism*, R. Howard Berman comments on the historical statements of principles for Reform Judaism and for Classical Reform Judaism. The following excerpt from these comments is noteworthy: "The 1976 Centenary Perspective adopted by the CCAR in San Francisco stated that the movement was called upon 'to probe the extraordinary events of the past generation'—particularly the Holocaust and the birth of the State of Israel—'and incorporate their significance into our lives.' The Centenary Perspective observed that Reform Jews would not abandon 'the ethics of universalism implicit in Judaism,' but it also charged that Reform 'must confront the claims of Jewish tradition.' In addition, it maintained 'that women have full rights to practice Judaism.'"[16]

In 1999 Richard Levy, as president of the CCAR, was commissioned to draft a statement in on Reform Judaism and its relation to traditional Jewish teachings would be closed to Reform Jews. Levy's proposal was approved by the CCAR and became known as the 1999 Pittsburgh Statement of Principles. In contrast to the Pittsburgh Platform of 1885, in which Reform rabbis convened to determine the initial principles of Reform Judaism, the 1999 Pittsburgh Statement of Principles asserted, in tones reminiscent of Franz Rosenzweig: "Through Torah study, we are called to *mitzvot* [sacred obligations], the means by which we make our lives holy.... Some of these *mitzvot* have long been observed by Reform Jews, others, both ancient and modern, demand renewed attention."[17]

In 2008 a group of leading Jewish intellectuals formed the Society for Classical Reform Judaism (SCRJ). Its mission was to "both affirm diversity within the movement and preserve and creatively nurture 'the historic ideals of Classical Reform Judaism' and its 'rich intellectual foundations and distinctive worship traditions.'"[18] The following statements in the SCRJ platform emphasize the pluralistic basis in Classical Reform and its emphasis on outreach to all who wish to practice or participate in Judaism:

> The SCRJ has sought to clearly define the distinctive perspective and alternative it offers, in its founding Statement of Principles, adopted in February 2008. While affirming the dynamic development and

---

[16] Berman, W. Gunther, in Plaut, *Growth of American Reform Judaism*, 377.

[17] Levy, 1999 Pittsburgh Statement of Principles, *CCAR Press Newsletter*, May 1999, reprinted in Levy, *Vision of Holiness*, xv, cited in Plaut, *Growth of Reform Judaism*, 379.

[18] Society for Classical Reform Judaism, "Principles of the Society for Classical Reform Judaism," cited in Plaut, *Growth of Reform Judaism*, 379.

continuous innovation that must mark any progressive religious vision, the Society's commitments echo the ideals of Reform's pioneers: a focus on the primary spiritual essence of Judaism; an embrace of the universalistic, prophetic mandate of ethical values as the major expression of religious commitment; the centrality of the American experience for Jewish identity in a free, open, pluralistic society; and a conscious and unconditional support of diversity in today's Jewish community.[19]

We affirm a broad, inclusive pluralism, which reflects the full diversity within today's changing Jewish community, and welcome all those who share our ideals. We are particularly committed to an active outreach and warm unconditional welcome for interfaith and multicultural families in the belief that the universal spiritual values of Classical Reform are uniquely meaningful and empowering for this ever growing number of our young people.[20]

Berman points out that the SCRJ was an alternative voice. The mainstream of Reform, he says, is expressed in the 1999 Pittsburgh Statement of Principles:

The ideology contained in the Statement of Principles is surely dominant in modern-day Reform, and the movement's newest prayer book, *Mishkan T'filah* (2007), edited by Rabbi Elyse Frishman and her CCAR committee, is consonant with these principles[:] . . . social justice, feminism, Zionism, distinctiveness, and human challenges. In the words of Rabbi Elaine Zecher, [it is] "an integrated theology" that invites the full participation of people who have different convictions and levels of faith while establishing a fixed text that promotes community and a shared Reform identity. The future of the Reform Movement depends in no small measure upon the realization of this vision and the ongoing creativity and meaning that Reform worship will generate.[21]

Commenting approvingly on this statement, Berman noted several

---

[19] Society for Classical Reform Judaism, "Principles of the Society for Classical Reform Judaism," cited in Plaut, *Growth of Reform Judaism*, 400.
[20] Society for Classical Reform Judaism, "Principles of the Society for Classical Reform Judaism," cited in Plaut, *Growth of Reform Judaism*, 402.
[21] Berman, ?, 380.

statements of principle that were adopted by the CCAR at the 1999 Pittsburgh Convention:

> We affirm that every human being is created [*b'tzelem Elohim*], in the image of God, and that heretofore every human life is sacred.[22]
>
> We are committed to the ongoing study of the whole array of [*mitzvot*] and to the fulfillment of those that address us as individuals and as a community. Some of these [*mitzvot*], sacred obligations, have long been observed by Reform Jews; others, both ancient and modern, demand renewed attention as the result of the unique context of our times.[23]

This statement reaffirms elements in R. Alexander Schindler's 1978 address to the board of trustees of the UAHC, in which he outlined a new vision for Reform Judaism:[24]

> As important as Jewish education is, in the context [of intermarriage], I believe that there are other steps we can — and must — take if we are to deal realistically with the threat which intermarriage presents to our survival. And it is on three such steps that I want to focus my attention.
>
> The first of these has to do with the conversion of the non-Jewish, partner-to-be. It is time for us to reform our behavior towards those who become Jews-by-Choice, to increase our sensitivity towards them and, thereby, to encourage growth in their numbers.
>
> We do not offer them [converts] help in establishing a Jewish home, in raising their children Jewishly, in grappling with their peculiar problems, in dealing with their special conflicts. More important still, we do not really embrace them, enable them to feel a close kinship with our people.
>
> On the contrary: if the truth be told, we often alienate them. We question their motivations (since only a madman would choose to be a Jew, the convert is either neurotic or hypocritical). We think them less Jewish (ignoring that they often know more about Judaism than born Jews).

---

[22] Levy, 1999 Pittsburgh Statement of Principles, cited in Plaut, *Growth of Reform Judaism*, 396.

[23] Levy, 1999 Pittsburgh Statement of Principles, cited in Plaut, *Growth of Reform Judaism*, 397.

[24] Schindler, speech to the Board of Trustees of the Union of Reform Judaism, cited in Plaut, *Growth of Reform Judaism*, 409.

Unto the end of their days, we refer to them as converts.[25]

A colleague of mine recently received a letter from one who elected to become a Jew:

> Dear _____:
>
> I know that I personally resent being referred to as a convert — a word that by now is alien to my heart. My conversion process was nearly ten years ago — I have been a Jew for a long time now. I think, eat and breathe Judaism. My soul is a Jewish soul though I am distinctly aware of my original background and birthright. This does not alter my identity as a Jew. If one is curious about whence I come or if indeed "am I really Jewish," the answer is categorically, "Yes, I'm really Jewish — a Jew-by-Choice." I shall continue to grow and search as a Jew. My "conversion process" was just that — a process which ended with the ceremony. From then on I was a Jew.

It is time for us to stop relating to the new Jews as if they were curiosities, or as if they were superficial people whose conversion to Judaism reflects a lack of principles on their part, a way of accommodating to their partners-to-be. Newcomers to Judaism, in short, must embark on a long-term naturalization process, and they require knowledgeable and sympathetic guides along the way, that they may feel themselves fully equal members of the synagogue family.[26]

Let there be no holding back. It was Maimonides himself, answering a convert's query, who wrote:

> You ask whether you, being a proselyte, may speak the prayers: "our God and God of our Fathers" and "Guardian of Israel who has brought us out of the land of Egypt," and the like.
> Pronounce all the prayers as they are written and do not change a word. Your prayers and your blessings should be the same as any

---

[25] Schindler, speech to the Board of Trustees of the Union of Reform Judaism, cited in Plaut, *Growth of Reform Judaism*, 410.

[26] Schindler, speech to the Board of Trustees of the Union of Reform Judaism, cited in Plaut, *Growth of Reform Judaism*, 410.

other Jew. This above all: do not think little of your origin. We may be descended from Abraham, Isaac and Jacob, but your descent is from the Almighty Himself.[27]

Maimonides, in this *Letter to Obadiah the Proselyte*, established the equality in Judaism of a born Jew and a proselyte. This clear statement is characteristic of his lenient decisions in specific situations.

Plaut explains that according to Schindler, the dignity of a convert takes precedence over a strict interpretation of halakhah:

> Schindler continued his address with the statement that Reform must look beyond conversion alone because most of the non-Jewish partners do not convert to Judaism. Two out of three intermarriages involve a Jewish husband and a non-Jewish wife. Only one out of four wives converts to Judaism. In the third of the Jewish marriages between a Jewish wife and a non-Jewish husband, the conversion rate is much lower than one in four. Schindler tells the board that everything possible must be done to bring the non-Jewish spouse into Jewish life. This will make it more likely that they will desire to become Jewish. It will be more likely that their children will be reared as Jews.[28]

The Jewish partner needs to be considered. She may have been rejected by her community, even by her own parents. She may feel guilty, resentful, and ambivalent about her involvement in the community. She may feel inhibited by her partner's feelings or by fear that the community will not accept her spouse. Schindler expressed these thoughts in 1978. The concerns remain today; acceptance of those who are intermarried and of converts is more likely but not certain.

The inclusion of women as rabbis and congregational leaders continues to affect Reform Judaism. The ordination in 1972 of Sally Priesand as the first woman rabbi in Reform epitomized the move to a more egalitarian denomination. By 2015 more than 670 women had become rabbis. Half the rabbinic students at HUC-JIR were women. Their influence reflected the changing values in the United States and the increasing influence of

---

[27] Schindler, speech to the Board of Trustees of the Union of Reform Judaism, cited in Plaut, *Growth of Reform Judaism*, 411–12. Schindler quotes Maimonides, *Mishneh Torah*, chapters 13–14.

[28] Plaut, *Growth of Reform Judaism*, 367–68.

women in all facets society. The impact of sociological changes in the United States on both Jews and non-Jews began to reverse the historical male domination over rabbinic leadership, Jewish institutions, the interpretation of texts, and the creation of prayer books. The traditional prayer that concluded "Thank God that I am not a woman" was excised from Reform prayer books.

Demographics of American Jewry

The issues of conversion and of who defines who is Jewish are more salient now than ever before. One of the reasons is that intermarriage has increased dramatically. Among Jewish respondents who have married since 2000, nearly 60 percent have a non-Jewish spouse, whereas among those married before 1970, 17 percent have a non-Jewish spouse.[29]

Reform has become the largest denomination, twice the size of Conservatism and four times the size of Orthodoxy. Orthodoxy was small and insecure sixty years ago. It was expected to continue to decline. Instead it strengthened, gained confidence, distanced itself from Reform in the United States, and aggressively attempted to delegitimize Reform in Israel. Conservatism has lost members. It follows Orthodoxy in observing halakhah, and it follows Reform in liberalism. The fastest-growing group of Jews are those who profess to belong to no denomination. They represent 30 percent of the Jewish population in America.[30]

There were 14,511,000 Jews in the world on Israel's seventieth anniversary, in 2018, according to the Israeli government. In 1939 there were 16,600,000 Jews. During the Holocaust these numbers were reduced to 11,500,000.[31]

Israel had 450,000 Jews in 1939, and at the time of Israel's seventieth anniversary it had 6,589,000 Jews, 43 percent of world Jewry. Israel's Jewish population was 74.5 percent of its total population. Israel's 1,849,000 Arabs were 20.9 percent of Israel's population. When the state was established, there were only 806,000 residents.[32]

The 5,700,000 Jews in the United States in 2018 are the next-largest

---

[29] "American Jewry Today – Jewish Population Statistics."
[30] Goodstein, "Poll Shows Major Shift in Identity of U.S. Jews."
[31] DellaPergola, "World Jewish Population, 2018."
[32] Ibid.

Jewish population in the world. There are 1,500,000 Reform Jews, half that many Conservatives, and a quarter that many Orthodox. The "nones" are the fastest growing. These numbers are not as precise as they may appear. Jews enter and leave denominations, participate and do not participate, and have different religious practices and beliefs than their denomination.[33]

In his article "A Policy of *Giyyur* for Our Time," Zvi Zohar argues that in order for American Jews to maintain or to increase their numbers, they must adopt a policy of welcoming converts and create a legitimate process for conversion that both conforms to tradition and is not unnecessarily onerous. His concern is that Jewish birthrates are insufficient to maintain a stable population. Drawing on the Pew Research Center's 2013 report *A Portrait of Jewish Americans*, Zohar observes that as of 2013, the Orthodox in the United States continued to comprise 10 percent of the Jewish population even though their birthrate was 4.1 children in each family. Jewish adults ages forty to fifty-nine had an average of 1.9 children, while the replacement level was 2.1 children per couple. Jews who had left Judaism made up 25 percent of the Jewish denominational population. Consequently, the effective rate of replacement was actually 1.65.[34]

The defection of 25 percent was less than the 28 percent of those who were leaving other religions. Jewish outreach and the attractiveness of Judaism have been effective but they have not been sufficient to stop the decline in Jews in the United States. Zohar points out:

> If Protestants who have changed their religious affiliation within Protestantism are included, then 44% of Americans have changed their religious affiliation at least once.[35]

> The Pew Survey finds that constant movement characterizes the American religious marketplace, as every major religious group is simultaneously gaining and losing adherents. Those that are growing as a result of religious change are simply gaining new members at a faster rate than they are losing members. Conversely, those that are declining in number because of religious change simply are not attracting enough new members to

---

[33] Ibid.
[34] Cooperman et al., *Portrait of Jewish Americans*, 5, cited in Zohar, "A Policy of *Giyyur* for Our Time."
[35] Cooperman et al., *Portrait of Jewish Americans*, 1, 10, cited in Zohar, "A Policy of *Giyyur* for Our Time."

offset the number of adherents who are leaving those particular faiths.[36]

Zohar argues that the problem of the decline in the Jewish population in America is that Jews have been averse to receiving converts. This policy follows a historical aversion that was designed for survival and was a response to the danger that conversion posed to the convert, to those who performed the conversion, and to those who accepted the convert. "The authorities of the dominant faiths reacted violently to members of their group who opted for another religion, taking vengeance both upon the convert and those who accepted him."[37]

These numbers are not as precise as one might believe. Americans enter and leave denominations, participate and do not participate, and have different religious practices and beliefs than the denominations with which they identify. Surveys cannot reflect accurately the number of Jews in each denomination and the number in alternative practices. The reported results of surveys are in that sense fictitious. Qualitative studies can reflect these differences. They are closer to a specific truth than the surveys are to an accurate generalization. Most quantitative studies are not conducted in sufficient depth to be more than anecdotal, and they are not always conducted by capable psychologists. Some of the questions asked in surveys are based on the very same questions Pew asked decades ago. They are retained for comparison to more recent surveys both by Pew and in other researchers, but the comparisons are questionable. Although the questions have not changed, American culture has. Many of the questions mean something different to respondents now than they meant to respondents when the questions were first were created. The respondents are no more able to locate themselves in the questions now than they were decades ago. The questions have a meaning to each researcher and to each respondent. These meanings are not necessarily identical. Multivariate analysis and other statistic methods cannot rationalize or summarize the varieties of human experience and human meaning that are expressed in responses to polls.

These problems with surveys and their impact on the American mind were the subject of a recent book by Robert Wuthnow on the polling industry published in 2015, two years after the Pew study. Wuthnow questioned the accuracy and meaning of the dominant view of American religion and

---

[36] Cooperman et al., *Portrait of Jewish Americans*, 7 (cf. 16, 18, 32–33, 122), cited in Zohar, "A Policy of *Giyyur* for Our Time."

[37] Zohar, "A Policy of *Giyyur* for Our Time," 3.

of the surveys that, he argues, created it. After the following summary Pew's *Portrait of Jewish Americans*, I will offer a more detailed exposition of Wuthnow's criticism of religious surveys.

A PORTRAIT OF JEWISH AMERICANS: PEW

A Portrait of Jewish Americans was the most current, extensive survey available when I was writing this book. It cost much more than other recent polls and pursued responses from its selected respondents relentlessly. Pew screened 142,000 people for the survey, of whom it selected 71,151 for screening interviews. The final number of Jews by religion who participated was 2 percent of the 142,000 and thus 4 percent of those chosen to be interviewed.[38]

The portrait began with several findings about Jews and Jewish identity. American Jews overwhelmingly said they were proud to be Jewish and had a strong sense of belonging to the Jewish people. But the survey also suggested that Jewish identity was changing in America, where one in five Jews (22 percent) described themselves as having no religion: "Jews of no religion comprise 22% of the adult Jewish population and Jews by religion comprise 78%. Jews of no religion have increased to 32% among Millennials, those born after 1980, from 7% among the Greatest Generation, those born between 1914 and 1927."[39]

The Pew survey found that changes in Jewish self-identification mirrored changes in U.S. culture. Gary Zola[40] of HUC-JIR has long argued that the changes in Reform in Germany and in the United States were driven in large part by the prevailing culture. He believes that changes in American culture, and consequently changes in American Reform Judaism, are accelerating. The Pew study described this process as follows.

> This shift in Jewish self-identification reflects broader changes in the U.S. public. Americans as a whole — not just Jews — increasingly eschew any religious affiliation. Indeed, the share of U.S. Jews who say they

---

[38] Cooperman et al., *Portrait of Jewish Americans*, 124.
[39] Cooperman et al., *Portrait of Jewish Americans*, 3.
[40] R. Gary Phillip Zola is the executive director of the Jacob Rader Marcus Center of the American Jewish Archives (AJA) and the Edward M. Ackerman Family Distinguished Professor of the American Jewish Experience and Reform Jewish History at HUC-JIR.

have no religion (22%) is similar to the share of religious "nones" in the general public (20%), and religious disaffiliation is as common among all U.S. adults ages 18–29 as among Jewish Millennials (32% of each).[41]

Secularism has a long tradition in Jewish life in America, and most U.S. Jews seem to recognize this: 62% say being Jewish is mainly a matter of ancestry and culture, while just 15% say it is mainly a matter of religion. Even among Jews by religion, more than half (55%) say being Jewish is mainly a matter of ancestry and culture, and two-thirds say it is not necessary to believe in God to be Jewish.[42]

The survey indicates that ancestry and culture are the most important determinants of Jewish identity. Eighty-three percent of Jews of no religion, the largest growing segment of the Jewish population, selected ancestry/culture, and 55 percent of Jews by religion did so. Seventeen percent of Jews by religion selected religion as the primary determinant of being Jewish. Twenty-six percent of Jews by religion selected ancestry/culture.

Intermarriage had increased substantially, and the rate of intermarriage was increasing among all denominations except the Orthodox. Intermarriage was much more common among secular Jews in the survey than among Jews by religion: Jews of no religion had married a spouse who was not Jewish in 79 percent of the cases. Jews by religion had married a spouse who was not Jewish 36 percent of the time. Among Jewish respondents who had married since 2000, nearly six-in-ten had a non-Jewish spouse. Among those who married in the 1980s, roughly four in ten had a non-Jewish spouse at the time of the survey. Among Jews who were married before 1970, 17 percent had a non-Jewish spouse.

It is not clear whether being intermarried tends to make U.S. Jews less religious, or being less religious tends to make U.S. Jews more inclined to intermarry, or some of both. Whatever the causal connection, the survey finds a strong association between secular Jews and religious intermarriage.[43]

The survey also shows that Reform Judaism continues to be the largest

[41] Cooperman et al., *Portrait of Jewish Americans*, 3.
[42] Ibid., 59, 74–75.
[43] Ibid., 5.

Jewish denominational movement in the United States. One-third (35%) of all U.S. Jews identify with the Reform movement, while 18% identify with Conservative Judaism, 10% with Orthodox Judaism and 6% with a variety of smaller groups, such as the Reconstructionist and Jewish Renewal movements. About three-in-ten American Jews (including 19% of Jews by religion and two-thirds of Jews of no religion) say they do not identify with any particular Jewish denomination.[44]

Though Orthodox Jews constitute the smallest of the three major denominational movements, they are much younger, on average, and tend to have much larger families than the overall Jewish population. This suggests that their share of the Jewish population will grow. In the past, high fertility in the U.S. Orthodox community has been at least partially offset by a low retention rate: Roughly half of the survey respondents who were raised as Orthodox Jews say they are no longer Orthodox. But the falloff from Orthodoxy appears to be declining and is significantly lower among 18-to-29-year-olds, 17%, than among older people.[45]

The change in denominational affiliation reversed in the last century. The Conservative movement had been the choice of immigrants who wanted to retain their religious practices and at the same time to become Americans. Conservatives were the largest denomination, Orthodoxy was small and declining, and Reform was stable. The trends began to change in the middle of the twentieth century. Switching between denominations became more prevalent. Most of the switching was toward less traditional Judaism. The survey found that approximately 25 percent of people who were raised Orthodox had since become Conservative or Reform Jews, while 30 percent of those raised Conservative had become Reform Jews, and 28 percent of those raised Reform had left Judaism entirely. Much less switching was reported in the opposite direction. For example, just 7 percent of Jews raised in the Reform movement had become Conservative or Orthodox, and just 4 percent of those raised in Conservative Judaism had become Orthodox.

The Pew survey explores what it means to be Jewish. Remembering the Holocaust and leading an ethical/moral life were selected by more than two-thirds of the respondents. Working for justice/equality was selected by slightly more than half. Being part of a Jewish community was selected by

---

[44] Ibid., 48.
[45] Ibid.

28 percent, and observing law by 19 percent. Remembering Jewish history and leading a moral life were essential for most American Jews.

INVENTING AMERICAN RELIGION: ROBERT WUTHNOW

In 2015 Robert Wuthnow, the Gerhard R. Andlinger '52 Professor of Sociology and director of Princeton University's Center for the Study of Religion, published *Inventing American Religion: Polls, Surveys, and the Tenuous Quest for a Nation's Faith*, a critique of the polling industry and the picture of American religion that it had created. In it he argued that our view of American religious demographics, beliefs, and practices was a creation of the polling industry. Wuthnow points out that the polling industry has impacted American religion through its creation of an entity called American religion that has influenced and distorted our view of religion in America:

> The polling industry's impact on American religion has been more significant than easy acceptance or quick dismissals would allow. As a nation, we know far more than previous generations did about what people believe, what they do to nurture those beliefs, and how those beliefs influence their opinions on important issues of the day. At the same time, polls are ill suited to capture the most meaningful aspects of our personal lives, let alone the depth, superficiality, and complicated relationships we may have with religious traditions and practices. They rarely probe in depth the experiences underlying religious beliefs or the narratives through which those experiences become personally meaningful. The intent, rather, is to generalize and thus reinforce the otherwise tenuous idea that the religion of an entire nation can be aptly and succinctly described.[46]

My argument is that the polling industry has influenced — and at times distorted — how religion is understood and portrayed, particularly in the media but also to some extent by religious leaders, practitioners, and scholars. To have been influenced does not mean that religion has been fundamentally changed. But some perceptions of religion were reinforced while others were not. The evidence comes largely from scholars

---

[46] Wuthnow, *Inventing American Religion*, 5.

of religion carrying on a constructive dialogue that included criticisms of what they were doing. When polls suggested that Americans unanimously believed in God, closer investigation showed that doubt in varying degrees prevailed as well and that there were markedly different views of God. Tacit generalizations about "American" religion were shown to pertain mostly to white middle-class Protestants.... Additional concerns focus on what counts as religion, whether counting it is the appropriate metaphor, and if it is, whether adequate attention is given to the political and ideological forces that may be shaping the counting.[47]

Later Wuthnow writes, "It was a kind of civil religion ... Robert N. Bellah would argue a few years later, similar to the one Rousseau had suggested, religious belief would be especially conducive to mutual happiness and tolerance."[48]

In a review of Robert D. Putman's *Bowling Alone: The Collapse and Revival of American Community* (2000), Wuthnow raised three major issues for discussion. The first concerned social capital. Religion was considered to be a form of positive social capital that put people in contact with others. The second concerned the questions that were asked in past polls and continued in order to maintain a continuity of responses. Were these questions relevant to respondents who grew up in a society in which their values and society's values had changed significantly? The third question concerned the accuracy of the methods used to determine the results of surveys. Statistical methods were used infrequently. Mathematical methods such as multivariate analysis predominated. The adage of early computer programmers, "Garbage in, garbage out," became relevant.

The second topic concerned the specific questions available in polls and surveys. In order to chart a decline in social capital, it was necessary to use questions that had been asked periodically for several decades. That meant using questions that reflected the habits and social norms of the 1950s, 1960s, or early 1970s, but that perhaps no longer captured how people interacted with one another. Questions about hosting dinner parties for friends and neighbors, participating in bowling leagues, mailing letters to public officials, and holding membership in Kiwanis, for example, might suggest that civic involvement was in serious decline.

[47] Ibid., 13.
[48] Ibid.

But the story might be different if questions were asked about newer forms of participation, such as having lunch together with friends and coworkers, participating in meet-up groups, e-mailing public officials, and doing volunteer work with Habitat for Humanity.[49]

The discussion of which questions to ask and how to interpret them had implications for polls and surveys about religion. Was it any more appropriate to measure religious involvement only with a question about attendance at worship services than it was to assess social capital with questions about dinner parties and bowling leagues? Studying religion that way suggested that it was one-dimensional.[50]

The questionable accuracy of polling is captured by Wuthnow's inference that the reason for the popularity of Gallup's polls was their optimism. The salience of religious faith in the polling industry is captured in a statement by George Gallup, who founded his profitable polling company in 1935. "Surveys are a very important tool in God's work, Gallup told Dart [The religious correspondent for the New York Times]."[51] Wuthnow argues that the public's view of religion in America, to which Reform Judaism is no exception, is a construct of the polling industry and of the media's interpretation of the meaning of the polls. We should be aware of this construct and its influence on our understanding of Judaism in America. The polls may not reflect the true number of members, the variations in participation, and the meaning that participation has for members. Rabbis and laity in American Judaism think about and practice Judaism in many diverse ways. They think about and act toward converts and conversion in many diverse ways. Polls have difficulty capturing the diverse thoughts and feelings and the diverse attitudes toward converts and conversion.

---

[49] Ibid., 142.
[50] Ibid.
[51] Ibid.

CHAPTER 7

Circumcision and Moral Universalism

Circumcision for Jews has a religious value that has led to the continuation of the practice since the time of Abraham. It began as a biblical command, the sign of the covenant between God and Israel. It became one of the 613 commands, mitzvot, in Jewish law, halakhah.

In defending male circumcision, Richard A. Shweder, the Harold H. Swift Distinguished Service Professor of Human Development at the University of Chicago, quoted a blog: "Call me a fundamentalist but like my father and the hundreds of generations that preceded me, there is only one reason why I am circumcised: it's a mitzvah [the moral law derived from a divine commandment]. From Abraham down to me, it is a basic belief. That the world can't seem to get that is beyond me."[1] The practice of circumcision in the Jewish tradition began when God instructed Abraham to circumcise himself and all his descendants as a symbol of an everlasting covenant between God and the Jewish people.

> "And I will give unto thee, and to thy seed after thee, the land of thy sojournings, all the land of Canaan, for an everlasting possession; and I will be their God." And God said unto Abraham: "And as for thee, thou shalt keep My covenant, thou, and thy seed after thee throughout their generations. This is My covenant, which ye shall keep, between Me and you and thy seed after thee: every male among you shall be circumcised. And ye shall be circumcised in the flesh of your foreskin; and it shall be a token of a covenant betwixt Me and you. And he that is eight days old shall be circumcised among you, every male throughout your generations, he that is born in the house, or bought with money of any foreigner, that is not of thy seed. He that is born in thy house, and he that is bought with thy money, must needs be circumcised; and My covenant shall be in your flesh for an everlasting covenant." (Genesis 17:8–13)

Today some liberal Jewish parents question the practice of circumcision. Some question the involuntary nature of circumcision and the lifelong

---

[1] Shweder, "Shouting at the Hebrews," cited in Shweder, *Thinking through Cultures*, 265.

change it makes on the body. They question if it is moral to make that decision for a child. Some non-Jews vehemently object to the practice.

Shweder writes of the Italian physician of the late nineteenth century whose opening words are the source of the title of Shweder's article "Shouting at the Hebrews": "I shall shout and shall continue to shout at the Hebrews, until my last breath: Cease mutilating yourselves: cease imprinting upon your flesh an odious brand to distinguish you from other men: until you do this you cannot pretend to be our equal. As it is, you, of your own accord, with the branding iron from the first days of your lives, proceed to proclaim yourselves a race apart, one that cannot, and does not care to, mix with ours."[1]

The vehemence of the Italian physician's entreaty is matched by the vehemence of protests in the Western world against female genital modification. Lost in the discussion of, or diatribe against, circumcision and female genital modification is the fact that a large number of African males and African females value both practices. These practices take place not after birth but in the child's early teens and are often called rites of passage. For male members of tribes in cultures such as those of Papua New Guinea and West Papua, the practices are accompanied by a requirement of surviving in the wild for a month, learning the secrets of the tribe and of manhood, and scarring of the body. Salt is rubbed in the wounds to enhance the visibility of the scars after the wound has healed.

Shweder asked a Kenyan professor who teaches in the United States, "Were you circumcised?" The professor responded, "I was thirteen years old and physically mature and it was the season for circumcising an age set of boys and transforming them into men. My older cousins were going to be circumcised but the senior adults thought I was too young. So I threw a fit and demanded they let me be circumcised too, which they did."[2] Shweder asked, "Was it painful?"

> "Painful," he exclaimed. "It was the most painful thing I have ever experienced in my life. It took a month to fully recover. But during that time they taught us so many things — about the history of my people, about what it means to be a man, about how to treat women, about how to have sex ... how to own property, how to brace up to painful ordeals in life and be fearless. And during that month we bonded with each other. I feel closer to those men who were circumcised with me ... than

---

[1] Shweder, *Thinking through Cultures*, 5, 248.
[2] Gilman, "'Barbaric' Rituals?," 53, cited in Shweder, *Thinking through Cultures*, 5, 247.

anyone else in the world."[3]

Fuambai Ahmadu, an anthropologist who is a native of the Kono people of Sierra Leone, wrote on the cultural psychology of male and female circumcision in Sierra Leone. Here is his statement on female genital modification: "It is difficult for me — considering the number of these ceremonies I have observed, including my own — to accept that what appear to be expressions of joy and ecstatic celebrations of womanhood in actuality disguise hidden experiences of coercion and subjugation. Indeed, I offer that most Kono women who uphold these rituals do so because they want to — they relish the supernatural powers of their ritual leaders over against men in society, and they embrace the legitimacy of female authority and, particularly, the authority of their mothers and grandmothers."

I spoke recently with a Kenyan man who emigrated to the U.S. fifteen years ago. He spoke disparagingly about female genital modification and said that the practice was declining in Kenya and throughout Africa.

Circumcision and Ethical Universalism

Shweder points out that circumcision, a cultural custom practiced differently in many societies around the world,[4] is compatible with moral universalism: "Moral universalism does not require uniformity in cultural customs. To the extent the distribution of power is such that different peoples have a capacity to defend the way of life they value and protect themselves from cultural domination the world is likely to remain multicultural."[5] Shweder points out that autonomy is not the only dominant value in moral systems in a culture.

> It is worth considering as well that while autonomy is surely a key moral value it is not the only foundation of genuine moral systems. In the type of case that disturbs Brian Earp (childhood male circumcision, as practiced by Jews and Muslims for example) there are many moral values at

---

[3] Shweder, "Equality Now in Genital Reshaping," 146.

[4] According to Shweder, 20–30 percent of all males in the world are circumcised, 60–80 percent of American males are circumcised, and over 90 percent of South Koreans are circumcised. After the Korean War, the Koreans wanted to emulate the American soldiers, most of whom were circumcised.

[5] Shweder, "Equality Now in Genital Reshaping," 144.

play, including the value of religious freedom plus the value of allowing parents to raise their children as they see fit, with the option of raising them in accordance with the long-standing traditions of their ancestral group. . . . This is one of the reasons we have many traditions of belief and value.[6]

He stresses the necessity of considering social context and history when evaluating religious practices: "The idea of an impartial observer may be an inviting abstraction. Nevertheless there are limits to how far one can remove oneself from social context and history. One does not practice religion, one practices a religion. One does not inherit tradition; one inherits a tradition. . . . Tolerance for Jewish and Muslim childhood circumcision grounded in religious belief amounts to respecting the sincerity of the person who holds the belief and the centrality of the belief to that person's identity and way of life."[7]

Shweder originated a higher-order principle that he derived from a consideration of the claims of liberalism and the claims of value pluralism. The principle is a frame of reference that is helpful in considering both a culture and a religious practice.

The claims of liberalism and the claims of value pluralism (which taken together result in the doctrine of liberal pluralism or permissive liberalism) are both legitimate because liberalism and value pluralism have their common foundation in a single underlying, universal and paradoxical truth about the relationship of human minds to the knowable world. That fundamental truth defines a higher order principle from which both liberalism and pluralism can be jointly derived.[8]

The higher order principle is this one: that for each and every human being the knowable world is incomplete if seen from any one point of view, incoherent if seen from all points of view at once, and empty if seen from nowhere in particular.[9]

One point of view is through the lens of liberal values. Another is through

---

[6] Ibid.
[7] Gilman, "'Barbaric' Rituals?," cited in Shweder, *Thinking through Cultures*, 264.
[8] Shweder, *Thinking through Cultures*, 5, 247.
[9] Gilman, "'Barbaric' Rituals?," cited in Shweder, *Thinking through Cultures*, 264.

the lens of illiberal values. Shweder discusses the Jewish understanding of the conflict between liberal and illiberal values concerning circumcision.

> By the lights of liberal pluralism the voice (and claims) of individual autonomy (demanding, for example, that parents not circumcise their children when the child is very young and that the decision-making process be delayed until the child is old enough to exercise freedom of choice) is always entitled to a moral hearing. Nevertheless that voice and its claims are also potentially refutable; and a balance must be struck between liberal and illiberal values to sustain any particular way of life. The Hebrews long ago recognized that truth, and they have struggled with it for millennia; which is one reason this liberal pluralist does not shout at the Hebrews. Jomo Kenyatta, the leader of the Kenyan national liberation movement against tyrannical imperial liberal British rule (he was also the first President of a postcolonial Kenya), once famously compared the intimate circumcision scars of East African men and women to Jewish ones and described those bodily signs "as the condition sine qua non of the whole teaching of tribal law, religion and morality."[10]

In his review of Webb Keane's book *Ethical Life: Its Natural and Social Histories*, Shweder connects moral absolutes with moral intuitions and with self-evident rules of moral reason.

> By moral absolutes I mean the undeniably valid and genuinely self-evident rules of moral reason that some moral philosophers call "intuitions." Moral absolutes of the sort I have in mind are self-evident in the sense that reason requires of them no further justification or deliberation. . . . With respect to genuine moral intuitions the fact that they deserve to be honored simply goes without saying. They possess their categorical, objective, imperative, fast, and spontaneous force largely because they are constitutive of moral reason itself.[11]

Possible examples of these self-evident rules of moral reason include the following: That one ought to give every person their due, treat like cases alike and impartially apply rules of general applicability (justice);

---

[10] Shweder, *Thinking through Cultures*, citing Kenyatta, *Facing Mount Kenya*, 133.
[11] Shweder, "Channeling the Super-natural Aspects," 478.

that one ought to speak the truth (veracity); that one ought to requite benefits received as gifts or patronage (reciprocity); that one ought to protect those who are vulnerable and in one's charge (beneficence); that one ought to respond to the urgent needs of others if the sacrifice or cost to oneself is slight; that one ought to pursue the more certain of two equal goods; that one ought to select a greater good in the future over a lesser good now (if both are equally certain); that one ought to never pursue a lesser good over a greater good (prudence).[12]

Ontologically speaking, moral absolutes of the sort just illustrated are widely experienced as meta-physical ahistorical norms.... The anthropologist Raymond Firth ... nicely captures this in his summary of the ethical life of the Tikopia people ...: "The spirits, just as men, respond to a norm of conduct of an external character. The moral law exists in the absolute, independent of the Gods."[13]

The Native's View of Morality

Shweder instructs us that we need to know the "natives'" view of morality in order to understand their values and their practices. He demonstrated this through his pathbreaking analysis of the responses to the same scenarios requiring moral choices by Brahmans residing in Oriya, India, and by residents of the Hyde Park neighborhood in Chicago: "Cultural anthropologists have discovered ... that moral judgments around the world are ubiquitous, passionate, motivating, truth asserting and divergent; and that in all cultures there is some sense of natural moral law and the development of some kind of normative language of rights, duties, obligations or values for regulating and justifying action."[14]

Shweder uses common categories of moral values, universal and particular, absolute and relative, to expand on this thought.

Universalism without the uniformity is one way to describe the relativism

---

[12] Ibid.
[13] Ibid., 479.
[14] The Brahmans in India are the highest social class or caste. The people of Oriya are known now as the people of Odie. The State of Orissa became the State of Odisha in 2011.

characteristic of all these proposals. [My] "Big Three," for example, proposes that the human self or subject can be represented and experienced as either an autonomous preference structure seeking to maximize the satisfaction of its wants; or as an office holder or social status bearer in a bounded community (a family for example) defined by role based and often hierarchically interdependent duties and responsibilities; or as a free will or spirit whose capacities to initiate action and experience things of value derives from some kind of elevating connection to something that is inherently higher, dignified, pure or divine. These pictures of the self are probably present in some degree in all cultural groups but they are emphasized to different degrees and made manifest or institutionalized in different ways. So too the values associated with them: the moral goods favored by the ethics of autonomy and by many liberal societies (harm, rights, justice, self-governance and equality for example) are not those favored by the ethics of community (duty, hierarchy, loyalty, interdependence, personal sacrifice) or by the ethics of divinity (sanctity, pollution avoidance, purity, cleanliness).[15]

The illiberality of a cultural practice is not necessarily an index of its immorality.[16]

On a worldwide scale, the argument-ending terminal goods of deliberative moral judgments privileged in a cultural community are rich and diverse, and they include such noble ends as autonomy, justice, harm avoidance, loyalty, benevolence, piety, duty, respect, gratitude, sympathy, chastity, purity, sanctity, and others. Several proposals have been advanced in the social sciences for classifying these goods into a smaller set, such as the three ethics of autonomy, community, and divinity.[17]

Shweder points out that there are universal moral values and that many have objectively valuable ends. However, there are too many of them for all of them to form a coherent system of morality for a specific society. Consequently, Shweder labels himself as a "universalist without the uniformity," which makes him a pluralist.

---

[15] Shweder, *Why Do Men Barbecue?*, 19.
[16] Ibid., 33.
[17] Ibid., 38.

We know from research in cultural psychology that moral judgments around the world are ubiquitous, passionate, motivating, truth-asserting, and divergent.[18]

I am a universalist, but the type of universalism to which I subscribe is universalism without the uniformity, which is what makes me a pluralist. In other words, there are universally binding values, just too many of them. Those objectively valuable ends of life are diverse, heterogeneous, irreducible to come common denominator such as "utility" or "pleasure," and inherently in conflict with each other.[19]

Thus, one can be a pluralist and still grant that there are true and universally binding values and undeniable moral principles—for example, "cruelty is evil," "you should treat like cases alike and different cases differently," "highly vulnerable members of a society are entitled to protection from harm." One of the claims of pluralism, however, is that values and principles are objective only to the extent they are kept abstract and devoid of content. A related claim is that no abstract value or principle, in and of itself, can provide definitive guidance in concrete cases of moral dispute. In other words, it is possible for morally decent and rational people to look at each other's practices, emote, and say, "Yuck!"[20]

Our immediate interest is the nexus of autonomy. Most American Reform Jews are included in this category. The salient values in autonomy are harm, rights, and justice. The individual is a preference structure. Obligations come from being a person. Personal agency is essential. Human dignity and human responsibility, both in individuals' behavior toward themselves and toward others, are paramount. One can think of Hillel two thousand years ago: "If I am not for myself, who will be? If I am only for myself, what am I? If not now, when?"[21]

One can think of Martin Buber a few decades ago: "And in all seriousness of truth, listen: without It a human being cannot live. But whoever

---

[18] Ibid., 36.
[19] Ibid.
[20] Ibid., 39.
[21] Avot (Ethics of the Fathers) 1:14.

lives only with that is not human."[22] One can think of Donniel Hartman more recently, citing Deuteronomy 22:1–4: "You may not remain indifferent . . . [toward the needs of your fellow man]."

Shweder explains how different cultures try to promote human dignity by specializing in different ratios of moral goods. He elaborates on the three nexuses of values as follows.

> The first cluster (the ethics of autonomy) relies on regulative concepts such as harm, rights, and justice. The second cluster (the ethics of community) relies on regulative concepts (such as duty, hierarchy, interdependency and souls). The third cluster (the ethics of divinity) relies on regulative concepts such as sacred order, natural order, sanctity, and tradition.[23]

> The ethics of autonomy aims to protect the zone of discretionary choice of individuals and to promote the exercise of individual will in the pursuit of personal preferences. Autonomy is usually the official ethic of societies in which individualism is an ideal. The ethics of community, in contrast, aims to protect the moral integrity of the various stations or roles that constitute a society or a community, where a "society" or "community" is conceived of as a corporate entity with an identity, standing, history, and reputation of its own. Finally, the ethics of divinity aims to protect the soul, the spirit, the spiritual aspects of the human agent and nature from degradation.[24]

> Presupposed by the ethics of autonomy is a conceptualization of the self as an individual preference structure, where the point of moral regulation is to increase choice and personal liberty. Presupposed by the ethic of community is a conceptualization of the self as an office holder. The basic idea is that one's role or station in life is intrinsic to one's identity and is part of a larger interdependent collective enterprise with a history and standing of its own. Presupposed by the ethics of divinity is a conceptualization of the self as a spiritual entity connected to some sacred or natural order of things and as a responsible bearer of a legacy that is elevated and divine. Those who regulate their life within the terms

---

[22] Buber, *I and Thou* (trans. Gregor-Smith), 85. In *I and Thou*, "It" (capitalized in English translations) has a technical sense for Buber.
[23] Shweder, *Why Do Men Barbecue?*, 97.
[24] Ibid.

of an ethics of divinity do not want to do anything, such as eating the flesh of a slaughtered animal, that is incommensurate with the nature of the spirit that joins the self to the divine ground of all things.[25]

The three thematic clusters introduced in this chapter may be thought of as culturally co-existing discourses of morality. Experience is often so complex that its tactility is sometimes better described by one discourse and sometimes by another.[26]

For example, in the United States today we are experts on the topic of the ethics of autonomy. We have extended the idea of "rights" to different domains such as education and health care. We have extended the class of rights holders to include children and animals.... We have stretched the notions of rights, autonomy, and harm even as we wonder nostalgically how we lost our sense of community and divinity and struggle to find a way to recover them.[27]

Moral Absolutes: Self-Evident Intuitive Truths

Shweder expresses his view of moral absolutes and the corresponding intuitions in his article "Channeling the Super-natural Aspects of the Ethical Life."[28]

> Any natural or social history that is entitled to be called a history of the ethical life must be a history framed, traced, and ultimately justified by reference to moral absolutes.[29]

The idioms used for acknowledging moral absolutes may vary across history and cultures. Nevertheless an experiential core is recognizable: The feeling of being under the command of God or bound by some force greater than the self; the experience of guilt, dread, shame, or a loss of

---

[25] Ibid., 100.
[26] Ibid., 100.
[27] Ibid., 102.
[28] For other passages by Shweder on moral absolutes from "Channeling the Super-natural Aspects," see the quotations above to which notes NN and NN are attached.
[29] Shweder, "Channeling the Super-natural Aspects," 478.

sanctity; the experience of a compulsion or constraint superior to the ego; Freud's super-ego, Kant's categorical imperative.[30]

Ontologically speaking, moral absolutes of the sort just illustrated are widely experienced as meta-physical ahistorical norms. Like mathematical truths or the laws of logic they have a transcendental quality precisely because their status in reality is not biological, psychological, or social. The anthropologist Raymond Firth . . . nicely captures this in his summary of the ethical life of the Tikopia people, who express their (very human) metaphorical engagement with a reality populated with ultimate values this way. "The spirits, just as men, respond to a norm of conduct of an external character. The moral law exists in the absolute, independent of the Gods."[31]

Twenty-three years earlier, in 1993, Shweder and Haidt (a former student of Shweder's who was then a professor at the University of Virginia) wrote an article on the future of moral psychology in which they posited that the emotions are "the gatekeeper to the moral world." For emotional responses to given situations often involve instantaneous, unconscious cognitive judgements. Shweder and Haidt state that the fast and slow mental processes that Kahneman calls System 1 and System 2 are both emotional and cognitive and that these cognitive appraisals are similar to the self-evident truths of morality that are universal moral categories.[32]

Emotional responses, it is now generally thought, involve rapid automatic, and unconscious cognitive appraisals of the significance of events for personal well-being.[33]

A second attractive feature of cognitive intuitions is that they make it possible to acknowledge the difference between fast and slow cognitive processes, without assimilating this difference to the distinction between "affect" and "cognition." Moral reasoning, like any other kind of explicit and conscious problem solving, is slow. Yet moral intuition, like all

---

[30] Ibid., 479.
[31] Ibid.
[32] Shweder and Haidt, "Future of Moral Psychology," 364.
[33] Ibid.

intuitive knowledge, is rapid and introspectively opaque.[34]

Crucially, many of the cognitive appraisals that have been postulated as casual conditions for an emotional experience are quite similar to the self-evident truths of morality. Anger is about injustice and the perception of a demeaning personal insult. Sympathy is about harm and suffering. Shame and guilt are about the right and the good. Disgust is about degradation and human dignity.[35]

Shweder relates these thoughts to the human processes that create moral judgments. He finds that moral judgments include elements that are both affective and cognitive. They quickly produce powerful feelings that motivate action. This notion is congruent with Kahneman's view that much human action is caused by our unconscious. It is also congruent with the view that our emotions are a window into our unconscious even if they create actions that we do not intend consciously nor whose genesis we cannot express accurately. Shweder writes, "Moral judgments are experienced as aesthetic and emotive judgments and not solely as cognitive judgments. Despite the fact that moral judgments ('that's good,' 'that's wrong') are experienced as judgments about some domain of moral truth, such judgments resemble aesthetic and emotive judgments ('that's ugly,' 'that's disgusting'). They occur rapidly and without the assistance of deliberative reason, indeed without much need for conscious reflection at all. Moreover, moral judgments motivate action largely because they produce powerful feelings of ugliness, repugnance, guilt, indignation, or shame."[36] This is a succinct statement of a current prominent psychological theory of the genesis of moral thought and action.

HUMAN RIGHTS ARE OBJECTIVE AND INALIENABLE

Shweder discusses human rights in a later article.

Ontologically speaking, what is a human right? Presumably it is something which everyone is entitled to simply by virtue of being a human

---

[34] Ibid.
[35] Ibid.
[36] Shweder, *Why Do Men Barbecue?*, 37.

being. Whatever it is, it is objective and inalienable and associated with a third-person point of view. If that is the case then it is an entitlement that derives not from who you are in particular or from what you have accomplished in life. And it is not an entitlement whose authority derives from the will of some person or group who decides or elects to honor the things called rights. A natural or inalienable right, in the strong sense, must be something transcendental or overarching, something that we may discover but not something we simply make up or invent, either individually or collectively; for then the right would be subjective (expressive of some person's or group's first- or second-person point of view), not objective, and it would not be universally binding.[37]

Jonathan Haidt: The Moral Mind

In the above-mentioned article on the future of moral psychology, Haidt and Shweder posited that emotion, one's immediate moral judgment, would come to be seen as the expression of the heart, which in their view is a cognitive organ. They believed that this view "makes it possible to acknowledge the difference between fast and slow cognitive processes, without assimilating this difference to the distinction between 'affect' and 'cognition.' Moral reasoning, like any other kind of explicit and conscious problem solving, is slow. Yet moral intuition, like all intuitive knowledge, is rapid and introspectively opaque."[38]

Haidt and Craig Joseph later redefine Shweder's three nexuses of values — autonomy, community, and divinity — into five sets of intuitions or innate characteristics of human beings: harm/care, fairness/reciprocity, ingroup/loyalty, authority/respect, and purity/sanctity. They find that their "five foundations fit perfectly with Shweder's three ethics: the Harm and Fairness foundations give rise to the discourse of the ethic of autonomy; the Ingroup and Authority foundations support the ethic of community; and the Purity foundation supports the ethic of divinity."[39] Haidt and Joseph link their five foundations to the need for human beings historically to adapt to challenges for which they engage one or more moral emotions.

---

[37] Shweder, *"Channeling the Super-natural Aspects,"* 481.
[38] Shweder and Haidt, "Future of Moral Psychology," 363.
[39] Haidt and Joseph, "Moral Mind," 387.

These are the "foundations of intuitive ethics—the psychological primitives that are the building blocks from which cultures create moralities that are unique yet constrained in their variations." The authors adopt the view that the moral mind is partially structured in advance of experience . . . and that their five foundations are likely to become moralized during the development of the child.[40]

Haidt and Joseph point out that when the moral domain is defined as "justice, rights, and welfare," as it is in most Western cultures,

> then the psychology that emerges cannot be a true psychology of morality; it can only be a psychology of judgments about justice, rights, and welfare. And when the domain of morality is narrowed in this way, then overly parsimonious theories of moral psychology flourish.[41]

> But in most cultures the social order is a moral order, and rules about clothing, gender roles, food, and forms of address are profoundly moral issues. . . . In many cultures the social order is a sacred order as well. Even a cursory look at foundational religious texts reveals that, while the gods do seem to care about whether we help or hurt each other, they care about many other things besides.[42]

As an example, Haidt refers to Shweder's early study of the responses by Indians and by Americans to scenarios that had an important moral consideration.

> Shweder's Oriya [Indian] subjects—adults and children—gave responses that revealed a very different moral domain from his comparison sample of adults and children in Chicago. The American respondents saw harm and rights violations in many of the actions (e.g., a husband beats his wife for disobedience), and moralized them accordingly. The Oriya respondents, in contrast, revealed a broader moral world in which issues of respect and hierarchy (e.g., a wife's obedience to her husband) and spiritual purity/sanctity (e.g., not eating spiritually polluting foods at proscribed times) seemed to be at least as important as issues of harm,

---

[40] Ibid., 384.
[41] Ibid., 372.
[42] Ibid., 373.

rights, and justice.[43]

This observation is important to keep in mind when we're thinking about the moral values embedded in a specific community or society.

Individualism and Autonomy: Robert N. Bellah

In order to understand the place of moral universalism in a discussion of conversion and dignity in the Jewish tradition, we should consider the viability of individualism in the United States, because our culture strongly associates respect for human dignity with respect for human individuality. Robert N. Bellah and his coauthors considered the role of individualism in U.S. culture in *Habits of the Heart: Individualism and Commitment in American Life.* Addressing the same concerns about democracy and community that preoccupied Alexis de Tocqueville in 1835 in his *Democracy in America*, the authors recognized that the integration of autonomy and community is an abiding American issue. On the one hand, Americans prize autonomy, as does the liberal Jewish community in America, seeing a high valuation of autonomy as consistent with their tradition's affirmation of human dignity.[44] Yet on the other hand, Americans also value community, and the issue of the relationship between autonomy and community continues to be a divisive one in American culture. It may be more divisive currently than it was during de Tocqueville's time and in prior Jewish history. How to maintain a balance between individual dignity and the spiritual pull of community thus poses a critical challenge to American Jewry. Historically, it is a challenge that gave birth to Reform Judaism and one that gains a particular poignancy when Jews are called upon to welcome converts into the House of Israel.

---

[43] Ibid., 377.
[44] It's clear that Shweder, too, sees autonomy and human dignity as related, for the nexus of values that he labels autonomy presumes that human dignity is a metavalue.

Epilogue: Reflections

"You Jews don't know what a treasure you have."

Thus a recent convert to Judaism opened our conversation — one of a hundred dialogues with rabbis, rabbinical students, and converts to Judaism that motivated this book. The book is addressed to all Jews in the hope that it will help them welcome converts to the journey of Jewish learning, so that converts, thus embraced, can better negotiate with their family, friends, and community the implications of their new identities.

The book defends the view that American Reform Judaism is a legitimate practice of Judaism and an authentic interpretation of the Jewish tradition. Reform is a continuation of the thought and values that are expressed in the Bible — including the Prophets — thoughts and values that have been adapted to the existential needs of Jews in each generation. I have posited that human dignity, as the metavalue in Reform Judaism, is the preeminent value concerning conversion and converts and, as such, should instruct our dialogue among ourselves and with others. I have also critically analyzed the "treasures" of Judaism and Jewish thought while acknowledging that "these and these" are the words of the living God. There is no single text or interpretation of a text that constitutes the essence of Judaism. The texts and interpretations of texts examined in the book have been selected and interpreted through a liberal Jewish lens, the lens of American Reform Judaism.

In the writing of this book, I have reflected on lessons I've learned from friends, family, teachers, and mentors. I hope that these lessons will be helpful to converts, too.

My parents, Jacob and Lillian Kaufman, taught me to practice and to honor Judaism and its history and traditions. They also taught me to be dignified and compassionate in my relationships with others.

R. David Hartman taught me that the Jewish tradition — including the Talmud and interpretation of texts — belongs to all Jews. He taught me that a Jew must act with dignity toward himself and herself and toward others. He helped me understand an Orthodox Jew's love of God and of halakhah.

Donniel Hartman taught me that I should not remain indifferent to fellow Jews or to any fellow man or woman. He taught me that I should define Jewish identity as broadly as I can and that I should accept with few exceptions those who wish to be Jewish. He taught me to think carefully about the demands of the God I worship.

Paul Mendes-Flohr taught me by example and by word that human dignity is essential to Judaism and to life. He taught me to emulate God's loving-kindness through supererogatory acts of loving-kindness in my actions toward others. He helped me understand that the conditions that Martin Buber postulated are necessary to achieve an authentic relationship with another. He explained how God is present in an authentic dialogue. He made me aware that Buber believed we cannot know God, but we can speak with him.

Richard Shweder taught me the value of using multiple lenses to view converts, conversion, and the Jewish tradition. He taught me that each community has a nexus of metaethical values that may be different from those of another community. Some of these values, such as the value of life and protecting the weak, are universal and are shared by most communities. Some, such as circumcision, are particular and are shared by few other communities. He taught me that there are many values that are praiseworthy and that the number of praiseworthy values is too abundant for any one community to embrace them all.

Avi Sagi and Zvi Zohar taught me that the predominant rabbinic paradigm for conversion to Judaism welcomes the convert, minimizes questioning the convert's motivation, and ignores the possible future lifestyle of the convert. Conversion is deemed a rebirth, and as such it is irreversible.

David Nussbaum helped me learn from reading Daniel Kahneman and other psychologists that our unconscious feelings and attitudes instruct our conscious thoughts and actions. The reasons we give for our thoughts and actions are often confabulations that do not express the unconscious feelings and attitudes that actually inform them. Our thought and feelings about conversion and converts are generated in a similar manner.

Chris Argyris taught me that there is a gap between our espoused values — the values that we say instruct our thoughts and actions — and the values that actually direct our thoughts and actions. Because of this gap, it is important for us to recognize biases in our selection and reading of Jewish religious texts. An appreciation of this gap is essential as we develop our thoughts about conversion and interact with converts. The gap can be reduced, if we wish.

The propositions that this book explores are found to be salient in the Jewish tradition. Human dignity is the foundational consequence of being created in the image of God; creation in God's image grants us agency and responsibility that we are expected to exercise in a caring manner in our relations with converts.

Human dignity, again, is the overarching metavalue of Reform Judaism. Although it is a metavalue of traditional Judaism, Reform Judaism places it at the center of its spiritual life and its conception of service to God.

It is not unreasonable to think that American Reform Judaism will create a new interpretation of the Talmud that incorporates both tradition and modernity, one that is more relevant to the existential and axiological reality of American Jews. The Babylonian Talmud, which was composed in the diaspora, outside the land of Israel, is more comprehensive and more authoritative than the Jerusalem Talmud, which was redacted several centuries earlier. It is not unthinkable that the diaspora, and America in particular, will become a successor to Babylon from which will come a new Talmud that addresses the current existential concerns of American Jews and perhaps of all Jews.

Women will play a significant role in creating this Torah. The first woman rabbi was ordained in 1972 within Reform Judaism. Now one-half of the rabbinical students at Hebrew Union College–Jewish Institute of Religion are women. And women now hold major pulpits throughout the country. Students at HUC-JIR have different beliefs and different practices that range from modern Orthodox to liberal Reform. Their views on conversion range from strict to lenient interpretations of the tradition, leading some to accept and some to reject those who wish to become Jewish and leading many to reconsider the process of conversion to Judaism. Their wide range of thought and observance is an important ingredient in the development of a Judaism that meets the existential needs of contemporary Jews.

The future of Judaism in the United States and the future relationship between American and Israeli Jews and between Orthodox and Reform Judaism is unpredictable. The United States offers an example. In the middle of the twentieth century, Orthodox Jews were few and were expected to decline even more. The Conservative was the largest denomination and was expected to remain dominant. There were few Jews without a religious affiliation. Currently, Reform is the largest denomination, with slightly over a third of the Jews who affiliate with a congregation. Conservative has half as many members. Orthodox remains demographically constant, constituting one-tenth of the Jews who affiliate. Jews without a religious affiliation represent a quarter of the American Jewish population and are growing in number.

We do not know what the future will bring. We do know some of the ingredients that seem likely to enable the Jewish people to remain fruitful and multiply in future generations. I will conclude the book with two of them: American Jews should recognize the unconscious gap between their theories and their behavior toward conversion and converts. And American Jews should accept converts as fully Jewish, encourage conversion, welcome converts and their families, and treat them with the dignity that befits them as being created in the image of God.

APPENDIX I

Memories and Metavalues

Dr. Paul Mendes-Flohr

Professor Emeritus of Modern Jewish History and Thought at the University of Chicago Divinity School

Having worked closely with Dick for the past five years on his various academic projects, I should like to suggest that we honor his memory by reflecting on the issues that most engaged his ever-lively intellect and unyielding ethical concerns: To explore what constitutes human dignity from the perspective of Jewish tradition. He was alert to features of the tradition that did not enhance the dignity of certain members of the community (e.g., women and the physically and mentally infirm). By focusing on the biblical and rabbinic approach to conversion and converts, Dick sought to identify what he called "meta-values" of Judaism that provide a theological and ethical axis to allow the tradition to evolve in accord with contemporary sensibilities. And thus Dick sought to foster Judaism to realize more fully its divinely appointed responsibility to further our inter-personal and inter-communal life as reflecting that we are created in the "image of God."

Both in his M.A. and doctoral studies, Dick's overarching questions concerned Reform Judaism -- its legitimacy as an expression of traditional Jewish values. In his doctoral dissertation, which was devoted to conversion to Judaism, he sought to identify "meta-values" which determined and authenticated more specific values. The latter are often local and historically and socially contextual, whereas meta-values constitute the core sensibilities and attitudes of the ethical and spiritual universe of Judaism throughout the ages. The meta-value that exercised Dick most in his dissertation research was what he called "human dignity," a fundamental, uncompromising respect for the individual as a fellow human being created in the "image of God." In explicating what this attitude entailed, Dick drew upon Martin Buber's distinction between I-Thou and I-It relations. The latter attitude treats the Other person as an object -- of one's instrumental goals, of an example of some culturally, economically, politically construed category (a Christian, a woman, young person, a prospective costumer, political ally, a Jew, a convert, an African-American, a Muslim...). The I-Thou attitude does not reduce others to these categories, but rather acknowledges each individual independent of such categories, thus affirming him or her as a unique human being, such as we each, indeed, are.

From this perspective, Dick understood the meta-value of Judaism as inscribed in the commandment to love one's neighbor and stranger, as one would wish others to love oneself. When commemorating and honoring Dick's memory we affirm him as a Thou and a fellow human being whom we loved, and, indeed, continue to love!

Dick had the soul and passion of a seasoned scholar. He would continuously revisit and revise the premises and guiding questions of his dissertation. He was, indeed, his most severe critic. His resolute adherence to the exacting standards of scholarly integrity did not diminish his ultimate concern to enhance the experience of converts to Reform Judaism as an elevated spiritual process and a dignified rite de passage to the family of Israel. Dick was unfailingly attentive to the unimpeachable dignity of others, whomever they may be -- Jew and non-Jew, poor or privileged, or whatever distinguishing characteristic with which we often callously label one another. It was this quality of his nishomah - his spiritual and ethical soul -- that not only informed his dissertation but his very being. May his memory be an everlasting blessing to all whom he loved and to many who admired and loved him, as I did.

APPENDIX 2

Should Conversion be Promoted in Judaism?

Donniel Hartman

President of the Shalom Hartman Institute and holder of the Richard and Sylvia Kaufman Family Chair

In the twenty-first century the Jewish people are experiencing an unprecedented influx of non-Jews living as *de facto* members of the Jewish community either through marriage or immigration to Israel. Presently, most do not undergo formal conversion, either because of the monopoly of Orthodoxy over the process in Israel, or in North America because of an increased sense that religious affiliation and identity are individual choices, which do not require formal conversion. Nevertheless, there is a significant population of potential converts to Judaism, which raises serious theological, ideological and policy questions regarding Judaism's attitude toward conversion in general.

For much of Jewish history, conversion was at best a theoretical issue with marginal practical implications. As a minority under Christianity and Islam, Jews were principally concerned with their survival, and attempts to convert a Christian or Muslim were deemed a capital offense. We were content when we were not being persecuted. The idea that we could actually convert others was beyond imagination. In addition, given our low political status, almost no sane individual would even consider converting to Judaism. As a result, reticence toward conversion and converts was a logical approach.

As stated, this reality has changed. Whether as a sovereign majority in the land of Israel or as a powerful, beloved, and respected minority in North America, becoming Jewish is no longer a bizarre, almost insane act of masochism, but a reasonable decision. Given this new reality, should we pursue and encourage conversion or is such "outreach" alien to Judaism?

As is the case with most serious dilemmas, when we are asked to choose between either *a* or *b*, Judaism responds, "Yes." Both an approach of discomfort with conversion and one which embraces it have deep theological roots within the Jewish tradition. In fact, both attitudes can be traced back to the moment of Abraham's election in Genesis 12, where Jewishness and Jewish peoplehood were conceptually outlined and formed.

> And the Lord said to Abram go forth from your land, from your birthplace, and from your father's house, to the land that I will show you, and I will make of you a great nation and I will bless you, and I will aggrandize your name and you shall be a blessing; and I will bless those who bless you, and the ones who curse you I will curse, and all the families of the earth shall be blessed in you. (Gen. 12:1–3)

One reading of these verses sees the process of election as demanding a deep and profound separation from the world. As depicted at the end of Genesis 11, Abraham and his father Terah were already going to the land of Canaan, which served as the crossroads between Egypt and Syria. On the way, Terah dies and Abraham continues on the journey. With the divine commandment of "Go forth," God is in essence telling Abraham, "Stop." "Do not continue on your journey to the land of *your* choosing; but instead, go to the land that I, God, designate for you."

This journey is depicted as one of profound separation: separation from one's past, homeland, and family roots, all of which are to be replaced by a new relationship with God in the land that God will choose. In return for this commitment, God will bestow abundant blessings upon Abraham and his descendants: "I will make of you a great nation and I will bless you and will aggrandize your name. [...] I will bless those who bless you, and the ones who curse you I will curse, and all the families of the earth shall be blessed in you."

From this moment on, the Jewish Bible deals almost exclusively with God's relationship with the Jewish people, with God challenging them over and again to walk in God's ways, either rewarding or punishing them in accordance with their compliance with God's will. The Bible is almost solely the story of the relationship between God and the Jewish people; with others entering into the story only through their interaction and intersection with the Jewish people. While God is the God of creation, sovereign of the universe, the Jewish Bible is principally an account of God's particular story with a specific people.

There are some within the Jewish tradition who interpreted chosenness and the exclusiveness of the covenant as a sign and symptom of Jewish superiority. The Bible, however, explicitly rejects this notion. Over and again, the Bible refers to the children of Israel as a "stiff-necked people" (Cf. Ex. 32:9; Deut. 9:6) and explicitly states that the covenant is not based on any inherent Israelite qualities: "It is not because of your virtues and your rectitude that you will be able to possess their country" (Deut. 9:5).

The Bible does not begin with Genesis 12 and the covenant between God and the Jewish people, but rather with the story of creation, which establishes God's relationship with and investment in the whole universe and all humankind. In doing so the Bible defines all of humanity *qua* humanity as being equally created in the image of God, thus precluding any notion of a superiority of one group over another.

The election of Genesis 12 is a tale of separation, but not superiority. In Genesis 12, Jews begin to tell their own particular story of their relationship with God and, in so doing, elevate and legitimize the place of the particular in the formation of identity. While God may be the God of all, God's ultimate relationships with human beings are not through their general, universal identities, but with particular individuals within a context of their distinct collective identities.

Within this reading of the covenant — as the story of God's relationship with a particular people — there is no room or place for conversion, for others to join our story, unless through marriage, for Jewishness is simply "our family's" story. It makes no claim to preclude other possible covenantal relationships between God and others, as the prophet Amos famously declared: "To Me, O Israelites, you are just like the Ethiopians declares the Lord. True, I brought Israel up from the land of Egypt, but also the Philistines from Caphtor and the Arameans from Kir" (Amos 9:7).

Conversion is not an option, for it is unnecessary. Jews do not engage in missionary activity, not out of superiority or political fear, but rather, because Judaism sees itself as essentially one particular way to live with God and has no aspiration for an end of days when all will become Jewish. Judaism does yearn for a messianic era in which all of humanity will abandon idolatry and where the land will be filled "with devotion to the Lord as waters cover the sea" (Isaiah 11:9). However, their covenantal relationship will remain within the context of their particular collective identity and story.

Returning to the overall question of this essay, the fact that Judaism is now beloved and a potential object of adoration, does not change this essential perspective toward conversion. Jews do not aspire to "save others," by spreading our version of the "good word," for our belief is that others don't need Judaism for salvation, nor do they need Judaism in order to have a covenantal relationship with God.

An interesting question is whether this approach to conversion should also apply to those who have already become members of the Jewish people through marriage or immigrating to Israel. In these cases, conversion is not about outreach toward others or a transformation of identity, but rather a formal process, which religious law affirms an identity transformation that has already occurred. I will return to this point at the end of this essay.

***

A second reading of Genesis 12 focuses not on Abraham's journey of separation, but rather on his becoming a blessing to the world: "And you shall be a blessing [...] and all the families of the earth shall bless themselves by you." The covenant does not envision Abraham as a lonely man of faith; engaged exclusively with his own tribe, but rather as an individual who is chosen so that he can become a blessing to the world. Moses Maimonides, in the thirteenth century, rereads Genesis 12 through this lens. According to Maimonides, Abraham was not chosen by God. Abraham is the first enlightened monotheist who chooses God, and only because he does so, God enters into a relationship with him. Abraham was forty years old, Maimonides says, when he became aware of God's existence—when he "saw the light." This experience, while profoundly alienating Abraham from his surroundings, inspired Abraham to begin to share his truth with all those who surrounded him:

> He then began to proclaim to the whole world with great power and to instruct the people that the entire universe had but one Creator and that Him it was right to worship. He went from city to city and from kingdom to kingdom, calling and gathering together the inhabitants till he

arrived in the land of Canaan. There, too, he proclaimed his message, as it is said, "and he called there on the name of the Lord, God of the universe" (Gen. 21:33). When the people flocked to him and questioned him regarding his assertions, he would instruct each one according to his capacity till he had brought them to the way of truth, and thus thousands and tens of thousands joined him. These were the persons referred to the in the phrase, "Men of the house of Abraham." (Maimonides, Mishneh Torah, "Laws Pertaining to Idolatry," 1:3)

According to this reading of Genesis 12, there is no covenant, which is exclusive to the descendants of Abraham. The covenant is not founded on a particular family, but on a universal truth, which can and must be shared equally by the descendants of Abraham and those who choose to affiliate, not with them, but with the idea. For Maimonides, Jews are not the descendants of Abraham, but rather "a people who know God" (ibid.), and this people are constituted by Abrahamic descendants and converts alike.

This reading of the initial covenantal moment shapes a radically different approach to conversion. Conversion is an integral dimension of this covenant, for the "house of Abraham," the Jewish people, from their inception are a people of converts—a people committed to embodying an idea.

This idea knows no ethnic, territorial, or racial boundaries, but is rather open to all of humanity who are equally created in the image of God and equally called upon to embrace it. As a result, similar to Abraham, we too are commanded to share what we have come to know with all others. While forced to curtail these efforts when we were a persecuted minority, in the new reality of contemporary Jewish life we can free ourselves from these inhibitions. Conversion is not only something that should not be looked down upon, or even something that fosters an ambivalence, but rather an essential aspect of the covenant between God and the Jewish people.

One of the primary sources for contemporary Jewish ambivalence toward an activist approach concerning conversion is the fact that, as a minority, we Jews were often the objects/victims of such efforts. Enlightened Christians and Muslims, throughout our history, expended significant efforts to "save us." It has made us deeply suspicious of those who possess *the* truth for all of humankind. We often interpret missionary work as overt and subtle coercion. This has led to a greater affinity with the theological humility of the first reading of Genesis 12.

There is, however, a difference between sharing the truth and forcing others to embrace it, between teaching one's truth and indoctrination. Abraham did not embark on a holy war to bring "the truth" of monotheism to the world. In fact, nowhere in the Jewish tradition did the Jewish people ever embark on such a war. We fought to preserve our identity and left it to God and the end of days to take responsibility for the conversion of the whole world to faith in God. Abraham was simply a teacher, who taught those who of their own volition chose to engage with him and his teaching.

***

Regardless of whether we pick the first or second reading of Genesis 12, the current reality in Israel and North America has created a new opportunity and responsibility. Whether or not we believe that we ought to share Judaism with humanity at large, there are today millions of individuals who, either through immigration to Israel or marriage with Jews, have embraced either a partial or full Jewish identity. For these millions of individuals, I believe the Jewish community must shed its ambivalence and actively engage with them in a discussion regarding their potential conversion.

Whether a particular covenant for a distinct people or a universal idea given to a particular people with a responsibility to share it with humanity, we have today a new and unique responsibility toward individuals, who on their own have chosen to join us, some fully and some partially. We have a responsibility to ensure that a path is paved, and a door is opened toward their full integration within our people and tradition, as full-fledged and equal members.

APPENDIX 3

Does Love Require Christians To Convert their Neighbor?

Richard Mouw

President Emeritus, Fuller Theological Seminary

I have a little spiritual discipline that I engage in on early morning flights: I reflect on my favorite Psalm, number 139, where the psalmist begins by saying "O Lord, you have searched me and known me. You know when I sit down and when I rise up; you discern my thoughts from far away." And then, the reason why I think of it on an airplane: "If I take the wings of the morning and settle at the farthest limits of the sea, even there your hand shall lead me, and your right hand shall hold me fast" (vv. 9–10). The Psalmist is talking about the omnipresent God — that there's no place where we can go in the world and escape the presence of God. Later in the Psalm there comes a point when the psalmist gets somewhat arrogant, saying, "Do I not hate those who hate you, O Lord? And do I not loathe those who rise up against you? I hate them with perfect hatred; I count them my enemies" (v. 21–22). And then it is as if he stops and says, "uh oh, just a minute," and the very next line is, "Search me, O God, and know my heart; test me and know my thoughts. See if there is any wicked way in me, and lead me in the way everlasting" (v. 23–24).

There is a great Latin phrase that we live *Coram Deo* — before the face of God; we live our lives in the presence of God, and in no way can we escape that divine presence. The Psalmist gives us some of the most important words we can say when we are acutely aware of being in the presence of God: "Search me, O God, and know my heart; test me and know my thoughts. See if there is any wicked way in me, and lead me in the way everlasting." The meaning of the Psalmist's words — that sense of being in the presence of God, of humility, a radical self-critique under the gaze of God — really has to be at the heart of Christian-Jewish relations. Our starting point must be from under the gaze of the God of Abraham and Sarah. From there we ask God to search us together and to know us, and see if there are any wicked ways in us, and to find ways in which together we can be God's people in the world. Furthermore, only as we live *Coram Deo* can we Christians and Jews begin to see in one another those things that inspire us in the other to be led in the way everlasting.

Over a decade ago I was invited to speak about the 10 Commandments with my dear friend Rabbi Elliot Dorff at the UCLA Center for Jewish Studies. Although Rabbi Dorff has 613 commandments and I only have 10, we still agreed on the same basic idea: the good life has its departure in living under the gaze of God and hearing God's words of guidance for our lives. When Dorff introduced me to the predominantly Jewish audience, he said, "You know, we're friends and I really like Rich Mouw, and Rich Mouw is a Calvinist, but he's a good guy anyway." After my lecture (on the commandment of coveting), a middle-aged Jewish couple came up to me as I was getting ready to leave to thank me for what I had said. Then they asked, "But did the rabbi say you're a Calvinist?" "Yes," I said. "You really are?" they asked. "That kind of surprises us, because you seem like a nice guy." I was confused. "Why wouldn't I be a nice guy if I was a Calvinist?" And they said, "Well, don't you believe that God chooses some and not others?" And I said, "Yeah, God chose the people of Israel and not the Philistines or the Amelekites, or the Midianites." And they looked at me kind of strange and said, "Well, that gives us something to think about, doesn't it?"

I sense that those of us in the Christian world and the Jewish world have been in some sense chosen by God, chosen to learn from God how to act in the world — both within our own communities and together as Jews and Christians. In a book I wrote fifteen years ago I came up with an example to illustrate a point — an example that I have recently received responses from people saying, "You know, I read that book and wow, that seemed like a strange thing to write at the time." Suppose, I said, that somebody became President of the United States. All he (the "he" is apt in this case) ever talked about was how he had been chosen; how he had been elected. Every time this president gave an address to the nation, the only thing he wanted to talk about was the fact that of all the other people who ran for office, indeed of all the other people in the United States, he was the one who got chosen! He even commissioned people to study how he got elected; how he got chosen. And, as I said fifteen years ago, there would come a point when we would say to that person, "What did we choose you to do?" "What did we elect you to do?"

That sense of being the chosen people singled out by God entails complexities that I will not go into other than to simply state that this chosen-ness can never be separated from the fact that God wants to lead us in the way everlasting. God wants us as Jews and Christians — communities each identifying with that sense of chosen-ness in our own ways — to be a model to the larger human community. In these days of Christian-Jewish relations, we desperately need to be talking to each other about the ways in which we can walk in ways of justice and righteousness *together*.

One of the disturbing things in recent years is that Christian-Jewish relations have gotten very politicized and polarized in ways that are similar to what we are experiencing in the larger society. For many of my fellow evangelical Christians, it is all about supporting the political policies of the State of Israel while for more progressive Christians it is all about criticizing the political policies of the State of Israel. It is easy to see contemporary Jewish-Christian relations primarily if not exclusively through the filter of political categories — and only with that filter in place might some Christians and Jews begin to talk to each other about what we all might have in common. I want to challenge this primary political filter and suggest that there is a much deeper way that Christians and Jews should see one another. Where we should begin is with that sense of being under the gaze of God, and seeing things in the ways that God wants us to see things. From that starting point we have quite a lot to talk about including how we find the way, whom we trust along the way, and what our lives should look like as a result of God choosing us to be God's people.

One of the great declarations of John Wesley was "the world is my parish." Wesley wasn't saying his parish was his whole world nor was he talking about the ways in which many of us want to stay within a kind of ghettoized spiritual community removed from the world; rather, he was saying the world is like a parish. At the heart of that is the profound declaration that wherever we are, we're on sacred ground, and that whomever we meet are human beings who are created in the very image of the God of the Bible, the God of Torah. Encountering people on the sacred ground of God's creation is to encounter people who are created in the very image of the divine. This reality requires that as we walk the paths of righteousness, do the works of justice, and cultivate a spirit of humility before God, we see other people with a dignity endowed upon them by their Creator—an identity that is essential to who they are.

As the president of Grand Valley State University said, it's not altogether inappropriate for there to be a center for interfaith understanding at a secular university (referring to the Kaufman Interfaith Institute). In fact, it might be the case that the ability of people of faith to learn from one another and seek to walk in the ways of justice, righteousness, honesty, and humility together—even in spite of our differences—might serve as an example and lesson to the larger academic community and even to the larger human community.

Learning in the Midst of Theological Messiness

One of the necessary components of Christian-Jewish dialogue is the commitment to learning from one another. Although I have not mastered this in my own experiences with Christian-Jewish dialogue, I am very much committed to it and am willing to live with a little bit of messiness in my own theology in the midst of it. My acceptance of messiness goes hand-in-hand with the fact that I do not have all of this figured out. My own struggles with some of the theological messiness in Christian-Jewish relations is the same kind of messiness found in documents produced by the Catholic Church, especially *Nostra Aetate* from the Second Vatican Council in 1965 and recent documents reflecting on *Nostra Aetate*. One statement that goes back and forth in ways that I go back and forth was issued in 2015, 50 years after *Nostra Aetate,* by the Vatican's Commission for Religious Relations with the Jews: "The Gifts and Callings of God are Irrevocable" (quoting Romans 11:29). Theological messiness can be seen in the following excerpt from the statement: "From the Christian confession...there can only be one path to salvation, however, it does not in any way follow that the Jews are excluded from God's salvation because they do not believe in Jesus Christ as the Messiah of Israel and the Son of God." I want a little more clarification than that! Catholics must continue to focus on "the highly complex theological question of how Christian belief in the universal salvific significance of Jesus Christ can be combined in a coherent way with the equally clear statement of faith in the never-revoked covenant of God with Israel." And then it says, "It is the belief of the Church that Christ is the Saviour for all," closely followed by the claim that "there cannot be two ways of salvation." Despite all of the messiness that begs for clarification, this section of the statement ends with the result of these complex and seemingly contradictory claims: "Here we confront the mystery of God's work, which is not a matter of missionary efforts to convert Jews, but rather the expectation that the Lord will bring about the hour when we will all be united," and then, quoting *Nostra Aetate*, "when all peoples will call on God with one voice and 'serve him shoulder to shoulder.'"

Although I am not Catholic, I shy away from talk about converting the Jews to Christianity just as the writers of this statement have instructed the Catholic Church to do. The idea of attempting to convert Jews in this day has 2,000 years of largely violent history behind it. It is both disrespectful and immoral for any Christian to go from what they might believe they find in Scripture to the present day without realizing that there are 2,000 years between those. I want to say this very clearly: we Christians have been unspeakably cruel to Jews throughout those 2,000 years. We cannot deny that. This reality of Christian contempt for Jews and Judaism is critical for Christians to recognize. The way forward for Christians is for us to accept responsibility for the contempt within our tradition, maintain a commitment to repentance, and trust in the mercies of God—those same mercies that God also promised to the physical seed of Abraham. Horrible things have been done by Christians to Jews especially in the name of conversion, and in recent years some Christians—certainly in the evangelical community—have even used the language of "targeting Jews for evangelism." There is something so unspeakably insensitive about the use of the word "targeting" when we talk about evangelism towards Jews.

I have accepted the need to live with theological messiness—"mystery" as the Vatican Commission puts it. This mystery also seems to be what the Apostle Paul struggles with in Romans 11. During a recent trip to Western Theological Seminary I was reminded of my time there in graduate school. I received the only "F" in any course I have ever taken in a course on the Epistle to the Romans. The assignment responsible for that grade was to write an interpretative essay on Romans 11—the one where Paul struggles with the whole question of God's relationship to the Jewish people now that Jesus, who he believed to be the Messiah, had come. I simply could not write that paper because I could not figure out what in the world

Paul was trying to do. He goes back and forth: Yes, some Jews rejected Jesus and that is not a good thing, but has God given up on them? No, he hasn't; but on the other hand...and he keeps going back and forth. I could not bring myself to write a paper that waffled in the ways that I thought Paul was wobbling, and so I got an incomplete which turned into an "F." Much later I went back to that chapter and was struck by the beautiful way it ends. Having said, "Well, on the one hand and on the other hand," Paul concludes by singing a hymn: "For who has known the mind of the Lord? Or who has been his counselor?" (Rom 11:34). It is this wonderful hymn that professes the mysteries of a God who is far beyond our understanding — and it is this hymn which I believe instructs Christians to live with mystery regarding how they understand the theological relationship between Christians, Jews, and God in the present era.

What are the practical ramifications of this messiness? Is it a loving thing to try to convert my Jewish neighbor? I'm going to say, "No." Does that mean that as a Christian I recommend a posture of relativism and deny the importance of the theological issues between Christians and Jews? No, there's a lot for us all to talk about. But I think we're at a stage in Christian-Jewish relations, at least in my own North American context, where Christians have to do a lot of spiritual preparation — the kind of spiritual preparation I was just talking about: repentance, the sense of our own history, and the things that we want to say that are shaped by our historical experiences. I suggest two key ways (although much more could be added) that Christians can proceed in Christian-Jewish relations today:

1. Recognize the unique and frightening challenges presented by new manifestations of anti-Semitism. This specific form of hatred has been so horribly on display in the last couple of years, both here and across Europe, and has a history that we need to be very much aware of as we encourage our communities to find ways to resist it. The sin of anti-Semitism is a deeply spiritual sin that goes to the heart of who I am as a follower of Jesus Christ. Years ago, when I was president of Fuller Seminary, I decided to hold a seminar one evening on current manifestations of anti-Semitism. There had been some bombings of synagogues in France and other places, and my good friend Rabbi Dorff agreed to come speak to the Fuller community about those recent events. In preparation for our dialogue and his lecture, I decided to ask the student leader of the Peace and Justice committee at Fuller who was a Palestinian Christian to introduce the evening. In good spiritual fashion this student said, "I'll have to pray about this; I'm not sure." Although he

was a very strong pro-Palestinian in terms of Middle East policy, he came to me several days later and said, "It's not gonna be easy, but I'm going to do it." At the event, in front of a packed house of students and a significant number of people from local synagogues, he began by saying, "You know, this is a tough thing for me as a Palestinian Christian to talk about the dangers of anti-Semitism, but those dangers are very real." And he said, "As a follower of Jesus, I'm going to be very concerned about hatred forever up here, and as a human being I've got to be concerned about how human beings treat other human beings. I want to say this, as a follower of Jesus I have been compelled to read recently about the Holocaust, some of the horrible things that happened to the Jewish people," and he said, "I just want to say this very clearly, 'never again, never again, never again.'" At the end of the evening one of the local rabbis stood up and thanked me for arranging the evening with Rabbi Dorff. He said, "For me, the most powerful moment this evening was when the Palestinian said, "never again, never again, never again. And I hereby publicly invite him to speak at my synagogue next weekend" — an invitation the student accepted.

2. Jews should not be targeted for evangelism or conversion by Christians. Since the 1980's, I have worked very closely with the board of the American Jewish Committee (AJC) dealing with First Amendment issues. I was working on a paper on religious freedom for the AJC and they asked a younger rabbi to come to my office and he and I would work on drafting this statement together. I had never met him before. He showed up and we had a great time producing a draft. About a week later he wrote me a note and said, "I want to thank you for the fact that I felt safe in your office. I was raised in Minnesota in a rural village so there was no Jewish community except our families and we had to go to the next town over for our religious practices." And he said, "In those days, the teacher of the public school, and I'm talking about fifth grade, the teacher in the public school was always a Lutheran and she would always begin the day saying, 'Boys and girls, let's pray the prayer that our Lord Jesus taught us to pray.' And my rabbi...told me I wasn't to pray that prayer. So I just stood there silently while the other kids prayed it. I got bullied on the playground, acts of violence toward me on the way home from school, people yelling at me, 'You're a Christ killer!' It was a long time ago for me, but when I realized that I was going to meet the president of an evangelical Christian seminary, when I arrived on your campus I broke out in a cold sweat." And then he said, "I am so grateful that I spent that hour and a half with you."

And I felt the same.

We need to hear stories like these — stories which speak to the very real and deep wounds carried by Jews because of the words and actions of Christians. At the heart of listening to these stories is the need to form friendships built upon trust so that these stories have a context in which they can take place and bring about transformation. David Roush, an evangelical historian, makes a compelling plea: "I strongly recommend that dialogue be maintained and that evangelicals and Jews continue to get to know one another personally; this should occur not only at the leadership level, but also on the grassroots level." Interfaith engagement is for all people — not just those with theological degrees. And at the center of that engagement there will hopefully be significant friendships. "Friendship," as Roush says, "dispel[s] caricature, stereotype, and distorted views; such interaction should be nurtured, and misperceptions as to its efficacy should be laid to rest by a more knowledgeable evangelical leadership." A message that needs to be preached in both synagogues and churches is that we need to form more friendships between our communities — and not only friendships between leaders.

After I had been president for a couple years at Fuller Seminary, the head of the Southern California Council of Rabbis came to me and said, "Can we have an Evangelical-Jewish dialogue?" He said "We get mainline Protestants all the time, we get along fine and Catholics write all this good stuff; I need somebody we can argue with." So we set up a rabbi-pastor consultation that would meet four times per year, twice at Fuller Seminary and twice at local synagogues or the AJC headquarters in Los Angeles. We did not start off talking about Jesus. In one of the first sessions we simply talked about what's happening with the younger generations of our communities and explained our primary religious holidays to each other.

One of the most profound evenings that we had involved two Hollywood script writers. David McFadden, an evangelical Christian who was the producer and main script writer for Home Improvement, spoke that evening to rabbis and pastors saying, "You know, I'm gonna put this in theological terms although we would never have used this in the program. The consistent weekly theme of Home Improvement was covenantal fidelity: couples that love each other, and they could tease each other, they could make fun of each other, they could argue with each other, but they loved each other. They were faithful to each other, they loved their neighbors. That was the constant theme." The other speaker that evening was an

Orthodox Jew who was the main script writer for The New Adventures of Old Christine, another sitcom. It was fascinating to hear the dialogue between an Orthodox Jew writing humor and an evangelical Christian writing humor. The Orthodox Jew who could not watch his own program because it was on Friday evening talked about what it was like as an Orthodox Jew to use sexual humor in a sitcom. It was a profound discussion — the very kind of conversation that we all need to have.

Finally, after eight years of the Evangelical-Jewish dialogue, the co-organizer Rabbi Mark Diamond said, "You know, I think we're ready to talk about Israel." And we had a tough session on Israel. However, by the end of the night, the two antagonists — one a very strong Presbyterian and advocate for Palestinian rights and the other a very strong Jewish Zionist — hugged each other. Later, Rabbi Diamond said, "Almost nine years now, and we tackled Israel. I think we're ready to talk about Jesus." That was possible only because we had those years of preparation building trust, finding common interests, working on common projects, and sharing our stories.

My wife Phyllis and I went to the National Prayer Breakfast twenty-one years in a row (those who have gone know that there's not much prayer and there's not much breakfast!). Although the event is largely an evangelical Christian event in terms of its motivations, Protestants, Catholics, Jews, and Muslims attend. There are some seminars following the breakfast, and one of the last seminars I attended had to do with Muslims and Jesus. Two of the panelists were friends: one was an evangelical missionary to Lebanon trying to convert Muslims and the other a Muslim businessman from Lebanon. The Muslim businessman began by saying, "I want you to know that I'm a real Muslim; the Quran is my book. But I'm a Muslim lover of Jesus. Every week I try to spend at least a couple days a week reading the stories in the New Testament of Jesus because Jesus has helped me be a more loving and forgiving Muslim. Jesus has deepened my understanding of the way that I'm called to live by the Quran." The two panelists had a terrific dialogue but at the end, during the Q&A, an evangelical in the audience stood up and said, "I want to ask that guy who talked about loving Jesus: What about the cross? Do you believe in the cross? Because the Quran doesn't seem to think that Jesus really died on the cross." The Muslim businessman said, "Why do you folks always have to start there? I'm here to tell you that I love Jesus. I'm a Muslim, and I really learn a lot from Jesus about being a more loving and more forgiving person, and I tell you I'm reading the New Testament because I want to understand Jesus better in the way of Jesus, and you immediately come to me and say, 'either it's about the cross or it's not any good.' You know my friend here has been for ten years a missionary to Muslims in the Middle East and he's got 10 converts. If he had gone to the Middle East and said, 'You Muslims, you can learn a lot from Jesus about being a more loving and forgiving person,' he could have thousands of people reading the New Testament all the time; but immediately you have to jump in with 'what about the cross?'" These are big theological issues to talk about, but I found the question asked by the evangelical audience member to be very offensive. If I had engaged in conversation with that Muslim businessman I would have wanted to say, "Wow, isn't that neat that you're reading about Jesus and that you find that Jesus deepens your sense of being a more loving Muslim. I'd like to know more about that. What is it about that? How do you work all that out?" I would have wanted to talk about his journey and genuinely try to find out about what is going on with him, maybe to the point of sharing with him how I find myself challenged to be a more loving and forgiving person by the person of Jesus. We need these kinds of conversations — but they have to be conversations about our own journeys and our own stories rather than aggressively challenging each other which cuts the conversation off and makes communication and mutual understanding impossible.

The building of trust and the nurturing of friendships undergirded by an awareness of the mysterious ways in which God is at work among Christians and Jews is crucial for Christian-Jewish relations. Roughly fifteen years ago CNN did a one-hour special on what's happening in the (American) evangelical world. They flew me to Washington D.C. where I spent an hour and a half under hot lights answering questions — although the final hour-long production only included about four and a half minutes of me! CNN had also interviewed a young Southern Baptist girl around the age of twelve. They edited the segment in such a way that they would ask her a question and then they'd ask me a question. At a certain point they said, "Is Jesus the only way to Heaven?" and she said, "Yes!" And then they asked me and I said "That's what Jesus says — 'I am the way the truth and the life.'" And then they said to her, "Well what happens to people who don't believe in Jesus?" And with a smile on her face she said, "They go to hell." And then they asked me the question. I knew I was taking some risk as an evangelical for saying what I said: "I live with a lot of mystery about that. All I know is that the God who I consider to be the Father of Jesus Christ has a lot of mysterious ways about Him." I got some hate mail on that. However, when Billy Graham was interviewed in Newsweek magazine and asked a similar question about the eternal status of "good Jews, Muslims, Buddhists, Hindus or secular people," he had this to say: "Those are decisions only the Lord will make. It would be foolish for me to speculate on who will be there and who won't…I don't want to speculate about all that. I believe the love of God is absolute. He said he gave his son for the whole world, and I think he loves everybody regardless of what label they have."

We Christians and Jews are living in a new era of possibilities between our two communities and have a lot of new opportunities for working together for the sake of our own communities and the larger human community. I once heard a rabbi tell the story of a time in the nineteenth century in one of the Eastern European ghettos where the Council of Rabbis decided to appoint one young newly appointed rabbi to be the person whose sole job was to look for the Messiah. Every time there was a baby boy born in the Jewish community he would go check it out. Anything that was reported as unusual he was supposed to check out. After one year he came to the rabbi and said, "I want another job." The rabbi said, "Why?" He said, "Looking for the Messiah is boring; nothing much ever happens." And the rabbi said, "Look at it this way; at least you have steady work." We Christians do have steady work, and let's keep at it.

Bibliography

"American Jewry Today – Jewish Population Statistics – 2000 NJPS National Jewish Population Survey." June 11, 2009. Judaism.about.com.

anon. *The Scandal of the Forged Giyyurim*. The World Committee of Matters of Giyyur. Jerusalem. 1980.

Argyris, Chris. *Flawed Advice and the Management Trap: How Managers Can Know When They're Getting Good Advice and When They're Not*. Oxford: Oxford University Press, 2000.

———. *Increasing Leadership Effectiveness*. New York: Wiley, 1976.

———. *Knowledge for Action: A Guide to Overcoming Barriers to Organizational Change*. San Francisco: Jossey-Bass, 1993.

———. *Organizational Traps: Leadership, Culture, Organizational Design*. Oxford: Oxford University Press, 2012.

———. *Reasoning, Learning, and Action: Individual and Organizational*. San Francisco: Jossey-Bass, 1982.

———. *Strategy, Change, and Defensive Routines*. Boston: Pitman, 1985.

Argyris, Chris, and Donald A. Schön. *Theory in Practice: Increasing Professional Effectiveness*. San Francisco: Jossey-Bass, 1974.

Ariely, Dan. *The (Honest) Truth about Dishonesty: How We Lie to Everyone—Especially Ourselves*. New York: Harper Perennial, 2013.

Aristotle. *Poetics*. Translated, with introduction and notes, by Malcolm Heath. London: Penguin, 1996.

Augustine. *Confessions*. Translated by Henry Chadwick. New York: Oxford University Press 1991.

Axelrod, Gedalya. *The Halachic Value of a Certificate of Giyyur*.

———. *Observance of the Commandments as a Condition for [valid] Giyyur*.

Bacher, W. "Gamaliel II." In *The Jewish Encyclopedia*, edited by Isidore Singer and Cyrus Adler, 5:560–62. New York: Funk & Wagnalls, 1906.

Bazerman, M. H., and Tenbrunsel, A. E. *Blind Spots: Why We Fail to Do What's Right and What to Do about It*. Princeton: Princeton

University Press, 2011.
Bellah, Robert N., Richard Madsen, William M. Sullivan, Ann Swidler, and Steven M. Tipton. *Habits of the Heart: Individualism and Commitment in American Life*. Berkeley: University of California Press, 2007.
Bellows, M. N. "Yisrael by Choice: Contemporary Understandings of the Psychosocial Aspects of Adopting a Jewish Identity." Master's thesis, Hebrew Union College–Jewish Institute of Religion Graduate Rabbinic Program, 2004.
Belzer, Tobin. *Jewish Communal Transformation: A Look at What's Happening and Who's Making It Happen*. New York: National Jewish Center for Learning and Leadership, New Paradigm Spiritual Communities Initiative, 2016.
Berger, J. *Invisible Influence: The Hidden Forces That Shape Behavior*. New York: Simon & Schuster, 2016.
Berkowitz, Allan L., and Patti Moskovitz. *Embracing the Covenant: Converts to Judaism Talk about Why and How*. Woodstock, VT: Jewish Lights, 1996.
Berman, Howard A. Introduction to Plaut, *Growth of Reform Judaism*, 7–11.
Bernstein, Louis. *Challenge and Mission: The Emergence of the English Speaking Orthodox Rabbinate*. New York: Shengold, 1982.
Bleich, J. David. (1971). "The Conversion Crisis: A Halakhic Analysis." *Tradition: A Journal of Orthodox Jewish Thought* 11, no. 4 (2017): 16–42. http://www.jstor.org/stable/23256315.
Bloom, Paul. *Against Empathy: The Case for Rational Compassion*. New York: Ecco, 2016.
———. "The Empathy Trap." *Wall Street Journal*, December 3, 2016.
———. *Just Babies: The Origins of Good and Evil*. New York: Crown, 2013.
Borodowski, A. F. *Isaac Abravanel on Miracles, Creation, Prophecy, and Evil: The Tension between Medieval Jewish Philosophy and Biblical Commentary*. New York: P. Lang, 2003.
Borowitz, E. B. *Choices in Modern Jewish Thought: A Partisan Guide*. New York: Behrman House, 1983.
———. *Liberal Judaism*. New York: Union of American Hebrew Congregations, 1984.

Brand, Yitzchak b.Z. *Briti Yitzhak*. Bnei Brak, Israel: Institute for the Publication of the Writings and Lectures of Rabbi Y. Brand, 1982.

Breisch, M. Y. *Responsa Helkot Ya'akov*. Jerusalem: Machzikei Da'at, 1951.

Broyde, M. J. *A Concise Code of Jewish Law for Converts: Kitsur Shulhan Arukh Le-gerim*. Jerusalem: Urim, 2017.

Buber, Martin. *A Believing Humanism: My Testament*. Translated by Maurice Friedman. New York: Simon and Shuster, 1968.

———. *Between Man and Man*. Translated by Ronald Gregor-Smith. London: Routledge, 2002.

———. *Eclipse of God: Studies in the Relation between Religion and Philosophy*. Various translators. With an introduction by Leora Batnitzky. New York: Humanities Press, 1988.

———. *Hasidism*. Translated by Greta Hort. New York: Philosophical Library, 1948.

———. *Hasidism and Modern Man*. Translated by Maurice Friedman. New York: Horizon Press, 1958.

———. *I and Thou*. Translated by Ronald Gregor-Smith. New York: Scribner, 1958.

———. *I and Thou*. Translated by Ronald Gregor-Smith. With a postscript by the author. 2nd ed. Charles Scribner's Sons, 1967.

———. *I and Thou*. Translated by Ronald Gregor-Smith. New York: Scribner Classics, 2000.

———. *I and Thou*. Translated by Ronald Gregor-Smith. Mansfield Centre, CT: Martino Publishing, 2010.

———. *I and thou*. Translated by Walter Kaufman. New York: Simon & Schuster, 1996.

———. *Israel and the World: Essays in a Time of Crisis*. Translated by Olga Marx, Greta Hort, et al. Syracuse: Syracuse University Press, 1997.

———. *The Knowledge of Man: Selected Essays*. Translated by Ronald Gregor-Smith and Maurice Friedman. New York: Harper & Row, 1965.

———. *Martin Buber on Psychology and Psychotherapy: Essays, Letters, and Dialogue*. Edited by Judith Buber Agassi. With an introduction by Paul Roazen. New York: Syracuse University Press, 1999.

———. *On Judaism*. Edited by Nahum N. Glatzer. Translated by Eva

Jospe and others. New York: Schocken Books, 1996.
———. *On the Bible: Eighteen Studies*. Edited by Nahum N. Glatzer. New York: Syracuse University Press, 2000.
———. Oral greetings on the occasion of the dedication of the Liberal Synagogue in Jerusalem, April 11, 1962. First published by the World Union for Progressive Judaism. Reprinted in the *Central Conference of American Rabbis Journal* 9 (1961): 11–12.
———. *Tales of the Hasidim*. Translated by Olga Marx. New York: Schocken, 1991.
———. *Tales of the Hasidim: The Early Masters*. New York: Farrar, Straus and Young, 1947.
———. *Ten Rungs: Collected Hasidic Sayings* Translated by Olga Marx. London: Routledge, 2002.
———. *Two Types of Faith*. Translated by Norman P. Goldhawk. With an afterword by David Flusser. Syracuse: Syracuse University Press, 2003.
Buckser, Andrew, and Stephen D. Glazier, eds. *The Anthropology of Religious Conversion*. Lanham, MD: Rowman & Littlefield, 2003.
Central Conference of American Rabbis. *Guidelines for Rabbis Working with Prospective Gerim*. New York: Central Conference of American Rabbis, 2001.
Cohen, Arthur A., and Paul R. Mendes-Flohr, eds. *20th Century Jewish Religious Thought: Original Essays on Critical Concepts, Movements, and Beliefs*. Philadelphia: Jewish Publication Society, 2009.
Cohen, Arthur A., David Stern, and Paul R. Mendes-Flohr, eds. *An Arthur A. Cohen Reader: Selected Fiction and Writings on Judaism, Theology, Literature, and Culture*. Detroit: Wayne State University Press, 1998.
Cohen, Hermann. *Reason and Hope: Selections from the Jewish Writings of Hermann Cohen*. Translated by Eva Jospe. New York: Norton, 1971.
Cohen, Jack Simcha. "Conversion of Children Born to Gentile Mothers and Jewish Fathers." *Tradition: A Journal of Jewish Thought* 22, no. 4 (1987): 1–17.
Cohen, Steven M. "Engaging the Next Generation of American Jews: Distinguishing the In-Married, Inter-Married, and Non-Married." *Journal of Jewish Communal Service* 81, no. 1–2 (Fall/Winter

2005): 43–52. doi:10.1787/443173737885.
Cohen, Steven M., and Arnold M. Eisen. *The Jew Within: Self, Family, and Community in America*. Bloomington: Indiana University Press, 2000.
Cooperman, Alan, et al., eds. *A Portrait of Jewish Americans*. Washington, DC: Pew Research Center, 2013.
Cowan, Paul. *An Orphan in History: Retrieving a Jewish Legacy*. Garden City, NY: Doubleday, 1982.
Cowan, Paul, with Rachel Cowan. *Mixed Blessings: Overcoming the Stumbling Blocks in an Interfaith Marriage*. New York: Penguin, 1988.
Davidman, Lynn. *Tradition in a Rootless World: Women Turn to Orthodox Judaism*. Berkeley: University of California Press, 1991.
Davis, Moshe. "Mixed Marriage in Western Jewry." *Jewish Journal of Social Studies* 10 (December 1968).
Decety, Jean, and Thalia Wheatley, eds. *The Moral Brain: A Multidisciplinary Perspective*. Cambridge, MA: MIT Press, 2015.
de Lange, Nicholas, and Miri Freud-Kandel, eds. *Modern Judaism: An Oxford Guide*. Oxford: Oxford University Press, 2005.
DellaPergola, Sergio. "World Jewish Population, 2018." In *American Jewish Year Book 118*, edited by Arnold Dashefsky and Ira M. Sheskin, 361–449. Springer International, 2019.
Diamant, Anita, and Howard Cooper. *Living a Jewish Life: Jewish Traditions, Customs, and Values for Today's Families*. New York: HarperCollins, 2007.
Dorff, Elliot N., and Louis E. Newman, eds. *Contemporary Jewish Ethics and Morality: A Reader*. New York: Oxford University Press, 1995
Dorff, Elliot N., Daniel S. Nevins, and Avram I. Reisner. *Homosexuality, Human Dignity and Halakhah: A Combined Responsum for the Committee on Jewish Law and Standards*. New York: Committee on Jewish Law and Standards, 2006.
Dowling, William C. *Ricoeur on Time and Narrative: An Introduction to Temps et Récit*. Notre Dame, IN: University of Notre Dame Press, 2011.
Druckesz, Eduard. *Zur Biographie des Chacham Isaak Bernays*. Jahrbuch der jüdischen Literarischen Gesellscahft 5. Frankfurt a.M.: n.p., 1907.

Dweck, Carol S. *Mindset: The New Psychology of Success*. New York: Ballantine, 2007.
Edwards, Lisa A., Stephen J. Einstein, Lydia Kukoff, Hara Person, and Marjorie Slome. *Introduction to Judaism: A Sourcebook*. New York: UAHC Press, 1999.
Eichenstein, Zevi Hirsch, and Louis Jacobs. *Turn Aside from Evil and Do Good: Sur Mera Va'aseh Tov; An Introduction and a Way to the Tree of Life*. Littman Library of Jewish Civilization. London: Oxford University Press, 1995.
Eliade, Mircea. *Patterns in Comparative Religion*. Lincoln: University of Nebraska Press, 1996.
Elior, Rachel. *The Mystical Origins of Hasidism*. Littman Library of Jewish Civilization. Oxford: Oxford University Press, 2006.
———. *The Paradoxical Ascent to God: The Kabbalistic Theosophy of Habad Hasidism*. Translated by J. M. Green. Albany: State University of New York Press, 1993.
Elior, Rachel, Yudith Nave, and Arthur B. Millman. *Jewish Mysticism: The Infinite Expression of Freedom*. Littman Library of Jewish Civilization. Oxford: Oxford University Press, 2007.
Ellenson, David. Jewish Meaning in a World of Choice: Studies in Tradition and Modernity. Lincoln: University of Nebraska Press; Philadelphia: Jewish Publication Society of America, 2014.
Ellenson, David Harry, and Daniel Gordis. *Pledges of Jewish Allegiance: Conversion, Law, and Policymaking in Nineteenth- and Twentieth-Century Orthodox Responsa*. Stanford, CA: Stanford University Press, 2012.
Elshtain, Jean Bethke. *Sovereignty: God, State, and Self*. New York: Basic Books, 2008.
Emon, Anver M., Matthew Levering, and David Novak. *Natural Law: A Jewish, Christian, and Muslim Trialogue*. Oxford: Oxford University Press, 2014.
Epstein, Lawrence J. *Converts to Judaism: Stories from Biblical Times to Today*. Lanham, MD: Rowman & Littlefield, 2015.
Fackenheim, Emil L. "The Dilemma of Liberal Judaism." *Commentary*, October 1960, 301–10.
———. *To Mend the World: Foundations of Post-Holocaust Thought*. New York: Shocken Books, 1989.
Feinstein, Moshe. *Igerot Moshe*. New York: Kalshan, 1976.

Festinger, Leon. *A Theory of Cognitive Dissonance.* Stanford, CA: Stanford University Press, 1957.

Fine, Lawrence. *Physician of the Soul, Healer of the Cosmos: Isaac Luria and His Kabbalistic Fellowship.* Stanford, CA: Stanford University Press, 2003.

Fishbane, Michael A. *Sacred Attunement: A Jewish Theology.* Chicago: University of Chicago Press, 2008.

Fishman, Sylvia Barack. *Choosing Jewish: Conversations about Conversion.* New York: American Jewish Committee, 2006.

———. *Double or Nothing? Jewish Families and Mixed Marriage.* Hanover, NH: Brandeis University Press, 2004.

———. *Jewish and Something Else: A Study of Mixed-Married Families.* New York: American Jewish Committee, 2001.

———. *Jewish Life and American Culture.* Albany: State University of New York Press, 2000.

Freedman, Samuel G. *Jew vs. Jew: The Struggle for the Soul of American Jewry.* New York: Simon & Schuster, 2001.

Freud, Sigmund. *Civilization and Its Discontents.* Oxford: Benediction Books, 2011.

———. *The Future of an Illusion.* Mansfield Centre, CT: Martino, 2010.

Freud, Sigmund. *Moses and Monotheism.* Translated by Katherine Jones. New York: Vintage Books, 1955.

Fromm, Erich. *The Forgotten Language: An Introduction to the Understanding of Dreams, Fairy Tales, and Myths.* New York: Rinehart, 1962.

Geertz, Clifford. *The Interpretation of Cultures: Selected Essays.* New York: Basic Books, 1973.

———. *Local Knowledge: Further Essays in Interpretive Anthropology.* New York: Basic Books, 1983.

Geertz, Clifford, Richard A. Shweder, and Byron Good. *Clifford Geertz by His Colleagues.* Chicago: University of Chicago Press, 2005.

Gilbert, Daniel Todd. *Stumbling on Happiness.* New York: Vintage Books, 2007.

Gilovich, Thomas, and Ross, Lee. *The Wisest One in the Room: How You Can Benefit from Social Psychology's Most Powerful Insights.* New York: Free Press, 2015.

Goldstein, David, trans. *The Wisdom of the Zohar: An Anthology of Texts*. From Fischel Lachower and Isaiah Tishby's Hebrew translation of the original Aramaic with introductions and explanations by Isaiah Tishby. 3 vols. Littman Library of Jewish Civilization. Oxford: Oxford University Press, 1989–2002.

Goldstein, Rebecca. *Betraying Spinoza: The Renegade Jew Who Gave Us Modernity*. New York: Schocken, 2006.

Goodstein, Laurie. "Poll Shows Major Shift in Identity of U.S. Jews." *New York Times*, October 1, 2013. https://www.nytimes.com/2013/10/01/us/poll-shows-major-shift-in-identity-of-us-jews.html

Gray, John. *Isaiah Berlin*. Princeton: Princeton University Press, 1996.

Green, Arthur. *Ehyeh: A Kabbalah for Tomorrow*. Woodstock, VT: Jewish Lights, 2003.

———. *A Guide to the Zohar*. Stanford, CA: Stanford University Press, 2006.

———. *Menahem Nahum of Chernobyl: Upright Practices, the Light of the Eyes*. New York: Paulist Press, 1982.

———. *Radical Judaism: Rethinking God and Tradition*. New Haven: Yale University Press, 2010.

———. *Seek My Face: A Jewish Mystical Theology*. Woodstock, VT: Jewish Lights, 2003.

Greenberg, Irving, and Shalom Freedman. *Living in the Image of God: Jewish Teachings to Perfect the World*. Northvale, NJ: Jason Aronson, 1998.

Haidt, Jonathan. *The Happiness Hypothesis: Finding Modern Truth in Ancient Wisdom*. New York: Basic Books, 2006.

———. *The Righteous Mind: Why Good People Are Divided by Politics and Religion*. New York: Vintage Books, 2013.

Halbertal, Moshe, and Donniel Hartman. *Judaism and the Challenges of Modern Life*. London: Continuum, 2007.

Hartman, David. *Conflicting Visions: Spiritual Possibilities of Modern Israel*. New York: Schocken, 1990.

———. *From Defender to Critic: The Search for a New Jewish Self*. Woodstock, VT: Jewish Lights, 2013.

———. *A Heart of Many Rooms: Celebrating the Many Voices within Judaism*. Woodstock, VT: Jewish Lights, 1999.

———. *Israelis and the Jewish Tradition: An Ancient People Debating Its Future*. New Haven: Yale University Press, 2000.

———. "Israel, Judaism and Jewish Identity." Lecture, Shalom Hartman Institute, Jerusalem, June 2004.
———. *A Living Covenant: The Innovative Spirit in Traditional Judaism*. Woodstock, VT: Jewish Lights, 1998.
———. "Living in Relationship with the Other: God and Human Perfection in the Jewish Tradition." Lecture, Shalom Hartman Institute, Jerusalem, June 2004.
———. *Love and Terror in the God Encounter: The Theological Legacy of Rabbi Joseph B. Soloveitchik*. Woodstock, VT: Jewish Lights, 2001.
———. *Maimonides: Torah and Philosophic Quest*. Philadelphia: Jewish Publication Society of America, 1976.
———. "The Possibilities of Change." Lecture, Shalom Hartman Institute, Jerusalem, October 15, 2003.
———. "The Significance of Israel for the Future of Judaism." Lecture, Shalom Hartman Institute, Jerusalem, June 2004.
———. "Synopsis: Who Are the Jews? The Boundaries of Judaism." Lecture, Shalom Hartman Institute, Jerusalem, n.d.
———. "Who Is a Jew? Membership and Admission Policies in the Jewish Community." Lecture, Shalom Hartman Institute, Jerusalem, July 2004.
Hartman, David, with Charlie Buckholtz. *The God Who Hates Lies: Confronting & Rethinking Jewish Tradition*. Woodstock, VT: Jewish Lights, 2014.
Hartman, Donniel. *The Boundaries of Judaism*. London: Bloomsbury Academic, 2007.
———. *Putting God Second: How to Save Religion from Itself*. Boston: Beacon, 2016.
Haidt, Jonathan, and Craig Joseph. "Moral Mind: How Five Sets of Intuitions Guide the Development of Many Culture Specific Virtues, and Perhaps Even Modules." Chapter 19 in *The Innate Mind*, edited by Stephen Laurence, Stephen Stich, and Peter Carruthers, vol. 3. New York: Oxford University Press, 2007.
Hayes, Christine. *Gentile Impurities and Jewish Identities: Intermarriage and Conversion from the Bible to the Talmud*. Oxford: Oxford University Press, 2002.
Hazon Ish [Abraham Isaiah Karelitz]. *Yorea De'ah*. Jerusalem: L. Epstein, 1942.

Heberman, Joshua. "Martin Buber and Reform Judaism." *European Judaism: A Journal of the New Europe*, no. 12 (Winter 1978): 23–30.
Hechter, Michael. *Containing Nationalism*. Oxford: Oxford University Press, 2000.
Herberg, Will. *Protestant, Catholic, Jew: An Essay in American Religious Sociology*. Garden City, NY: Country Life Press, 1955.
Herman, Simon N. *Jewish Identity: A Social Psychological Perspective*. Beverly Hills, CA: Sage Publications, 1977.
Hertzberg, Arthur, and Aron Hirt-Manheimer. *Jews: The Essence and Character of a People*. San Francisco: Harper, 1998.
Herzog, Isaac HaLevy. *Responsa Heikhal Yitzhak*. Jerusalem: 1961.
Heschel, Abraham J. *God in Search of Man: A Philosophy of Judaism*. New York: Farrar, Straus & Cudahy, 1955.
———. *Man's Quest for God: Studies in Prayer and Symbolism*. Santa Fe, NM: Aurora Press, 1998.
———. *Moral Grandeur and Spiritual Audacity: Essays*. Edited by Susannah Heschel. New York: Farrar, Straus & Giroux, 1996.
———. *The Sabbath: Its Meaning for Modern Man*. New York: Farrar, Straus and Young, 1951.
Hicks, Donna. *Dignity: Its Essential Role in Resolving Conflict*. With a foreword by Desmond Tutu. New Haven: Yale University Press, 2013.
Hirsch, Samson Raphael. *Horeb: A Philosophy of Jewish Law and Observance*. Translated by I. Grunfeld. London: Soncino, 1962.
———. "Principles." The Torah im Derech Eretz Society. http://tidesociety.blogspot.com/p/principals-of-htide-and-ahtide.html.
Hoffman, Lawrence A. *The Way into Jewish Prayer*. Sydney: Readhowyouwant, 2014.
The Holy Scriptures Title. Edited by Max Leopold Margolis. Philadelphia: Jewish Publication Society of America, 1907.
Hyman, Meryl. *Who Is a Jew? Conversations, Not Conclusions*. Woodstock, VT: Jewish Lights, 1998.
Idel, Moshe. *Kabbalah: New Perspectives*. New Haven: Yale University Press, 1990.
———. *Messianic Mystics*. New Haven: Yale University Press, 1998.
Jacobs, Louis. *A Jewish Theology*. New York: Behrman House, 1973.

James, William. *The Varieties of Religious Experience: A Study in Human Nature*. Cambridge, MA: Harvard University Press, 1985.
Janvey, A., ed. *Identity: Young Jews Speak Out*. New York: American Jewish Committee, 2005.
Joas, Hans. *The Genesis of Values*. Chicago: University of Chicago Press, 2000.
JPS Hebrew-English Tanakh. Philadelphia: Jewish Publication Society, 1999.
Kadushin, Max. *A Conceptual Commentary on Midrash Leviticus Rabbah: Value Concepts in Jewish Thought*. Atlanta: Scholars Press, 1987.
———. *The Rabbinic Mind*. New York: Jewish Theological Seminary of America, 1952.
Kaufman, Andrew David. "The Searching Subject in Tolstoy's *The Cossacks*, *War and Peace*, and *Hadji-Murat*." PhD diss., Stanford University, 1998.
———. *Understanding Tolstoy*. Columbus: Ohio State University Press, 2011.
Kaufman, Debra R. *Rachel's Daughters: Newly Orthodox Jewish Women*. New Brunswick, NJ: Rutgers University Press, 1991.
Kaufman, Mike. "The Illusory Promise of Professional Success in the Shadow of Social Development: A 46 Year Longitudinal Study of Harvard College Students from Late Adolescence to Late Midlife." PhD diss., University of Chicago, 2014.
Kaufmann, Walter A. *Without Guilt and Justice: From Decidophobia to Autonomy*. New York: P.H. Wyden, 1973.
Keane, Webb. *Ethical Life: Its Natural and Social Histories*. Princeton: Princeton University Press, 2016.
Kellner, Menachem. *Maimonides' Confrontation with Mysticism*. Littman Library of Jewish Civilization. Oxford: Oxford University Press, 2006.
Knohl, Israel. *The Sanctuary of Silence: The Priestly Torah and the Holiness School*. Minneapolis: Fortress, 1995.
Kochan, Lionel. *The Jew and His History*. Chico, CA: Scholars Press, 1983.
Korn, Eugene. Review of *On the Relationship of Mitzvot between Man and His Neighbor and Man and His Maker*, by Daniel Sperber. *Meorot* 8 (2010).

Kosmin, Barry Alexander. *National Jewish Identity Report*. New York: Council of Jewish Federations, 1990.

Kramer, Kenneth, and Mechthild Gawlick. *Martin Buber's "I and Thou": Practicing Living Dialogue*. New York: Paulist Press, 2003.

Kugel, James L. *How to Read the Bible: A Guide to Scripture, Then and Now*. New York: Free Press, 2007.

Kuran, Timar. *Private Truths, Public Lies: The Social Consequences of Preference Falsification*. Cambridge, MA: Harvard University Press, 1995.

Lau-Lavie, Rabbi Amichai. "'Like a Broken Potsherd': The Inspirational Lesson of the [Oven of Aknai]." *The Lab Rabbi* (blog), March 8, 2006. http://labrab.blogspot.com/2006/03/like-broken-potsherd-inspirational.html.

Leadership and Crisis: Jewish Resources and Responses. Shalom Hartman Institute Lecture Series. Jerusalem: Shalom Hartman Institute, 2009. DVD.

Ledewitz, Bruce. "Hilary Putnam Misinterprets the Oven of Aknai Story." *Hallowed Secularism* (blog), September 2, 2011. http://www.hallowedsecularism.org/2011/09/hilary-putnam-misinterprets-oven-of.html.

Lehmann, Marcus. *Akiva: The Story of Rabbi Akiva and His Times*. Translated by Pearl Zucker. New York: Feldheim, 2003.

Leibowitz, Yeshayahu. *Judaism, Human Values, and the Jewish State*. Edited by Eliezer Goldman. Cambridge, MA: Harvard University Press, 1995.

Levinas, Emmanuel. *Difficult Freedom: Essays on Judaism*. Translated by Sean Hand. Baltimore: Johns Hopkins University Press, 1990.

Levine, Amy-Jill, and Marc Zvi Brettler, eds. *The Jewish Annotated New Testament: New Revised Standard Version Bible Translation*. Oxford: Oxford University Press, 2011.

Lévi-Strauss, Claude. *Structural Anthropology*. Translated by C. Jacobson and B. G. Schoepf. Rev. ed. New York: Basic Books, 1974.

Levy, Richard. 1999 Pittsburgh Statement of Principles. In *Vision of Holiness*.

Levy, Richard. *A Vision of Holiness: The Future of Reform Judaism*. New York: Union of Reform Judaism, 2005.

Lewis, Michael. *The Undoing Project: A Friendship That Changed Our*

Minds. New York: W.W. Norton, 2016.
Lieberman, Beth, and Hara Person, eds. *Honoring Tradition, Embracing Modernity: A Reader for the Union for Reform Judaism's Introduction to Judaism Course*. New York: Central Conference of American Rabbis, 2017.
Liebman, Charles S. *The Ambivalent American Jew: Politics, Religion, and Family in American Jewish Life*. Philadelphia: Jewish Publication Society of America, 1973.
Limon, Tayla, and Dionne Lipman. "Journeys to Judaism: The Convert's Perspective." Master's thesis, Hebrew Union College–Jewish Institute of Religion, 2000.
Lipschitz, Shlomo Zalman. *Responsa Hemdat Shelomo*. Warsaw: S. Munk, 1922.
Luban, David. "The Coiled Serpent of Argument: Reason, Authority, and Law in a Talmudic Tale." *Chicago-Kent Law Review* 79 (2004): 1253–88. Repr., Scholarly Commons, Georgetown Law, 2004. http://scholarship.law.georgetown.edu/facpub/151/.
MacIntyre, Alisdair C. *After Virtue: A Study in Moral Theory*. 2nd ed. Notre Dame, IN: University of Notre Dame Press, 1984.
Madden, Janet. "The Talmud Revisited: Tragedy and 'The Oven of Aknai.'" *Menorah Review*, no. 71 (Summer/Fall 2009): 21–29. https://scholarscompass.vcu.edu/cgi/viewcontent.cgi?article=1068&context=menorah.
Maimonides, Moses. *The Code of Maimonides, Book Fourteen: The Book of Judges*. Translated by Abraham M. Hershman. Yale Judaica Series. New Haven: Yale University Press, 1949.
———. *The Code of Maimonides*. Vol. 3, *The Book of Judges*. Translated by Abraham M. Hershman. New Haven: Yale University Press, 1977.
———. *Epistles of Maimonides: Crisis and Leadership*. Translated by Abraham S. Halkin. With discussions by David Hartman. Philadelphia: Jewish Publication Society, 1993.
———. *Ethical Writings of Maimonides*. Edited by Raymond L. Weiss and Charles E. Butterworth. New York: Dover, 1983.
———. *The Guide of the Perplexed*. Vol. 1. Translated by Shlomo Pines. Chicago: University of Chicago Press, 1963.
———. *The Guide of the Perplexed*. Vol. 2. Translated by Shlomo Pines. Chicago: University of Chicago Press, 1974.

———. *A Maimonides Reader*. Edited by Isadore Twersky. New York: Behrman House, 1989.
———. *Mishneh Torah* [Review of Torah]. Edited by Y. Kafih. Jerusalem: Mossad haRav Kook, 1987.
Margaliot, Reuven, ed. *Tikunei ha-Zohar*. Jerusalem: Mossad haRav Kook, 1978.
Margalit, Avishai. *The Decent Society*. Cambridge, MA: Harvard University Press, 1998.
Marty, Martin E. *Building Cultures of Trust*. Grand Rapids, MI: Eerdmans, 2010.
Massarik, Fred. *National Jewish Identity Report*. New York: Council of Jewish Federations and Welfare Funds, 1971.
Matt, Daniel C., ed. and trans. *The Zohar*. Pritzker edition. Stanford, CA: Stanford University Press, 2011.
———. *Zohar, the Book of Enlightenment*. New York: Paulist Press, 1983.
Mauss, Marcel. *The Gift: Forms and Functions of Exchange in Archaic Societies*. London: Routledge, 2002.
Mayer, Egon, and Amy Avgar. *Conversion among the Intermarried: Choosing to Become Jewish*. New York: American Jewish Committee, 1987.
Mayer, Egon, Kosmin, Barry A. Kosmin, and Ariela Keysar. "American Jewish Identity Survey." New York: Center for Jewish Studies, Graduate Center of the City University of New York, n.d. Retrieved February 09, 2017, from https://www.jewishdatabank.org/databank/search-results/study/488.
McAdams, Dan P. *The Stories We Live By: Personal Myths and the Making of the Self*. New York: Morrow, 1993.
Meir, Ayeh. *Twentysomething and Jewish: Personal Reflections on Jewish Identity*. New York: American Jewish Committee, 1994.
Mendelssohn, Moses. *Jerusalem, or On Religious Power and Judaism*. Translated by Allan Arkush. Hanover, NH: University Press of New England, 1983.
Mendes-Flohr, Paul R. "Love, Accusative and Dative: Reflections on Leviticus 19:18." Lecture presented at The B. G. Rudolph Lectures in Judaic Studies, Syracuse University, January 2007.
———. *Martin Buber: A Contemporary Perspective*. Syracuse, NY: Syracuse University Press, 2002.

Mendes-Flohr, Paul R., and Jehuda Reinharz, eds. *The Jew in the Modern World: A Documentary History*. New York: Oxford University Press, 1980.

Meyer, Michael A. *Ideas of Jewish History*. Detroit: Wayne State University Press, 1999.

———. *Response to Modernity: A History of the Reform Movement in Judaism*. New York: Oxford University Press, 1988.

Meyer, Michael A., and Plaut, W. Gunther, compilers. *The Reform Judaism Reader: North American Documents*. New York: UAHC Press, 2001.

Mill, John Stuart. *On Liberty*. New Haven: Yale University Press, 2003.

Miller, Avis, Janet Marder, and Steven Bayme. *Approaches to Intermarriage: Areas of Consensus*. New York: American Jewish Committee, 1993. http://www.bjpa.org/Publications/details.cfm?PublicationID=2962.

Mischel, Walter. (1981). *Introduction to Personality*. New York: Holt, Rinehart and Winston, 1981.

Mittleman, Alan L. *A Short History of Jewish Ethics: Conduct and Character in the Context of Covenant*. Chichester, UK: Wiley-Blackwell, 2012.

Moyn, Samuel. *The Last Utopia: Human Rights in History*. Cambridge, MA: Harvard University Press, 2012.

Muffs, Yochanan. *The Personhood of God: Biblical Theology, Human Faith and the Divine Image*. Woodstock, VT: Jewish Lights, 2005.

Newman, Louis E. *An Introduction to Jewish Ethics*. Upper Saddle River, NJ: Pearson Prentice Hall, 2005.

Niebuhr, R. (1992). *Love and Justice: Selections from the Shorter Writings of Reinhold Niebuhr*. Edited by D. B. Robertson. Louisville: Westminster/John Knox, 1992.

Nirenberg, David. *Anti-Judaism: The Western Tradition*. New York: W.W. Norton, 2013.

Nisbett, Richard E. *Mindware: Tools for Smart Thinking*. New York: Farrar, Straus and Giroux, 2015.

Nussbaum, Martha C. *Anger and Forgiveness: Resentment, Generosity, and Justice*. New York: Oxford University Press, 2016.

Pagels, Elaine H. *The Origin of Satan*. New York: Random House, 1995.

Pagels, Elaine H., and Karen L. King. *Reading Judas: The Gospel of*

Judas and the Shaping of Christianity. New York: Viking, 2007.
Pennebaker, James W., and Sandra Kûhr Beall. "Confronting a Traumatic Event: Toward an Understanding of Inhibition and Disease." *Journal of Abnormal Psychology* 95, no. 3 (1986): 274–81. https://doi.org/10.1037/0021-843X.95.3.274.
Pennebaker, James W., and John F. Evans. *Expressive Writing: Words That Heal*. Enumclaw, WA: Idyll Arbor, 2014.
Pennebaker, James W., and Janet D. Seagal. "Forming a Story: The Health Benefits of Narrative." *Journal of Clinical Psychology* 55, no. 10 (1999): 1243–54.
Pennebaker, James W., and Joshua M. Smyth. *Opening Up by Writing It Down: How Expressive Writing Improves Health and Eases Emotional Pain*. 3rd ed. New York: Guilford, 2016.
Phillips, Bruce A. *Children of Intermarriage: How "Jewish"?* Oxford: Oxford University Press, 1998. http://www.bjpa.org/Publications/details.cfm?PublicationID=2753.
———. *Re-examining Intermarriage: Trends, Textures and Strategies; Report of a New Study*. New York: American Jewish Committee, William Petschek National Jewish Family Center, 1997.
Phillips, Benjamin T., and Shaul Kelner. "Reconceptualizing Religious Change: Ethno-Apostasy and Change in Religion among American Jews." *Sociology of Religion* 67, no. 4 (2006): 507–43. doi:10.1093/socrel/67.4.507.
Plaut, W. Gunther. *The Growth of Reform Judaism: American and European Sources*. Edited by Howard A. Berman. 50th anniversary ed. Lincoln, NE: Jewish Publication Society, 2015.
———. *The Rise of Reform Judaism: A Sourcebook of Its European Origins*. 50th anniversary ed. Lincoln, NE: Jewish Publication Society, 2015.
Plotzky, Meir Dan Raphael. *Kli Hemdah*. Petah Tikvah: Yitzhak Bruch, 1997.
Polanyi, Michael. *Personal Knowledge: Towards a Post-critical Philosophy*. Chicago: University of Chicago Press, 2009.
Posner, M. *Responsa Beit Meir*. Jerusalem: Self-published, 1987.
Power, F. Clark, Ann Higgins, and Lawrence Kohlberg. *Lawrence Kohlberg's Approach to Moral Education*. New York: Columbia University Press, 1989.
Putnam, Hilary. *Jewish Philosophy as a Guide to Life: Rosenzweig,*

Buber, Lévinas, Wittgenstein. Bloomington: Indiana University Press, 2008.
Putnam, Robert D. *Bowling Alone: The Collapse and Revival of American Community*. New York: Simon & Schuster, 2000.
Rambo, Lewis Ray. *Religious Conversion*. New Haven: Yale University Press, 1993.
Raphael, Marc Lee. *Profiles in American Judaism: The Reform, Conservative, Orthodox, and Reconstructionist Traditions in Historical Perspective*. San Francisco, CA: Harper & Row, 1984.
Robbie, Erica. "Inclusive Conversation." *Aspen (Colorado) Times*, July 1, 2017.
Lau-Lavie, Rabbi Amichai. "'Like a Broken Potsherd': The Inspirational Lesson of the [Oven of Aknai]." *The Lab Rabbi* (blog), March 8, 2006. http://labrab.blogspot.com/2006/03/like-broken-potsherd-inspirational.html.
Rosenzweig, Franz, ed. and trans. *Ninety-Two Poems and Hymns of Yehuda Halevi*. Edited and with an introduction by Richard A. Cohen. Translated from German by Thomas Kovach, Eva Jospe, and Gilya Gerda Schmidt. Albany: State University of New York Press, 2000.
———. *On Jewish Learning*. Edited by Nahum N. Glatzer. Madison: University of Wisconsin Press, 2002.
———. *The Star of Redemption*. Notre Dame, IN: University of Notre Dame Press, 2014.
———. *Understanding the Sick and the Healthy: A View of World, Man, and God*. Translated by Nahum N. Glatzer. With an introduction by Hilary Putnam. Cambridge, MA: Harvard University Press, 1999.
Ross, Lee, and Richard E. Nisbett. *The Person and the Situation: Perspectives of Social Psychology*. Foreword by Malcolm Gladwell. London: Pinter & Martin, 2011.
Rubenstein, Richard L. *After Auschwitz: History, Theology, and Contemporary Judaism*. Baltimore: Johns Hopkins University Press, 1992.
Sacks, Jonathan. *The Dignity of Difference: How to Avoid the Clash of Civilizations*. London: Continuum, 2002.
———. *Future Tense*. London: Hodder & Stoughton, 2009.
———. *To Heal a Fractured World: The Ethics of Responsibility*. New

York: Schocken, 2005.

Sagi, Avi, and Statman, Daniel. *Religion and Morality*. Translated by B. Stein. Amsterdam: Rodopi, 1985.

Sagi, Avi, and Zvi Zohar. *Transforming Identity: The Ritual Transformation from Gentile to Jew; Structure and Meaning*. London: Continuum, 2007.

Sandel, Michael J. *Justice: What's the Right Thing to Do?* New York: Farrar, Straus and Giroux, 2009.

Sarna, Jonathan D. *American Judaism: A History*. New Haven: Yale University Press, 2004.

Schäfer, Peter. *Judeophobia: Attitudes toward the Jews in the Ancient World*. Cambridge, MA: Harvard University Press, 1997.

Schindler, Alexander. Speech to the Board of Trustees of the Union of Reform Judaism, Houston, Texas, December 2, 1978.

Scholem, Gershom. *Major Trends in Jewish Mysticism*. New York: Schocken, 1961.

———. *On Jews and Judaism in Crisis: Selected Essays*. Edited by Werner J. Dannhauser New York: Schocken, 1976.

———, ed. *Zohar: The Book of Splendor*. New York: Schocken, 1963.

Schön, Donald A. *Educating the Reflective Practitioner: Toward a New Design for Teaching and Learning in the Professions*. San Francisco: Jossey-Bass, 1987.

———. *Reflective Practitioner: How Professionals Think in Action*. New York: Basic Books, 2000.

Schwarz, Sidney. *Jewish Megatrends: Charting the Course of the American Jewish Future*. Woodstock, VT: Jewish Lights, 2013.

Shapira, A. D. C. *Devar Avaraham*. Jerusalem: Mesamhei Lev, 1999.

Shweder, Richard A. "Channeling the Super-natural Aspects of the Ethical Life." Review of *The Ethical Life: Its Natural and Social Histories*, by Webb Keane. *HAU: Journal of Ethnographic Theory* 6, no. 1 (2016): 477–83.

———. "Equality Now in Genital Reshaping: Brian Earp's Search for Moral Consistency." *Kennedy Institute of Ethics Journal* 26, no. 2 (2016): 145–54.

———. "Shouting at the Hebrews: Imperial Liberalism v. Liberal Pluralism and the Practice of Male Circumcision." *Law, Culture and the Humanities* 5, no. 2 (2009): 247–65. https://doi.org/10.1177/1743872109102491.

———. *Thinking through Cultures: Expeditions in Cultural Psychology.* Cambridge, MA: Harvard University Press, 1991.

———. *Why Do Men Barbecue? Recipes for Cultural Psychology.* Cambridge, MA: Harvard University Press, 2003.

Shweder, Richard A., and Jonathan Haidt. "The Future of Moral Psychology: Truth, Intuition, and the Pluralist Way." *Psychological Science* 4, no. 6 (November 1993): 360–65.

Shweder, Richard A., and Robert A. LeVine, eds. *Culture Theory: Essays on Mind, Self, and Emotion.* Cambridge: Cambridge University Press, 1984.

Society of Classical Reform Judaism. "The Principles of the Society of Classical Reform Judaism." Adopted February 1, 2008 (unpublished).

Sofer, Yosef Hayyim. *Menuhat Shalom.* Part 2. Jerusalem: Otzrot Shlomo, 2003.

Soloveitchik, Joseph B. *The Lonely Man of Faith.* New York: Doubleday, 1992.

Sorin, Gerald. *Tradition Transformed: The Jewish Experience in America.* Baltimore: Johns Hopkins University Press, 1997.

Sperber, Daniel. *On the Relationship of Mitzvot between Man and His Neighbor and Man and His Maker.* Jerusalem: Urim Publications, 2014.

Spiegel, Ya'akov Shemu'el, ed. *Magen Elohim.* Petah Tikvah, Israel: Self-published, 2014. First published 2007.

Spinoza, Benedictus. *Theological-Political Treatise.* Translated by Samuel Shirley. With and introduction and annotations by Seymour Feldman. 2nd ed. Indianapolis: Hackett, 2001.

Steele, Claude M. *Whistling Vivaldi: How Stereotypes Affect Us and What We Can Do.* New York: W.W. Norton, 2010.

Stendahl, Krister. *Meanings: The Bible as Document and as Guide.* Philadelphia: Fortress, 1984.

Telushkin, Joseph. *Jewish Literacy: The Most Important Things to Know about the Jewish Religion, Its People, and Its History.* New York: Morrow, 1991.

Thaler, Richard H., and Cass R. Sunstein. *Nudge: Improving Decisions about Health, Wealth, and Happiness.* New Haven: Yale University Press, 2008.

Tigay, Jeffrey H. *Deuteronomy: The Traditional Hebrew Text with the*

New JPS Translation. JPS Torah Commentary. Philadelphia: Jewish Publication Society, 1996.

Tobin, Gary A. *Opening the Gates: How Proactive Conversion Can Revitalize the Jewish Community*. San Francisco: Jossey-Bass, 1999.

Tobin, Gary A., and Katherine G. Simon. *Rabbis Talk about Intermarriage*. San Francisco: Institute for Jewish & Community Research, 1999.

The Tosefta. Translated by Jacob Neusner. 2 vols. Atlanta: Scholars Press, 1990.

Tucker, Gordon. *Halakhic and Metahalakhic Arguments concerning Judaism and Homosexuality*. New York: Committee on Jewish Law and Standards, 2006.

Uzziel, Ben-Zion. *Mishapati Uzziel*. 2nd ed. Jerusalem: Mosad HaRav Kook, 1950.

Vorspan, Albert. *Jewish Values and Social Crisis: A Casebook for Social Action*. New York: Union of American Hebrew Congregations, 1968.

Walzer, Michael, Menachem Lorberbaum, Noam J. Zohar, and Ari Ackerman, eds. *The Jewish Political Tradition*. New Haven: Yale University Press, 2000.

Walzer, Michael, Menachem Lorberbaum, and Noam J. Zohar, and Yair Lorberbaum, eds. *The Jewish Political Tradition*. Vol. 1, *Authority*. New Haven: Yale University Press, 2003.

Walzer, Michael, Menachem Lorberbaum, and Noam J. Zohar, and Ari Ackerman, eds. *The Jewish Political Tradition*. Vol. 2, *Membership*. New Haven: Yale University Press, 2006.

Washofsky, Mark. "M'nuchah and M'lachah: On Observing the Sabbath." In *Honoring the Tradition, Embracing Modernity*, edited by Rabbi Bet Lieberman and Rabbi Hara Person, 71–96. New York: Central Conference of Reform Rabbis, 2017.

Weber, M. *Ancient Judaism*. Translated by Hans H. Gerth and Don Martindale. Glencoe, IL: Free Press, 1952.

Weinberg, Yehiel Yaakov. *Serdie Eish*. 3 vols. Jerusalem: Mosad haRaKook, 1977.

Wertheimer, Jack. *A People Divided: Judaism in Contemporary America*. New York: Basic Books, 1993.

Whyte, William Foote. *Street Corner Society: The Social Structure of an*

Italian Slum. Chicago: University of Chicago Press, 1955.
Wiesel, Elie. *Night*. Translated by Stella Rodway. New York: Hill & Wang, 1960.
———. *Somewhere a Master: Further Hasidic Portraits and Legends*. New York: Schocken, 1982.
Wilson, Timothy D. *Redirect: Changing the Stories We Live By*. London: Penguin, 2013.
———. *Strangers to Ourselves: Discovering the Adaptive Unconscious*. Cambridge, MA: Belknap Press of Harvard University Press, 2002.
Wittgenstein, Ludwig. *Philosophical Investigations*. Translated by G. E. M. Anscombe. 2nd ed. Oxford: Blackwell, 1958.
Wuthnow, Robert. *After the Baby Boomers: How Twenty- and Thirty-Somethings Are Shaping the Future of American Religion*. Princeton: Princeton University Press, 2007.
———. *Inventing American Religion: Polls, Surveys, and the Tenuous Quest for a Nation's Faith*. Oxford: Oxford University Press, 2015.
———. *The Restructuring of American Religion: Society and Faith since World War II*. Princeton: Princeton University Press, 1988.
Yerushalmi, Yosef Hayim. *Zakhor: Jewish History and Jewish Memory*. Seattle: University of Washington Press, 1982.
Zarka, Sholom. *Menuhat Shalom*. 5 vols. Jerusalem, ca. 1876–1918.
Zohar, Zvi. "A Policy of *Giyyur* for Our Time." Unpublished paper. Late 1980s.